MOR
ASSEMBLIES
FOR
PRIMARY SCHOOLS

SUMMER TERM

Margaret Cooling

RMEP

First published in 2008 by RMEP
13-17 Long Lane, London EC1A 9PN

www.rmep.co.uk

RMEP (Religious and Moral Education Press) is a division of SCM-Canterbury Press Ltd.

A catalogue record for this book is available from the British Library.

ISBN 978-1-85175-358-1

Designed and typeset by Topics – The Creative Partnership, Exeter

Illustrations by Clive Wakfer

Printed and bound in Great Britain by Halstan & Co. Ltd

Contents

Assemblies by group   3
Alternative themes index   5
Acknowledgements   8

Introduction   9
Assemblies   15
Appendix   86

Assemblies by group

Title	Theme	
Group A Summer saints and festivals		
A1 Ascension Day	*Areas of care*	15
A2 Pentecost	*Rose petal day*	16
A3 Trinity Sunday	*Three and one*	17
A4 St Hervé and St Rivanon	*Passing on gifts*	18
A5 St Oswald	*Faith in Northumbria*	19
Group B Fun and games		
B1 Clowns and holy fools	*The gift of laughter*	20
B2 Snakes and ladders	*Right and wrong*	21
B3 Tiddlywinks	*The unexpected*	22
B4 Balloon fun	*Thanks and praise*	23
B5 Jelly babies	*Encouragement*	24
Group C Celtic Christian faith		
C1 The caim	*The circle of prayer*	25
C2 Creativity	*Poetry, music, art*	26
C3 The five-stringed harp	*The five senses*	27
C4 A prayer basket	*Prayer through the day*	28
C5 The boat	*Life as a sea journey*	29
Group D Tearfund assemblies		
Introductory page		30
D1 The bin twins	*Recycle*	31
D2 Two degrees	*Global warming*	32

D3	Veggies	*Nutrition*	33
D4	Borrowing and lending	*Lending fairly*	34
D5	Let's talk toilets	*Toilets for health*	35
D6	Water	*The gift of water*	36
D7	Be an angel	*Messengers of good*	37
D8	TB and Mr Medicine	*Combating TB*	38
D9	Lost childhood	*Child-parents*	39
D10	Trade injustice	*Justice in trade*	40

Group E **Faith and football**

E1	Fulham	*Church teams*	41
E2	Tottenham Hotspur	*Playing well*	42
E3	Southampton	*Changing things*	43
E4	Manchester City	*Persevere*	44
E5	Everton and Liverpool	*Reconciliation*	45

Group F **Values assemblies**

F1	Life in the pond	*Getting on with others*	46
F2	Michael Watson	*Forgiveness*	47
F3	Ruby Bridges	*Reconciliation*	48
F4	Three circles	*Love*	49
F5	Running over	*Generosity*	50
F6	More than waiting	*Patience*	51
F7	The seed	*Honesty*	52
F8	The wall	*Self-control*	53
F9	The quiz	*Wisdom*	54
F10	The difficult word	*Faith*	55

Group G **Mark Street**

G1	Mark Street assemblies	*Making the street*	56
G2	Mark the writer	*Good news*	57
G3	The herald	*John the Baptist*	58
G4	Catching?	*The man with leprosy*	59
G5	The story-man	*Parables: the sower*	60
G6	Just a carpenter?	*Ordinary celebrity*	61
G7	Who am I?	*Jesus' question*	62
G8	The eye of the needle	*Wealth and priorities*	63
G9	The question	*God and taxes*	64
G10	A cross and a cave	*Death and resurrection*	65

Group H **Famous scientists**

H1	The Lavoisiers (metric)	*Order in nature*	*66*
H2	Gregor Mendel (genes)	*Asking questions*	*67*
H3	Kathleen Lonsdale (crystals)	*Keep wondering*	*68*
H4	Francis Collins (the genome)	*Sharing knowledge*	*69*
H5	Jocelyn Bell Burnell (pulsars)	*Beautiful stars*	*70*

Group I **Faith in the high street**

I1	Clarks	*Setting an example*	*71*
I2	Dollond and Aitchison	*Freedom of faith*	*72*
I3	Boots the Chemist	*Medicine for all*	*73*
I4	Thomas Cook	*Healthy fun*	*74*
I5	Lloyds	*Trust and honesty*	*75*

Group J **Changing lives**

J1	Dr Kim Tan	*Sharing for change*	*76*
J2	Changing communities	*Business for change*	*77*
J3	Kuzuko game park	*Long-term change*	*78*
J4	Success and significance	*Being significant*	*79*
J5	Lord Chan	*Gentleness and justice*	*80*

Group K **Special places**

K1	The hill of crosses	*Hope*	*81*
K2	Iona	*Spiritual journey*	*82*
K3	The Black Madonna	*The flame of faith*	*83*
K4	Walsingham	*The 'holy house'*	*84*
K5	Bardsey Island	*Island of saints*	*85*

Alternative themes index

People

A4	St Hervé and St Rivanon	*18*
A5	St Oswald	*19*
E3	Southampton (Basil Wilberforce)	*43*

E4	Manchester City (Anna Cardwell)	44
F2	Michael Watson	47
F3	Ruby Bridges	48
G3	The herald (John the Baptist)	58
G6	Just a carpenter? (Jesus)	61
H1	The Lavoisiers	66
H2	Gregor Mendel	67
H3	Kathleen Lonsdale	68
H4	Francis Collins	69
H5	Jocelyn Bell Burnell	70
I3	Boots the Chemist (Jesse Boot)	73
I4	Thomas Cook	74
J1	Dr Kim Tan	76
J5	Lord Chan	80

Celtic Christianity

A4	St Hervé and St Rivanon	18
A5	St Oswald	19
C1	The caim	25
C2	Creativity	26
C3	The five-stringed harp	27
C4	A prayer basket	28
C5	The boat	29
K2	Iona	82
K5	Bardsey Island	85

Values

B2	Snakes and ladders (right and wrong)	21
B5	Jelly babies (encouragement)	24
D4	Borrowing and lending (lending fairly)	34
D10	Trade injustice (justice in trade)	40
E2	Tottenham Hotspur (playing well)	42
E4	Manchester City (persevere)	44
E5	Everton and Liverpool (reconciliation)	45
F1	Life in the pond (getting on with others)	46
F2	Michael Watson (forgiveness)	47
F3	Ruby Bridges (reconciliation)	48
F4	Three circles (love)	49
F5	Running over (generosity)	50
F6	More than waiting (patience)	51
F7	The seed (honesty)	52
F8	The wall (self-control)	53
F9	The quiz (wisdom)	54

F10 The difficult word (faith)   55
G8 The eye of the needle (wealth and priorities)   63
H4 Francis Collins (sharing knowledge)   69
I5 Lloyds (trust and honesty)   75
K1 The hill of crosses (hope)   81
K3 The Black Madonna (flame of faith)   83

Acknowledgements

The author and publisher thank the owners or controllers of copyright for permission to use the copyright material listed below. Every effort has been made to contact the holders of copyright material but if any have inadvertently been overlooked, the publisher would be pleased to make the necessary alteration at the first available opportunity.

The extract on page 69 from *When We Were Very Young* by A. A. Milne © The Trustees of the Pooh Properties. Published by Egmont UK Ltd London and used with permission.

The prayer on page 85 is the Short Proper Preface from The Order for the Celebration of Holy Communion in *Common Worship: Services and Prayers for the Church of England*, which is copyright © the Archbishops' Council 2000.

The photographs referred to on pages 34 and 36 are available for use with Assemblies D4 and D6 from RMEP's website, www.rmep.co.uk/summer, by permission of the photographer, © Richard Hanson/Tearfund.

The author would like to express her thanks to Tearfund and The Transformational Business Network for their help with the assemblies on pages 31–40 and 76–78, in particular to Ralph Catto for the idea for the assembly on page 79.

The author would also like to acknowledge the following.
Thank God for Football! by Peter Lupson, published by Azure, for the inspiration for the assemblies pages 41–45.

Mountains on the Moon by Michael Arthern, published by Crossbridge Books, for the inspiration for the assemblies on pages 66–70 and for general inspiration for assemblies on scientists that appear in this series.

The *How is all Began* series by Maurice E. Baren, published by Michael O'Mara Books. This series was the inspiration for the assemblies on pages 71–75.

With thanks to David Edden for the music on page 90.

Introduction

This book contains 70 'broadly Christian' assemblies for use in primary schools (ages 5–11). In England and Wales, the term 'assemblies' applies to the non-religious items such as the notices and recognition of pupil achievement, but here it is used to cover the religious element (collective worship) as it is still the most commonly used term.

Brand new assemblies

This new series of assemblies contains fresh material for today's teachers. Inevitably, a few themes reoccur, such as the Easter and Christmas stories, but very different assemblies have been built around them.

Four nations

These assemblies can be used by all four nations of the United Kingdom. In Scotland several assemblies can be combined to create a longer act of religious observance. For details of legislation of collective worship and religious observance see the following websites:

England
www.dfes.gov.uk
www.teachernet.gov.uk

Wales
www.collectiveworship.com
http://new.wales.gov.uk/topics/educationandskills

Scotland
www.ltscotland.org.uk/religiousobservance
www.scotland.gov.uk

Northern Ireland
www.deni.gov.uk

Broad Christian tradition

The material in this series of books draws on the breadth of the Christian tradition: from Quaker to Catholic, from the early Christians to modern aid projects, from African Christianity to Aboriginal Christian insights.

Multicultural

The assemblies draw on Christian examples from around the world. The majority of Christians live in the two-thirds world (formerly known as the 'third world') and these books reflect some of that change in Christian demographics. For more information see: M. Cooling, *Rethinking Spirituality: An Approach Through Christian Spiritual Traditions* (The Stapleford Centre).

Spirituality

Some of the assemblies draw on a variety of Christian spiritual traditions so that pupils can see the range of spiritualities within one faith. For more information see: M. Cooling, *Rethinking Spirituality: An Approach Through Christian Spiritual Traditions* (The Stapleford Centre).

Values and virtues

Each book in this series contains a number of explicit virtue/values assemblies, such as 'happiness' and 'forgiveness', as well as general assemblies that deal with virtues and values. These can be part of a wider programme to build a school ethos.

Variety

Assembly themes are varied, covering charities, saints, values, festivals, biography, music, Bible stories and many other subjects. This is deliberate, as it allows as many staff as possible to be involved. Most members of staff should be able to find something they are comfortable delivering.

Seasonal

The books have been organised into three seasons to help people locate seasonal material. Some schools operate on multiple terms, but much of the material can be delivered at any time. Up to twenty assemblies in each book are seasonal, but even some of these could be used on other occasions.

Creating a programme

The material in this book can form part of a larger school programme of assemblies. The nature of the school – whether church or community, perhaps – will decide how many of these Christian assemblies are included in the programme.

Series

Most of the assemblies have been written in series of five so that they fit a school week. These series could, however, be split and assemblies put together in different combinations. Some suggestions are given in the Alternative themes index on pages 5–7.

Order

The assemblies are not necessarily presented in the order in the term in which the subjects occur. They certainly do not need to be delivered in the sequence they appear. The 'Mark Street' assemblies, for example, by their nature include Easter material. As suggested above, teachers can pick out individual assemblies from a series to present at an appropriate time if they wish.

Layout/fonts

Instructions and directions for teachers are shown in this font.

Direct speech, to be addressed to the pupils, or something the pupils might join in saying, is shown in this font.

Assemblies cannot be completely scripted. Teachers will need to improvise around the direct speech to make the assembly appropriate for the age and aptitude of their pupils.

Historical heritage
Some historical content is included to familiarise pupils with the Christian heritage of Britain. Well-known saints, and saints associated with particular regions, are the subject of some assemblies.

Using images
In some assemblies it is suggested that images are used. If you have the facilities for using web images this will enhance the presentation, but such suggestions are always optional. Please check copyright on images that you plan to use.

Pastoral issues
Some assemblies deal with sensitive issues. These should be handled appropriately and adapted to your situation as necessary.

➢ Jesus' death needs sensitive handling. It is not advisable to use graphic images of the crucifixion with young children. The assembly on page 65 introduces the resurrection so that pupils do not think that Jesus' death is the end of story.

➢ Death is touched upon in some assemblies. It is up to teachers as to whether they mention this or omit it.

Miracles
Miracles are the subject of some assemblies, and these will need sensitive handling, particularly healing miracles. Miracles for Christians are about power and compassion and often come from a relationship of faith. They are not magic, which is about control. Miracles are understood within Christianity as signs pointing to the nature of God and Jesus, showing the power of the creator. Christians believe that, as creator, God has the power to temporarily suspend the 'rules of nature'. Christians differ in their attitude towards miracles; some believe in them while others do not. With younger pupils, concentrate on the motive for miracles (usually compassion) and miracles as signs, and do not overemphasise the supernatural element.

Prayers and reflections
Both prayers and reflections are included, so that teachers can choose what is right for their school – either or both can be used if appropriate. Pupils should only ever be *invited* to join in prayers, never *forced* to respond. One option is for the teacher to introduce the prayer – if they choose to – by saying:

I am going to say a prayer. If you wish you can join in with the Amen at the end. Or you can listen quietly. Amen means 'I agree'.

If you wish you could ask pupils (ones who would be comfortable with this) to read prayers.

A range of activities is used for prayer and reflections, sometimes active and fun, at other times quiet and thoughtful. Text shown in bold is for pupils to be invited to join in and say together. This may involve displaying the prayer in some way.

The following books are sources of prayers that can be adapted:

Prayers Encircling the World (SPCK, 1998)
A Procession of Prayers by John Carden *(Cassell, 1998)*
An African Prayer Book by Desmond Tutu *(Doubleday, 1995)*

Websites
Websites referred to in the text were live at the time of going to print. The websites do not necessarily represent the author's views. Please check copyright before you download any material.

Participation
The assemblies have been designed with participation in mind, and may involve pupils, other teachers, and school staff such as caretakers and meal supervisors. In some assemblies other community members and parents could be involved. The participation has been designed to be manageable in the context; either a few children are invited to take part, or all pupils do a small seated activity such as sign language.

British sign language
Some prayers and activities include signing. For this British sign language has been used. Signing is deliberately included to widen access and raise pupil awareness.

Health and safety
All activities must be carried out with due regard to health and safety, and teachers must act with reference to their health and safety documents. The lighting of candles should be done by adults, and candles should stand in a pot of damp play sand.

Preparation
These assemblies are easy to deliver but they do require some preparation and there may be some items you need to collect beforehand. You could delegate safe elements of preparation to older pupils, such as bringing in a football.

Assembly box
It is helpful to have a box containing basic items that are often needed for delivering assemblies. The assembly box should contain:

➣ Scissors (child and adult)
➣ Stick glue
➣ Paper (different sizes and colours including large sheets)
➣ Card (different sizes and colours)
➣ Felt pens/pencils/crayons

- String
- Rubbers
- Post-it notes (large size)
- Sellotape and double-sided tape
- Roll of lining paper or frieze paper

Each assembly begins with a 'You will need' section that lists specific items needed to deliver that assembly. This list does not include the contents of the assembly box, which are taken as present.

Printing the illustrations

Some assemblies require large versions of the illustrations in the Appendix. These can be photocopied and enlarged or they can be downloaded free as a PDF file for printing from RMEP's website: www.rmep.co.uk/summer.

Bible quotations

All Bible quotations have been paraphrased to make them accessible for the age group. The reference is given if teachers want to look up the original.

Music

Music is suggested for some assemblies. This can be obtained from music libraries, high street music stores or on-line outlets and resources.

Presenting Bible stories

Bible stories and stories from the Christian tradition need to be introduced carefully so that both staff and pupils feel comfortable. The following form of words might be helpful:

Today we are having a story that is important for Christians.

Today's story comes from the special/sacred book of the Christians, the Bible.

This leaves everyone free to decide whether to identify with the story or not. They can silently respond in their own personal way:

That's my story; we read that at home. We have that story at church.

Now I know why that is important for Christians.

It is important that pupils feel free to decide to make their own response to the story, as long as it is respectful.

What makes a good assembly?

A good assembly needs four things:

- Content
- Atmosphere
- Reflection
- Participation

The following factors are also helpful:

- Pay attention to the general ethos of the school and relationships, as this affects everyone and everything.
- Plan the way pupils enter and leave; this can set the tone.
- Create a relaxed but secure environment. Assemblies need an ordered atmosphere but the discipline does not need to dominate.
- Avoid having distracting noises, such as the clattering of pots and pans.
- Think about the way the room is arranged. How comfortable can you make it?
- Make decisions about the presence or absence of members of staff. If staff do not attend, what message does it send?
- Separate the notices from the act of worship, if they take place at the same occasion. Create a ritual for ending one and beginning the other. You might use music, light a candle or have a stilling activity.
- Create a focus for worship. You might use a candle, a picture or some flowers as a focus.
- Use poetry, music, art, drama and silence as well as speech.

Ascension Day

You will need

The name of your parish church. To find your local parish, go to www.acny.org. uk/parishmap.php and type in your school postcode.

Introduction

Draw a church in the centre of a large sheet of paper. Draw an irregular line around the church, close to the edge of the paper. Explain that a parish is an area of land around a church (often an Anglican one) and the people of that church help look after the people who live in that area. It is an area of responsibility or care. Inside the line pupils can draw some of the things that will be found in a parish: houses and shops, schools, etc.

Core material

On Ascension Day shoppers in the underwear department of Marks and Spencer in Oxford may be surprised, for on that day a group of choir boys and a procession of Christians from St Michael's Church enter that department of the store and start beating the floor with sticks, shouting 'Mark! Mark! Mark!' This ceremony happens in various places around the country every year on Ascension Day, which is the Thursday 40 days after Easter, or on one of the days between the previous Sunday and Ascension Day. The ceremony is called 'beating the bounds' and it is where the vicar and a group of people from a church walk round their parish boundary to mark where the boundary line is. As they walk round, the parish people stop at important places to pray and say blessings and sometimes mark the stopping places with a cross. In the days before maps, this ceremony was very common, and was needed so that people knew which parish they belonged to. Over the years some shops have been built over the parish boundaries, which is why beating the bounds in Oxford happens in Marks and Spencer and other shops.

It is appropriate that this ceremony happens on or around Ascension Day, for that is the time when Christians come together to remember Jesus returning to heaven and handing over to them the task of spreading his message of love and justice. For many Christians that starts with their parish. The vicar conducts christenings, weddings and funerals. There may be a playgroup and a club for the elderly. People from the church may visit those in hospital and help others with shopping. Find out what your local church does.

Reflection

Ask pupils what they think needs doing in their area to show love and justice.

Prayer (OPTIONAL)

If possible, arrange a prayer walk around the school, stopping to pray, place crosses or say a blessing at significant places. Or use the following prayer:

'Love and justice start at home, in our area. Help us, Lord, to see the needs close to home.'

Pentecost

You will need
> Something red, such as a scarf.
> Child-safe party trumpets.
> Red rose petal confetti or red tissue cut as petals.

Introduction
Show the red item, the trumpets and the confetti and ask where they might be used. Explain that they all form part of a Christian festival. Can the pupils guess which one?

Core material
Many Christian churches are decorated with red for this festival and sometimes people wear red on this day, which is called Pentecost. Pentecost is the festival when Christians remember the coming of the Holy Spirit, which is what they call God the invisible but real helper and friend, who guides them through life.

On the first Pentecost, the friends of Jesus were together in a room at the top of a house. They were waiting. Jesus had told them to wait, but they were not quite sure what they were waiting for. Suddenly there was a sound like a great rushing wind and what appeared to be flames above each person's head. No one was harmed; instead they felt filled with great power and able to talk to people of all races in their own languages. They were no longer afraid and they went out to talk to people about Jesus. *(Acts 2:1–13)*

This was the beginning of the Christian church. Since then, Christians have always celebrated the coming of the Holy Spirit 50 days after Easter Sunday. In Italy, Pentecost is called Pascha Rosatum (feast of roses) and red rose petals are scattered from the ceiling as a reminder of the flames in the story. Pupils can throw confetti. In France people blow trumpets as a reminder of the wind in the story. Pupils can demonstrate this.

Reflection
Listen to the sound of the trumpet and think about who helps you through life.

Prayer (OPTIONAL)
Blow the trumpet.

> 'Lord, as the trumpet sounds we remember the coming of your Holy Spirit. Be with us, Holy Spirit, lead and guide us through life.'

Blow the trumpet.

Trinity Sunday

You will need

A picture of a shamrock (ttp://commons.
wikimedia.org/wiki/Image:Shamrock.svg).

Introduction

This is a shamrock. How many leaves has it got? It is, in fact, just one leaf, made up of three parts. St Patrick, a Celtic saint *(C1, page 25)* used the shamrock to help explain the Trinity. *Note:* It is recognised that this does not fully represent the Trinity but it is useful as a starting point.

Core material

Trinity Sunday is the first Sunday after Pentecost. On this day Christians celebrate their belief that they can know God in different ways:

- Through creation they can get to know God the Father and creator of the world.
- By reading the Bible and praying, people can get to know Jesus. Christians believe that Jesus showed people what God was like by his teaching and how he lived.
- In daily life Christians get to know God through the Holy Spirit, God the real but invisible friend, helper and guide.

Christians believe that God the Father, the Son and the Holy Spirit are all one God. To remember this belief some Christians make the sign of the cross. A member of staff or a pupil could demonstrate making the sign of the cross. Practices vary; Catholic Christians cross from left to right, Orthodox Christians cross from right to left.

The thumb, index finger and middle finger of the right hand are held together as a reminder of the Trinity. The ring finger and little finger are tucked into the palm. The forehead is touched as the believer says 'In the name of the Father'. The breastbone is touched as 'and of the Son' is said. The left shoulder is touched then the right shoulder, as 'and of the Holy Spirit' is said.

Reflection

Christians use images like the shamrock to help them understand difficult ideas, such as the Trinity. What other ideas do you find difficult to understand? What helps you understand them?

Prayer (OPTIONAL)

If appropriate, make the sign of the cross as the Celtic prayer below is said:

'God the Father cherish us.
God the Son cherish us.
God the Holy Spirit cherish us, three all-kindly.' *(From the Carmina Gadelica)*

St Hervé (17 June) and St Rivanon (19 June)

You will need
Enlarged illustrations on jigsaw-shaped pieces of paper (see page 87).

Introduction
Please read the note headed 'Pastoral issues' (page 11). Follow the instructions on page 86 for creating the jigsaw. Ask some pupils to hold up each piece and say what it is and guess what it means. For example, what might the harp stand for?

Core material
As you read the following, ask pupils to select the correct piece of jigsaw and display it, fitting the pieces together one at a time.

1   St Rivanon and St Hervé (pronounced 'Ervay') are mother and son. They are popular saints in Brittany, one of the Celtic lands *(C1, page 25)* but their story starts in England.
2   Hervé's father was a bard (a singer-poet) who fled from England when the Saxons invaded in the sixth century, and went to Brittany. There he met and married Rivanon, who also sang beautifully. Their son, Hervé, was born blind and his father died when he was small.
3   Rivanon was poor and had little to give her son but she taught Hervé to love music and poetry. She also passed on to him her own love of God.
4   Hervé became a monk and a teacher. He did so well that he became head of the monastery. He was such a good teacher that the children used to swarm round him like bees. He did his best to pass on his knowledge of music and poetry and his love of God.

Reflection
Cup your hands as if they are full. Think about the invisible things that we can pass on to others. What we give to others cannot always be seen.

Prayer (OPTIONAL)
Pupils can create prayerful actions to go with this Celtic prayer.

> 'May the road rise to meet you.
> May the wind be always at your back.
> May the sun shine warm upon your face;
> The rains fall soft upon your fields and until we meet again,
> May God hold you in the palm of his hand.' *(Anonymous Celtic blessing)*

St Oswald

(9 August)

You will need
> Enlarged illustrations on jigsaw-shaped pieces of paper (see page 88).
> Images from the Lindisfarne gospels (http://commons.wikimedia.org/wiki/
> Image:LindisfarneFol27rIncipitMatt.jpg).

Introduction
Please read the note headed 'Pastoral issues' (page 11). Follow the instructions on page 86 for creating the jigsaw. Ask some pupils to hold up each piece and say what it is and guess what it means. For example, what might the 700 stand for?

Core material
As you read the following, ask pupils to select the correct piece of jigsaw and display it, fitting the pieces together one at a time.

1 Oswald was a Saxon prince who lived about 700 years after Jesus.
2 Oswald's father was King of Northumbria in northern England. His father was killed in battle and Oswald had to run away for safety, to an island called Iona, which is off the coast of Scotland. There the Celtic monks *(K2, page 82)* looked after him and taught him in their school.
3 Oswald learned about Christianity while he was on Iona and he became a Christian.
4 Many years later, Oswald also became King of Northumbria, like his father. He wanted his people to hear the Christian message, so he invited Celtic Christians from Iona to come to Northumbria. These Christians set up churches and soon Oswald's kingdom (country) became famous for its faith and learning. The Lindisfarne gospels were produced by Christians who lived in Northumbria. These are very beautiful copies of pages from the Bible, telling the story of Jesus. Each page is beautifully decorated with Celtic artwork.

Reflection
Look at an image or images of the Lindisfarne gospels.
The Christian Celts thought that it was important to make the gospels beautiful. Why do you think they did that?

Prayer (OPTIONAL)
If possible, look at an image from the Lindisfarne gospels in high magnification to show the beauty of the work. Pupils can pray silently.

> **'God of beauty, you give people skill to make beautiful things. May they use that skill to your glory.'**

Clowns and holy fools

You will need
> Clown face (see page 94).
> Clown items such as a hat or hooter or other safe noise maker (optional).

Introduction

Show the clown face and ask pupils who might look like this. **Once a year hundreds of clowns, wearing full costume, go to Holy Trinity Church in Dalston, London to take part in a service that thanks God for laughter.**

Core material

Clowns, or 'holy fools', have a long history. In the Middle Ages some kings had a form of clown called a 'jester' to make them laugh. One of these king's jesters, called Rahere, became ill with malaria and he prayed to God that he might get better. Rahere recovered, and he promised that he would build a hospital and church to thank God for his recovery. The hospital, in London, became known as St Bartholomew's and is still there today.

Jesters not only made kings laugh, they were allowed to say things to the king that other people couldn't without getting into trouble. One Russian holy fool, called Basil, dared to tell off the king, Ivan the Terrible, about his violence. That took great courage, as Ivan was not called 'terrible' for nothing! Surprisingly Ivan did not harm Basil; when Basil died, Ivan himself helped to carry the holy fool's coffin at the funeral. Later, a cathedral in the centre of Moscow was named after this brave clown. (Images of St Basil's are available online.)

Modern Christian clowns or holy fools try to tell others about life and faith using clowning. They fall over and they fall off things. Life is like that. We are sometimes foolish or we do wrong things. That is like falling over in life. Clowns also make people laugh by being successful at things, like walking a tightrope or riding a one-wheeled bike. We too have our successes. Christians believe that God is with people through their failures and their successes. Laughter is seen as a gift from God to help us get through life, and clowns celebrate the joy of the Christian life.

> There is a time to cry and a time to laugh. *(Ecclesiastes 3:4)*
> A cheerful heart is like good medicine. *(Proverbs 17:22)*

Reflection

Think about times when you have been sad or unwell. Have others ever cheered you up with laughter? Laughter at the right time and used in the right way can help us feel better.

Prayer (OPTIONAL)

The clown's hooter can be used where there is a *. Don't worry if the pupils laugh.

> Thank you, God, for the gift of laughter.* Thank you for jokes and funny programmes, for fun and giggles.* We give you our laughter as thanks.*

Snakes and ladders

You will need
> Snakes and Ladders board game.
> 24 large Post-it notes.

Introduction

Before the assembly, draw ladders on three Post-it notes, then add to each of these notes a good quality plus an instruction (see Core material for qualities). For example: 'Joy: go forward two squares'. Draw snakes on three more Post-it notes and add to each of these a negative characteristic plus an instruction (see Core material for characteristics).For example, 'Bad temper: go back four places'.

Show the board game. Explain that today we are going to play a version of it.

Core material

Snakes and Ladders used to be a very popular game and it was sometimes used to teach children about right and wrong. The ladders stood for the good qualities, the snakes stood for bad characteristics. Here are some of the things Christians would put on the ladders: love, joy, peace, patience, kindness, goodness, faithfulness, gentleness, self-control *(Galatians 5:22–23).* **Here are some of the things Christians would put on the snakes: jealousy, outbursts of rage, selfishness, hatred, causing trouble** *(Galatians 5:20–21).*

Make a floor version of the game, using the Post-it notes placed in an eight by three rectangle, distributing the snakes and ladders evenly. Leave enough space between the rows to walk along; pupils walk *beside* the notes not on them. Use the dice from the board game to decide moves and use pupils as 'counters'. When a pupil lands beside a snake or a ladder, read out the quality or characteristic, and ask them to make the move on the note. Ask other pupils to suggest an example of behaviour that expresses that quality/characteristic.

Reflection

Draw a large snake on a piece of paper, and invite pupils to suggest other behaviours that they think belong on the snake. Draw a large ladder and repeat this process.

Prayer (OPTIONAL)

Pupils can do appropriate actions as the prayer is said.

> **'Holy Spirit, help us to climb the ladder of goodness, for we cannot climb alone. Stop us sliding into doing wrong.'**

Tiddlywinks

You will need

Tiddlywink counters and a pot.
A large circle of coloured card or paper (optional).

Introduction

Ask pupils to demonstrate how Tiddlywinks is played. Can they get the counters in the pot? Staff can also demonstrate their skill at the game. Point out that the counters do not always go in the direction you want; you aim for the pot but the counters might go off in a different direction.

Core material

In life there might be certain things we want to do, but life does not always go as planned and sometimes we end up going in a different direction. Like the Tiddlywinks counters that go all over the place, the unexpected or the unplanned sometimes happens. Christians believe that God is with them whatever happens. In the Bible it says that God is with people wherever they go:

Lord, you are my safe place; guide me in the way you want me to go. *(Psalm 31:3)*

When you pass through deep waters of difficulty I will be with you.
When you go through times of great troubles they will not overcome you. *(Isaiah 43:2)*

I will be with you always, even to the end of the world. *(Matthew 28:20)*

Reflection

Listen to the sound of the Tiddlywinks as they jump. Sometimes they land in the pot, sometimes they miss. Sometimes things will go according to plan, sometimes they won't; that is part of life. If we expect life always to run smoothly we will soon get upset. Sometimes we learn things through the unexpected. Sometimes the unplanned turns out to be better than what we planned.

Prayer (OPTIONAL)

Flip some Tiddlywinks. Ask pupils to listen to the sound and think about those times when the unexpected happens. Alternatively, write the prayer on the large circle of paper or card (Tiddlywink), read it aloud then display it.

'For the times when life goes well, we thank you, God.
For the times when life goes off plan, be with us.
Help us to learn what we can in the situation, knowing that you are there with us.'

Balloon fun

You will need
> Two balloons of different colours.
> Spare balloons for each class to take away afterwards.

Introduction
Talk with pupils about when they might have balloons. Explain that today we are going to look at how balloons can be used as reminders.

Core material
We are going to explore praise and thanks. See if you can answer the following questions.

- **What is praise?**
- **Whom do we praise?**
- **Who has been praised recently?**
- **What is thanks?**
- **When do we say thank you?**
- **Whom do we thank?**

Encourage staff and pupils to share how they praise and thank others. Write 'Thank you' on one balloon and 'Praise' on the other. After the assembly, take the balloons back to your classroom as a reminder.

Christians praise and thank each other. They also give thanks and praise to God *(see Prayer)*. **They praise God for being great and they thank him for what he has done.**

Reflection
Invite some pupils to form a line at the front. Pat the 'Praise' balloon to the first pupil, who catches it and pats it to the next person in line, while saying something in praise of someone else. For example, 'Mrs Bellamy is really helpful'. At the end of the row the balloon is patted back to a member of staff. Repeat this with a different row of pupils using the 'Thank you' balloon. In this case each pupil pats the balloon to the next person down the row while saying something they are grateful for. It might help to give pupils a few moments' thinking time before you start this activity.

Prayer (OPTIONAL)
Use the same activity as for the Reflection, but ask pupils to say a 'Praise' or a 'Thank you' prayer to God.

> **'I think you are great, God.'**
> **'God, you are clever and wise.'**
> **'God, you are good.'**
> **'Thank you, God, for my friends.'**
> **'Thank you, God, for playtimes.'**
> **'Thanks, God, for food.'**

Jelly babies

You will need
 Jelly babies (preferably free of artificial colours and flavours).
 Running clothes (optional).
 A bottle of water.

Introduction
Demonstrate jogging. Some pupils can do a gentle jog on the spot. Ask pupils what you need when you go running: good shoes, water for if you get thirsty, appropriate clothes. Explain what a marathon is, or ask pupils to explain. If you have any staff or parents who are runners they might share experiences.

Core material
Sometimes people run in races or events that raise money for charity. It is very hard to keep going for a long race like a marathon, which is over 26 miles (42 km). It would be easy to give up. To keep the runners going, friends line the route and shout encouragement. Some people hand the runners jelly babies to give them energy.

Living your life well can sometimes feel as difficult as a long run. It may be tempting to give up trying to do the right thing and just do the easy thing instead. That is when we need to support each other – like the friends who shout encouragement and hand out jelly babies. The Bible says: 'Strengthen those people whose hands and knees shake with tiredness. Encourage those who feel like giving up.' *(Isaiah 35:3)*

Reflection
Show the jelly babies and ask pupils to think of people who encourage them to live their lives well. Who stops them giving up? How could they encourage others?

Prayer (OPTIONAL)
Pupils can say the following prayer while walking on the spot:

 'As we travel through life, help us to encourage each other to keep going, to keep living well, to keep putting faith into action in daily life.'

If appropriate, when they are back in class pupils can have a jelly baby to remind them to encourage others. (Provide an alternative for diabetics and others who can't eat sweets.)

The caim

You will need
> A large box with a lid, such as an archive box.
> A small soft toy.
> Celtic music (http://allsaintsbrookline.org/celtic/celt_music.html).

Introduction
Demonstrate 'place' by using the soft toy. Place the box on the table and ask a pupil to position the soft toy in the right place as you say each of the following:

Beside	**Above**
Before (in front)	**Beneath**
Within (inside)	**To the right**
Behind	**To the left**

Core material
Long before the time of Jesus, the Celts were people who lived all over Europe. Slowly the amount of land that they held was reduced and by the time of Jesus they lived largely in northern France, England, Wales, Scotland and Ireland. Some people who live in these areas today are descended from the Celts.

The Celts became Christians. They were especially aware of God's presence; they felt that God was all around them. Refer to the introductory activity. **Celtic Christians believed that God was with them wherever they went. He was in front and behind them, he was to the right and to the left. They believed that God was everywhere and they were never alone.**

They sometimes drew a circle around themselves as a way of remembering that God was all around. Hold out your right arm and forefinger and turn in a circle clockwise. **This circle was called the caim. It was not magic; it was a reminder for Celtic Christians that they could never move out of the circle of God's love. It also reminded them of these words from the Bible:**

> **Nothing can separate us from the love of God.** *(Romans 8:38)*

> **If I go to the highest heaven you are there. If I go to the darkest depths, you are there.**
> **If I go east or west you are there and you hold my hand.** *(Psalm 139:8–10)*

Reflection
Pupils can think about what they have heard, while they listen to some Celtic music.

Prayer (OPTIONAL)
Ask pupils to draw a circle on the palm of one hand with the forefinger of the other hand, while part of the prayer of St Patrick is said (see page 89). Introduce the caim prayer (see page 89); pupils can suggest their own caim prayers.

Creativity

You will need
> Examples of pupil art, music and poetry.
> Examples of a Celtic knot (see page 90).
> Celtic music (http://allsaintsbrookline.org/celtic/celt_music.html).
> Some musical instruments: recorders and glockenspiel (optional).
> The music of Pachelbel's *Canon* (see page 90).

Introduction

Pupils can share their art, music and poetry. Explain that Celtic Christians were good at art, music and poetry and expressed their faith this way.

Core material

Pupils can trace their finger round an enlarged version of a Celtic knot (or go to http://commons.wikimedia.org/wiki/Image:Celtic-knot-basic-linear.svg).

The Celtic knot never ends; it goes round and round, and is a reminder of the never-ending love of God. The Celts loved music; they probably played pipes, harp and drum. They also had a great love of nature and nature occurs a lot in their poems and songs. Listen to this prayer, which is also a poem and a song. What parts of nature can you hear? In this poem the writer is wishing the peace of Jesus and God's creation to others.

> **Deep peace of the soft white dove to you;**
> **Deep peace of the pure green grass to you;**
> **Deep peace of the pure blue sky to you;**
> **Deep peace of the pure brown earth to you;**
> **Deep peace of the pure white moon to you;**
> **Deep peace of the Son of Peace to you.**

> (adapted from *The Dominion of Dreams: Under a dark star*
> by Fiona Macleod, nineteenth-century Celtic)

Christians read Jesus' words about peace in the Bible.

> **Jesus said: 'My peace I leave with you'.** *(John 14:27)*

> **The peace of God, which is beyond understanding, keep your hearts and minds safe in Jesus.** *(Philippians 4:7)*

Reflection

Listen quietly as the poem is read again while either some quiet Celtic music is played, or pupils can play Pachelbel's *Canon* (see page 90).

Prayer (OPTIONAL)

Pupils can add their own lines to the Celtic prayer-poem. The poem can be sung as a prayer to the tune of Pachelbel's *Canon*, omitting the word 'Deep' in each line.

The five-stringed harp

You will need

A stringed instrument.

Items for the five senses (see the Introduction below).

Five picture labels, one for each of the five senses (see page 92).

Introduction

Show the stringed instrument and invite pupils to pluck the strings to hear the different sounds. Ask pupils to name the five senses and match the items to the picture labels. Make sure that no one is allergic to the food items.

➢ Orange (smell)
➢ Picture (sight)
➢ Chocolate (taste)
➢ Rosary, or soft fabric (touch)
➢ Musical instrument (sound)

Core material

Celtic Christians thought of the person as a five-stringed instrument. We have five senses: taste, touch, sight, hearing and smell. And Celtic Christians thought of worship as 'tuning the five-stringed harp'. Christians can worship using all their senses.

Sight – pictures, flowers, stained glass.
Hearing – music and singing.
Touch – an action such as kneeling, using a rosary or making the sign of the cross *(A3, page 17)*.
Taste – taking a small piece of bread and sip of wine at communion.
Smell – sweet-smelling incense is sometimes used in worship.

Reflection

What helps you to reflect? Do you like having a candle lit or music playing?

Prayer (OPTIONAL)

Look at the picture:
'Father, we thank you for a beautiful world; may we never take sight for granted.'
Touch your fingertips together:
'When our fingers touch things we remember those who comfort us when we are upset.'
Think of a favourite smell:
'As we recall our favourite smells, we thank you for a world of interesting smells.'
Pluck the strings of the musical instrument:
'Father, we are glad that we live in a world of sound and we pray for those who cannot hear.'
Think of your favourite foods:
'As we think of our favourite foods we remember those who have little food to eat.'

A prayer basket

You will need
> A basket lined with a serviette or cloth.
> Ribbons.

Introduction
Ask a few pupils to describe and role-play a day: getting up, having a wash, eating breakfast, going to school, playing with friends, watching TV, etc.

Core material
Celtic Christians saw all of life as belonging to God. They thought that God was interested in all of life. Celtic Christians would pray when reading the Bible and when milking the cow. They would pray when washing and when lighting the fire. They had prayers for all occasions and all parts of the day: prayers for getting up, prayers for going to bed, prayers for getting dressed and prayers for going on journeys. They made up blessings and prayers for every part of their day. Here are some Celtic prayers (drawing on the *Carmina Gadelica*, a nineteenth-century collection of Celtic prayers and poems):

> **A prayer for lighting the fire**
>
> **I will light my fire this morning in the presence of God and all his angels.**
> **O God, light a flame of love in my heart for my neighbour and my enemy.**

> **A prayer on getting up**
>
> **I come before God at the start of the day.**
> **I bring all I am and all I have done and seen,**
> **And ask the kindly Three to shelter me;**
> **From the crown of my head, to the soles of my feet.**

If the early Celtic Christians had possessed computers, they would have had a prayer for turning on the computer. Ask pupils to suggest activities during the day and make up prayers for them. Write the prayers on coloured paper, then roll them up, tie with ribbon and place them in the prayer basket. For example, they could make up prayers for playing and prayers for washing, prayers for going to school. Label the outside of each prayer scroll. Some ready-made prayers can be found on page 89.

Reflection
Think through your own day. What is your favourite part? Do you have a part of the day when you stop and think?

Prayer (OPTIONAL)
Pupils can choose a prayer to read out.

The boat

You will need
>   A toy boat, or a small, clean margarine tub.
>   A bowl of water.

Introduction

Ask pupils about their experiences of being in boats. Has anyone ever been in a boat when the water was rough?

Core material

The Celts were good at handling boats. For going short distances, they used a coracle, which is a little, light, round-bottomed rowing boat. (www.coracle-fishing.net/society/index.htm) They also had bigger boats for greater distances. Sometimes the Celtic Christians would sail to a new country to share the Christian message, but would not plan where they would land. They sometimes let their boat drift on the water, and where it landed was the place where they started sharing their faith. Before they started out on any sea journey, Celtic Christians would say prayers. This is a practice that continued among Celts.

> Lord of sky and water, carry us over the surface of the sea.
> Bless our boatmen and our boat,
> Bless our anchors and our oars.
> Be our compass and our chart, be your hand on the rudder,
> So that we may return home in peace.
>
> *(adapted from the Carmina Gadelica)*

Celts thought that life was like a sea journey: it could get stormy when troubles came, but they believed that God was with them. Today we sometimes feel that life is difficult, it just gets too much for us, and this feeling is sometimes called being 'all at sea'. Some people pray when they feel 'all at sea'.

Reflection

The Celts thought about life as a sea journey. How would you describe life?

Prayer (OPTIONAL)

This is a Breton (Celtic France) fisherman's prayer for when life gets stormy:

> 'Dear God, be good to me: the sea is so wide and my boat is so small.'

Write the prayer on a piece of paper and place it in the boat. Put the boat in the water. Swirl the water.

At other times life is like a calm sea. Then Christians pray a different type of prayer:

> 'Thank you, God, for your peace that spreads deep inside, making me quiet within, at rest in you.'

Write this prayer on a piece of paper and place it in the boat. Still the water.

Tearfund assemblies (Teacher information)

The following ten assemblies are based on information supplied by Tearfund and the author would like to express her thanks to Tearfund for this material. Tearfund is a leading relief and development agency working with a global network of local churches to overcome poverty and offer whole-life transformation.

Each assembly deals with an issue that is part of Tearfund's work, either a particular campaign or a section of their website, details of which teachers can find on page 91. The campaigns may change but the issues are likely to be ongoing, and relevant material should continue to be available on the Tearfund website and the websites of other aid agencies (see below). Tearfund and other aid agencies supply packs (many of them free) complete with children's material, visuals, posters, etc. The work of other agencies on the relevant issues can be incorporated into the assemblies.

A schools pack containing material useful for the following assemblies can be downloaded free from the Tearfund website: http://youth.tearfund.org/webdocs/website/youth/schoolspack.pdf

Web addresses of other aid agencies:

CAFOD www.cafod.org.uk
Christian Aid www.christian-aid.org.uk
Oxfam www.oxfam.org.uk
Action Aid www.actionaid.org.uk
Unicef www.unicef.org.uk

Important note
It is easy for children to feel overwhelmed by information about disasters and disease and to feel that they or their family are threatened, or to think that nothing can be done. It is important to reassure children and to deliver these assemblies in a positive way, emphasising that we can change things. If you have very young pupils in the assembly, choose material that will not worry them. Some assemblies, such as the one on child-parents, may be better done with older pupils.

The bin twins

You will need
  Brown paper.
  A heart-shaped piece of paper.
  Safe, clean items of 'rubbish' in a bag:

- Newspaper
- Card
- China plate
- Recyclable plastic bottle
- Polystyrene cup

- Aluminium can
- Piece of fabric
- Tin foil
- Stuffed toy
- Glass bottle

Introduction
Two pupils can dress as bins using the brown paper. Attach labels to them: 'Rubbish bin' and 'Recycle bin'. Explain that they are twins, but are always arguing over the rubbish – the 'bins' can demonstrate this. Pull the items of rubbish out of the bag one at a time and ask pupils to decide which item goes in which bin. (Polystyrene, stuffed toys and china can't be recycled.)

Core material
In Britain seven out of ten items in our bins could be recycled, but we only actually recycle about two out of ten. If rubbish isn't recycled it has be stored, and stored rubbish gives off a gas that contributes to climate change. Sometimes we don't recycle because we feel that the problem is so big that we cannot make a difference or change things, and we lose heart and give up trying. Yet we can do something about climate change and recycling is one thing that helps. All the small actions add up.

Christians read these words in the Bible: 'Let us not get tired and give up doing good, for we shall see the results of what we do if we do not lose heart.' *(Galatians 6:9–10)*

We can encourage each other so that we don't 'lose heart' (give up). Christians remind themselves that God notices the small actions, and this helps to encourage them. Tearfund works alongside small local groups of Christians to try to tackle climate change and to help people affected by it. They help with recycling projects, conserving water, building dykes, and adapting farming so that people whose lives are trapped by poverty can break free. (For more information see page 91.)

Reflection
Write 'Don't lose heart' on the heart and display it for pupils to think about.

Prayer (OPTIONAL)
Read out this prayer then write it on the heart.

  'Father, help us to encourage each other so that we do not lose heart.'

Two degrees

You will need

Different ways of measuring and a variety of things to measure (see Introduction below).

An ice cube.

Introduction

Ask pupils to demonstrate how they measure the items.

➤ The length of a piece of string (centimetres).
➤ The weight of an apple (grams).
➤ A cup of water (millilitres).
➤ How warm a room is (degrees).

Core material

Scientists use special instruments to measure the temperature of the world in degrees Celsius. Some parts of the world are very hot (over 40°C); other parts are very cold (below zero), and these parts are covered in ice. Generally our world is getting warmer. If the world gets too warm, some of the ice melts, and then the seas rise and flat countries get flooded. Show the ice cube and leave it out to melt. If the world gets too warm, some other places will get so dry that food will be difficult to grow. Just a 2°C rise could harm our planet. But this does not have to happen. We can change the future. (Reassure pupils.) We can help to stop it by simple actions:

• Switch off lights when they are not in use.
• Shut the fridge door – leaving it open wastes energy.
• Walk, when it is safe to do so, rather than go by car.

The Bible describes Christians as being like a body, with each part needing all the others: the foot needs the hand and the eye needs the ear *(1 Corinthians 12:12–20)*. In a similar way the peoples of the world need each other. It is not a case of some countries saying, 'We are all right. We will not be flooded because we are not flat.' We all need to work together to change things. Tearfund works with everyone from small groups of local Christians to governments to change life for some of the world's poorest communities/people, including countries such as Bangladesh, which will be affected by a rise in sea levels. (For more information see page 91.)

Reflection

As you watch the ice cube melt, think about what you can do. It does make a difference.

Prayer (OPTIONAL)

'Father, as the ice cube melts we remember those who will be most affected by global warming. Help us, by our small actions, to play our part in preventing this.'

Veggies

You will need
>   Food to represent different meals (see Core material).
>   Some washed potatoes.
>   A plate.
>   Birthday candles and holders, and matches (teacher only).
>   A tray of damp play sand.

Introduction
One or two pupils can dress up as 'veggie police' (just wear labels) and 'arrest' a few members of staff and question them about how much fruit and vegetables they eat. Explain that today's assembly is about fruit and vegetables.

Core material
Ask a few pupils to sort the food into breakfast, lunch and dinner items, and label each one. Now replace all the food with potatoes. **What would it be like to eat potatoes for breakfast, lunch and dinner? In parts of Bolivia that is exactly what happens. As a result of not having a balanced diet, many of the children are not healthy and do not grow properly. Children (and adults) need the vitamins in fruit and vegetables, but because much of Bolivia is made up of high mountains and the weather is cold, it is difficult to grow them. The answer is simple: greenhouses, which the people can build themselves. The greenhouses keep the plants warm and so fruit and vegetables can grow to improve people's health.**

The people learn from advice given by other local people: a doctor, a cook, a pastor and a gardener. In the Bible it says that God gives people different gifts and those gifts are for serving others *(1 Corinthians 12:4–5).* **In this project different people share their gifts. The gardener shares his knowledge of how plants grow. The cook shows people how to cook the vegetables. The pastor works with people to create better relationships. The doctor helps people to be healthy. People across the UK give money to Tearfund – a Christian charity which supports the gardener, the cook, the doctor and the pastor. There are thousands of people around the world who Tearfund helps like this, offering the chance for life to be changed for the better.** (For more information see page 91.)

Reflection
Stand the plate on the tray of damp play sand. A few pupils can place the potatoes on the plate. Place a candle in each potato. As the candles are lit, ask pupils to think about using their gifts to serve others.

Prayer (OPTIONAL)
As the candles are lit, the following prayer can be said:

> **'Father, we thank you for the people of Bolivia, who share their gifts and use them to help each other. Help us to share our gifts with others.'**

Borrowing and lending

You will need
> Some money (coins).
> Some possessions to seize (see Introduction below).
> Coin-shaped pieces of paper (optional).

Introduction

Role-play borrowing and lending money charging high rates of interest. Borrowers explain that they need money to feed their family. One person might borrow £1, then is charged £1.50 when they return to pay it back. If they can't pay the interest you seize some of their goods (e.g. pencil case, coat). Explain that the money lent is called a 'loan'. (For more information see page 91. For a picture of Saleha go to www.rmep.co.uk/summer)

Core material

In many of the poorer countries of the world people have to borrow to survive. It is not something they choose to do. Saleha is one of these people, and she lives in Bangladesh. In Bangladesh many people do not own enough land to grow all the food they need to feed their families. Saleha and her husband have enough land to feed their family for only half of the year. This sometimes means that people like Saleha have to borrow money. Some money-lenders charge high rates of interest, which means that they ask for much more money back than was originally borrowed. If the person cannot pay the extra, the money-lender may take their land in place of money.

A project called 'Heed Bangladesh' (supported by the Christian charity Tearfund) lends people money at a low rate of interest. People like Saleha who want to start their own business either save small amounts of money each month with Heed Bangladesh until they have enough, or Heed lends them the money they need. Saleha borrowed some money to buy hens, and sells the eggs at the local market. She paid back the loan, and now Saleha uses the money she makes to feed her family and send her children to school.

In the Bible Christians read that God cares about borrowing and lending as well as about whether people are able to live free from poverty: 'It is good to be generous and fair when you lend.' *(Psalm 112:5)*

Reflection

Hold up the coins and let them drop. As they hear the sound ask pupils to think about lending money at a fair rate and the difference that can make.

Prayer (OPTIONAL)

Add pupil prayers to coin-shaped pieces of paper. Include the two prayers below, by Bangladeshi women.

> 'These loans are a gift from God; pray that we use them properly.' *(Florence)*
> 'Pray that our children will have an education and a good life.' *(Sheuly)*

Let's talk toilets

You will need
  Toilet signs.

Introduction
Show the toilet signs and ask pupils where they would expect to see them. Make a list with pupils of where you find toilets. Stand three pupils in a line. **How many out of every three children in the world do not have access to toilets? The answer is one in every three.**

We find toilets at home, in shops and restaurants, in schools and at stations. We take them for granted. Lack of toilets can lead to disease, as waste left lying around spreads germs. Toilets, like those at school, are expensive and many people in the world are not able to afford them.

Core material
Tearfund works with local churches, groups and individuals so that local people can solve this problem themselves. This is what happens:

- It starts with a walk round the village to meet people and talk about the problem and see what is already happening.
- The local community meet together to discuss the issue and to decide what they want to do.
- People design their own toilets using the materials they have locally: bamboo, wood, jute.
- People who already have toilets, or can afford to build them, help those who don't have toilets or give them the materials to build their own.

Many people would be surprised to find that toilets are mentioned in the Bible, but in Deuteronomy 23:12–13 there are instructions on going to the toilet so that the people stay healthy. Christians believe that God cares about all aspects of life, and that includes toilets. Christians thank God for toilets. (For more information see page 91.)

Reflection
Show the toilet signs. **Toilets are so much part of our life that we take them for granted. But in many parts of the world they are a luxury.**

Prayer (OPTIONAL)

'Thank you, God, for toilets, and for all the normal everyday things that we do not notice. We pray for people who work across the world to bring clean toilets to those who cannot afford them. Encourage them in their work as they bring health to whole communities.'

Water

You will need

A means of measuring 500 metres.
A small, clean beach bucket of water and a
cloth for spills.
Some kilogram weights.

Introduction

Ask pupils to list the different things they use water for:

- Washing
- Cleaning teeth
- Cooking

- Watering plants
- Washing clothes
- Washing up

Imagine that you have to walk to fetch all the water that you use in your home and carry it back. Just a small bucket weighs quite a lot. In some countries people carry as much as 25kg of water at a time. Imagine carrying enough for a bath! Pupils can handle a weight to feel what 1kg feels like. Ask several pupils to try carrying the bucket of water a short distance without spilling any. Wipe any spills up immediately.

Core material

Christine lives in Uganda; she is a mum with six children. Christine has to walk for two hours each day to get water. Across the world there are many people like Christine. It is often women who do this heavy work, and girls too, who have to miss school to do it. Tearfund works with local organisations who try to bring water supplies close to where people live. Their aim is to have safe (drinking) water within 500 metres of people's homes in the areas where Tearfund partners are working. Safe water nearby means people can have enough to drink, wash properly, and water their plants so that food can grow. As a result, people's health improves.

In the Bible water is seen as a gift of God *(Deuteronomy 8:7)* and something that is precious. Jesus said that giving a child a cup of water is a deed that would be rewarded by God *(Mark 9:41)*. Giving someone a drink of water was an important act of kindness where Jesus lived as it was (and still is) a hot country. (For more information see page 91. For a picture of Christine go to www.rmep.co.uk/summer)

Reflection

Measure between 100 and 500 metres in the playground if it is fine, and take the pupils on a silent walk (whatever distance is appropriate for their age). Ask them to imagine doing this with a bucket of water for 500 metres. Many people walk much further than this. If it is cold or wet, work out how many times round the hall 500 metres would be and ask pupils to reflect on carrying water that distance.

Prayer (OPTIONAL)

Silent prayers can be said on the walk as above.

Be an angel

You will need
> An angel costume (optional).
> A tinsel halo, tissue wings.
> A strip of gold or silver paper.
> £5 in change (optional).

Introduction

Talk with the pupils about the part of the angel in a nativity play. If possible dress someone up in an angel costume.

Core material

Many of us have images of angels in our minds. In the Bible angels are special beings, who come with messages from God. They often look just like everyone else. The word 'angel' just means 'messenger'. Angels are also described as helpers *(Hebrews 1:14)* **who help people in difficult times. Ordinary people can be 'angels', bringing messages of hope and comfort to people who are in need. There are lots of ways of sending important messages out to other people. For example, Tearfund supporters pray, they give money and they spend time talking to people telling them about the problems of poverty around the world.**

Ask the pupils for suggestions about how they could 'be an angel' around school. Ask them for ways in which people could be rewarded for 'being an angel', such as little halo badges. You need ideas that will appeal to boys and girls.

If appropriate, use some of the ideas from the Tearfund or other aid agency websites for raising money or raising awareness (see pages 30 and 91). See page 92 for what can be done with different amounts of money up to £5. Pupils can enact the different parts holding the appropriate amount of money.

Reflection

Pass a halo along a line of three pupils as the reflection is read.

Pupil 1: **Be an angel: bring someone a message of hope, comfort, and love. Say something good to someone else.**

Pupil 2: **Be an angel: help someone out. Give them a helping hand in difficult times.**

Pupil 3: **Be an angel: an everyday angel, An angel who wears trainers, an angel who dances, plays football. Be an angel today.**

Prayer (OPTIONAL)

Write the following prayer on a strip of paper and display as a halo.

> **'Lord, thank you for all those who have "been an angel" to us; help us to "be an angel" for others.'**

TB and Mr Medicine

You will need

Some balloons (and pumps if possible).

A 'stick' made from rolled-up paper with dots on to look like tablets.

Two paper bag puppets.

Introduction

Blow up the balloons, some with more air in than others. Do not tie them; give them to pupils to hold. Some balloons should be only half full of air. Stand the pupils holding the balloons in a row and ask them, on a given signal, to let them go (away from the pupils). Which balloon went furthest? Explain that the more air in the balloon, the further the balloon goes. Air gives the balloon energy. **Today's assembly is about an illness called TB, which affects people's lungs so they don't work properly. Our lungs are a little like balloons, they fill with air as we breathe. If the lungs can't get enough air people feel ill and tired.** As before, reassure pupils. TB is not a problem in this country and is curable.

Core material

The following can be performed by pupils using paper bag puppets.

TB: **My name is TB. I am a killer germ. I get into people's airways and make them poorly. I work in poor countries and make lots of people ill.** *(Boo, hiss)*

MM: **I'm Mr Medicine. I have the medicine on my stick** (tablets) **that will stop that nasty TB. My medicine is powerful. I can stop TB completely.** *(Cheer)*

TB: **That silly Mr Medicine won't stop me. Lots of people can't afford to buy his medicine.** *(Boo)*

MM: **Not so fast, TB. People around the world give money so that other people can afford to buy my medicine. Then local people use motorbikes to take the medicine where it is needed.** *(Cheer)*

They chase each other until MM knocks TB out with his medicine stick. (For more information see page 91.)

Christians believe that they should follow Jesus' example of caring for those who are ill. This is why Tearfund provides medicine for those who need it and also works to help people stay healthy and avoid dangerous diseases like TB. Jesus healed the sick and comforted the sad, telling his followers to do the same. People with TB are sick and often sad, but they don't have to be. It is a disease that can be easily cured.

Reflection

Blow up a balloon and slowly release the air. As the balloon deflates, ask pupils to think about what they have heard, or to listen to the prayer below.

Prayer (OPTIONAL)

'Father, we thank you for the local people around the world who are tackling TB. We pray for them; for strength and support as they seek to wipe out this disease.'

Lost childhood

You will need
> Some children's toys and games.
> A rucksack.
> Post-it notes (optional).

Introduction

Ask some pupils to demonstrate the toys and games and to talk about what they like to play. Interview some staff about what they played as a child. You can ask them to bring in toys that they still have or to demonstrate playground games they used to play.

(*Note:* This assembly involves talking about the death of parents. Please read the note headed 'Pastoral issues' (page 11). The children referred to in this assembly lost their parents through HIV/AIDS, but this is not mentioned specifically as it is too sensitive an issue for the age group. Do reassure pupils, as some children worry.)

Core material

Childhood is a time for learning and playing, but not for some children like Rachel in Uganda. For Rachel childhood is a time of hard work and worry. Rachel's parents died when she was eight and since then she has been looking after the six younger children in her family. At the age of thirteen Rachel is both mum and dad and instead of going to school and playing, she cooks, cleans and grows food for the family. Tearfund helps local churches to support children like Rachel, providing her with medicine, training, and money for education. People from the local churches help share Rachel's load, for Rachel is carrying a load of work and worry that is far too much for her.

In the Bible it talks about 'bearing one another's burdens' or loads *(Galatians 6:2)*. This does not mean literally helping to carry a rucksack or a load of some other sort – though it may mean that on some occasions. It means sharing some of the work and worry that other people have. (For more information see page 91).

Reflection

Using the rucksack as a focus, ask pupils to think about 'bearing one another's burdens'. The burdens are the work and worries other people have; sometimes just a small action can help.

Prayer (OPTIONAL)

Write prayers by the pupils on Post-it notes and stick them to the rucksack.

> 'Father, we remember Rachel and all children who have lost their childhood. Thank you for all who share their burdens. Help us to share each other's burdens.'

Trade injustice

You will need

Items for some unfair games (see
Introduction below).
A basket of cotton wool (or mostly
newspaper with cotton wool on top).
A good T-shirt and a clean, old T-shirt.

Introduction

Play some games that are unfair with the pupils. For example, hold a walking race
with one person having to start further back. Organise an egg and spoon race using
Duplo bricks instead of eggs, with some people being allowed to hold their eggs
while others are not.

Core material

Sometimes we get upset when games are not fair. We have a feeling deep inside of
us that things ought to be fair. Trade is sometimes unfair. Trade is when one person or
country sells things to another person or country. For example, Malawi sells the cotton
that it grows to other countries who make it into T-shirts. If trade was fair, the people
of Malawi would get a good price for their cotton, and they would not be always
poor. The people who grow the cotton often get paid very little, while most of the
money is made by the factories and shops. People can help themselves by trade, but
unfortunately trade is not always fair.

Demonstrate unfair trade with a group of pupils, the cotton wool and the good T-
shirt. The cotton farmer sells a basket of raw cotton for 37p to a factory owner in
Europe who makes it into a T-shirt. The factory owner might sell the T-shirt to a
shop for £5. The shop might sell it to the customer for £10.

Organisations like Tearfund work to make the rules of trade fairer, so that countries
like Malawi can get a good price for their cotton. Christians believe that God is fair
and just and is concerned about fairness and justice in the world. In the Bible it says:
'Let justice flow like a river that never runs dry' *(Amos 5:24).* Christians believe
that they have a part to play in making the world a fairer, better place. (For more
information see page 91.)

Reflection

Cut the care label out of the old T-shirt and read it out. What sort of care label could
we write for the people who made it?

Prayer (OPTIONAL)

Write pupil prayer suggestions on the old T-shirt, or use the prayer below.

> 'God of justice, help us to make our world a fairer place. Give the poorer nations
> the chance to trade fairly so that they can help themselves. Help us to make others
> aware of this.'

You will need
 A Fulham strip or appropriate images (www.fulhamfc.com).
 A football.
 Photocopy the numbered points below (see Core material) and tape them to
 the football.

Introduction
Show the Fulham football strip (a pupil can wear it). Does anyone know which
football club it is? Ask pupils how they think a football club might start.

Core material
Arrange four pupils in a line with space in between them. The football can be
gently kicked to each one in turn. The pupil stops it, picks it up and reads one of
the numbered pieces of information about the founding of Fulham football club.
Introduce this activity by saying:

**Not many people know that some football clubs were started by churches (though most
no longer have church connections). About one in three of the Premier league clubs
were once church clubs and in the next few assemblies we will find out about some of
them. Fulham is one example; at least eight clergymen were involved in the early days
of Fulham (1879–1898), and we are going to find out a little about four of them.** (Note
that Christian origins do not imply that the modern club has a religious affiliation.)

1 **My name is John Cardwell, and I am the vicar of St Andrew's, Fulham. Like many
 other parts of London, the area around my church is very poor and young people
 have little to do. I started a football club with help from people in the church. I am
 president of the football club. We decided to call our team 'St Andrew's', but later
 the name was changed to 'Fulham'.**
2 **I'm Peregrine Propert, a young vicar at nearby St Augustine's. I play cricket and
 football. I got involved with the football club at St Andrew's and sometimes play for
 the team. I set up a gym for local lads and encouraged boxing. I think it helped that I
 am a champion rower and a record-breaking swimmer and I like rock-climbing as well.**
3 **I am the Reverend Gilbert Hall. I play for the team sometimes. I have won awards
 for football.**
4 **I am the Reverend William Muriel. I became president of the club after John Cardwell.**

Reflection
Think about your ideas of what a vicar does. Does it include being involved in
starting a football club?

Prayer (OPTIONAL)
Read out the following prayer, then attach it to the football and display it.

 **'Almighty God, we thank you for football. Today we remember those people who
 started the clubs so that people could have fun and friendship.'**

Tottenham Hotspur

You will need
> A Spurs strip or appropriate images (www.tottenhamhotspur.com).
> A football.
> A red card and a yellow card.

Introduction
Show the Spurs football strip (a pupil can wear it). Does anyone know which football club it is? Demonstrate forms of bad play in football (appropriate for assembly) that get a yellow or red card. Make sure these are done safely. You may need to put mats down.

Core material
In 1882 a group of teenagers got together to form a football club. They called it 'Hotspur'. They played on some open land, where before each match they had to carefully mark out the pitch. That was when the trouble started. Bigger lads also wanted to play football in the area, and when they found a pitch all marked out by the Hotspur players, they just pushed the Hotspur lads off the pitch and used it themselves. The boys were worried that they would have nowhere to play, then they thought of someone who might help them. Most of the boys went to a Bible class at All Hallows' Church run by John Ripsher. They went to him for advice, and John helped them to start a proper club and get it organised. He helped them find a ground to play on, with somewhere to change, and he became the president, often supplying equipment when it was needed. Sometimes a team would be able to afford only one ball for the whole season. If the ball burst or was lost the games had to stop. The players were no angels but John Ripsher continued to stand by the team. Under him the club not only gained a reputation as a good team, it also got a name for playing fairly. Fifty years after it was formed the club still had this reputation. Sometimes players behaved badly, but they would not wait to be sent off by the referee; they would discipline themselves and leave the field. If a player did behave badly on the pitch he was called before the board and told that there was no place for him on the team.

In the Bible it says: 'We do not have anything to do with deceitful or dishonest ways … that way others will be sure we can be trusted.' *(2 Corinthians 4:2)*

(Note that Christian origins do not imply that the modern club has a religious affiliation.)

Reflection
Ask pupils to think about sports personalities who behave well in their sport.

Prayer (OPTIONAL)
Hold up the red card and ask pupils to think about times when they have found it difficult to play fairly. The prayer can be written on the red card and displayed.

> 'Lord of all truth, help us to behave well in sport and be honest and fair in the way we play.'

Southampton

You will need
> A Southampton strip or appropriate images (www.saintsfc.co.uk).
> A football.

Introduction

Show the Southampton football strip (a pupil can wear it). Does anyone know which football club it is? **Since 2001 Southampton football club have played in a new stadium, which bears the name of a church, St Mary's. At the opening of the stadium, the rector (vicar) of St Mary's gave a blessing before the first match. The man who started the Southampton football club over a hundred years ago was also the rector of St Mary's. He came from a family who were famous for changing things.** Ask pupils to suggest things that we can change easily (clothes, hairstyle, etc.). Explain that today's story is about a difficult change.

Core material

Basil Wilberforce, rector of St Mary's, was the grandson of a very famous man, William Wilberforce, who led the movement to stop the slave trade. Basil Wilberforce went to work in one of the worst places in Southampton. The people who lived in the area around the church of St Mary's were very poor, didn't have much education and were often hungry. Wilberforce did what he could to change things.

- **He opened three kitchens that offered free food.**
- **He started clubs for men and women.**
- **He ran a Sunday school that taught reading.**
- **He taught a night school.**

Basil was the president of the church football club, which had started just before he came to work at the church. Other people in the church were involved, too: one curate (vicar-in-training) helped to organise the club and another played for the team. Over a hundred years later, in 2001, Southampton remembered how the team got started by naming its new ground after the church. The team are appropriately called 'the saints'. Basil Wilberforce saw that there were things that could be changed and decided to change them. Football was part of that movement for change, giving people a healthy activity.

Many Christians pray for courage to change the things they can. They pray for the ability to accept what cannot be changed. *(Based on a prayer by Reinhold Niebuhr.)*

(Note that Christian origins do not imply that the modern club has a religious affiliation.)

Reflection

Think about something that can't be changed. Think about something that can be changed. It is better to focus on things that can be changed.

Prayer (OPTIONAL)

Use the prayer above. Write it on a Post-it note and display it on the football.

Manchester City

You will need
> A Manchester City football strip or appropriate images (www.mcfc.co.uk).
> A football.

Introduction
Show the Manchester City football strip (a pupil can wear it). Does anyone know which football club it is? Explain that Manchester has two leading football teams. Demonstrate not giving up by jogging gently around the hall while saying how determined you are to keep going. Speak your thoughts out loud about not wanting to give up.

Core material
Manchester City, like many clubs, started life as a church club, but it is unusual because it owes its existence to a woman. Anna Connell was a vicar's daughter; her father was the vicar of St Mark's, West Gorton, Manchester. At the time she lived, in the 1850s, West Gorton was an area where many factories were being built. Thousands of people were coming to Manchester from the countryside around to work in the factories. They lived in very crowded housing; sometimes there were only two toilets for 250 people. Young men sometimes fought in the streets and many people were hurt. Anna was determined to do something. She had already started activities for women, but now she felt it was time the men had something to do besides drinking and fighting. Anna started a working men's club. Although only three men came to the first meeting, she did not give up, and with the help of some men from the church she got the club going. Football was one of the club's activities. The St Mark's team played on waste land until they got a proper ground. In 1894 the name of the team became Manchester City and they went on to great success.

It would have been easy for Anna to give up when she saw so much poverty and need, but she carried on even when she had little support. Anna would have read these words in her Bible: 'We are surrounded by so many good examples, let us rid ourselves of everything that slows us down, and press on with determination so that we can run the race of life. We need to keep our eyes on Jesus ... who did not give up.' *(Hebrews 12:1–2)*

(Note that Christian origins do not imply that the modern club has a religious affiliation.)

Reflection
Think of times when you have felt like giving up. What kept you going?

Prayer (OPTIONAL)
Pupils can say the response below (in italics). The prayer can be written and placed on a football and displayed.

> 'Father, when we feel tired, *help us to keep going.*
> When we feel fed up, *help us to keep going.*
> When nothing seems to work, *help us to keep going if what we are doing is right.'*

Everton and Liverpool

You will need

Liverpool and Everton strips or appropriate images (www.liverpoolfc.tv and www.evertonfc.com).
A football.

Introduction

Show the two football strips (pupils can wear them). Whose strips are these? Ask pupils where they go if they want a game of football. Explain that these two clubs are rivals and that rivalry goes back a long way. The rivalry can be role-played.

Core material

Ben Chambers was the minister at St Domingo's Methodist Chapel in 1877. He was concerned about the boys in his church as there was nothing much for them to do. He started cricket and football teams and they played in the local park. After a while the team changed its name from St Domingo's to Everton and some time later they decided to get a strip. It was a while, though, before the famous blue and white was decided upon. John Houlding – a wealthy local businessman – became their first president and he found them a football ground at Anfield where they were a great success. John had plans for the club but some of the Everton players and members of St Domingo's were not happy with these plans. The two sides could not agree. John Houlding then decided to start his own team, just called 'Liverpool'. Everton was forced to move from Anfield, and there was a lot of bad feeling on both sides.

A member of the chapel found a new site for Everton called Goodison Park and for the next 50 years St Domingo's played a large part in the development of Everton football club. In 1902 John Houlding died. As an act of forgiveness and reconciliation between the two teams, his coffin was carried by three Everton players and three Liverpool players. The flags at both clubs flew at half-mast.

Reconciliation means bringing people together in friendship when they have been separated by some hurt or wrong. It's about making up after a wrong has been forgiven. For Christians reconciliation is something they are told to do by Jesus: 'Jesus reconciled us to himself, making us friends with God; he gave us the work of reconciling others.' *(2 Corinthians 5:18)*

(Note that Christian origins do not imply that the modern clubs have a religious affiliation.)

Reflection

Think of a time you have had an argument with a friend. How did you make it up again?

Prayer (OPTIONAL)

The following prayer can be attached to the football and displayed.

'Thank you, God, for the example of the Everton and Liverpool teams; we pray that we might be reconcilers too.'

Life in the pond

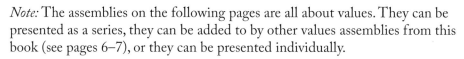

You will need
 A large sheet of blue frieze or sugar paper.
 Brown and green tissue paper.
 Paper/card in a variety of colours.

Note: The assemblies on the following pages are all about values. They can be presented as a series, they can be added to by other values assemblies from this book (see pages 6–7), or they can be presented individually.

Introduction

Introduce the 'life as a pond' metaphor, explaining any difficult words. You could use role-play to show what happens when one 'fish' behaves badly. **Life/school is a little bit like life in a pond, where all the creatures have to get on, in the space they share, in order to make a happy pond. To do so they need certain qualities and ways of behaving. We are going to create a 'pond'. In the pond we will put lots of different fish. Each fish will have something to teach us or a story to tell.**

Pupils can help create the pond, starting with a large piece of blue paper. Weeds can be made from crumpled green tissue. Brown tissue can make the mud at the bottom of the pond. Have paper fish of different sizes and colours ready cut. Pupils can write a name on each fish from the list below. Fix the fish by making horizontal slits in the pond and slotting the bottom fin or 'belly' of the fish into the slits.

In each assembly pupils locate the appropriate fish and write the name of the value for that day on the other side of the fish. They can use this to introduce the assembly; for example, 'This is Fergus, he reminds us that forgiveness is important.'

➤ Fergus (forgiveness)
➤ Rachel (reconciliation)
➤ Lucy (love)
➤ Gizela (generosity)
➤ Pedro (patience)
➤ Henry (honesty)
➤ Simon (self-control)
➤ Wendy (wisdom)
➤ Fidel (faith)

Reflection
Think for a moment. In what way is life/school like a pond?

Prayer (OPTIONAL)
The following prayer can be written on the pond.

> **'Lord of all life, help us to live together in harmony. Help us to develop the characteristics we need to live together in peace.'**

Michael Watson

You will need
> A large sheet of paper.
> Fergus fish.

Introduction
Use Fergus the fish to introduce this assembly (F1, page 46, Core material). Invite one of the pupils to mime boxing and ask the others to guess what sport it is. Explain that today's story is about a boxer who had the strength to forgive. (For more information go to www.michaelwatsonmbe.co.uk/photofile/index.php and www.theforgivenessproject.com/stories/michael-watson.)

Core material
Michael Watson was a boxer at super middle weight. He was near the end of his fight with Chris Eubank in 1991 when he collapsed in the ring and he was rushed to hospital. Michael was in a coma for 40 days. Before his accident Michael believed in God but he was more interested in money and fast cars. Eventually Michael came round from the coma, but he had to face being unable to talk or walk, which was very difficult for someone who was used to being super-fit. Michael wasted no time, though, and as soon as he woke up he asked God for help. He prayed for strength and he prayed for Chris Eubank. He wondered how Chris was feeling about what had happened. Although it was an accident, he knew that Chris must be feeling terrible. Instead of feeling angry, Michael felt a deep peace that came with forgiving Chris.

For Michael it was a long road to recovery but he said his inspiration was Jesus' words from the cross: 'Father, forgive them, for they don't know what they are doing.' If Jesus could forgive his enemies, Michael decided that he could forgive an accident. Michael had many operations and over the next twelve years he slowly regained his speech and the ability to walk. Michael described this as the greatest fight of his life. In 2003 he took part in the London marathon. Top runners do this in less than three hours; it took Michael six days. Every day the crowds cheering him on got bigger. Michael had other people running with him, and on the last day Chris Eubank ran alongside him. They crossed the finishing line together, a living example of forgiveness.

Reflection
Think of a time when you may have been hurt accidentally. How did you feel when it happened? Create a thought scatter to show the range of feelings. Ask pupils to lightly colour the emotions in different colours. Talk about ways of changing feelings. You can change the colours as you talk.

Prayer (OPTIONAL)

> 'Lord, help us to deal with the feelings we have when someone accidentally hurts us. With the help of the Holy Spirit, may we change those feelings so that we can forgive others.'

Ruby Bridges

You will need
> Information from www.rubybridges.com/story.htm.
> Rachel fish.

Introduction
Use Rachel the fish to introduce this assembly (see F1, page 46, Core material). Ask one pupil to lead a group of about three other pupils on a route around the hall. Repeat this activity but add a second group, who must walk in a different direction and stay away from the first group. **The person we are looking at today helped two groups of people who lived separately and often did not get on, to begin to come together.**

Core material
Fifty years ago in the USA, many white and black Americans led separate lives (refer to introductory activity). **They ate in separate cafes and went to separate schools. The two communities did not get on. Through the work of Martin Luther King and others this situation began to change. The schools became mixed. Ruby Bridges was six years old when this happened. Ruby got ready to go to her new, mixed school where she would get a good education. But some people were not happy with this change, and tried to stop it. They thought that Ruby should not go to this school, and lined the road all the way to the school and shouted horrible things at her. It was so bad that Ruby had to have an escort of four US marshals (policemen) every day.**

The crowd thought that Ruby would give up, but she didn't, and days turned into weeks and weeks into months. Still Ruby kept going. Ruby loved her new teacher, the first white lady she had known. Mrs Henry was not like the bullies, neither were the white people who helped to protect her family, or the white people who went to school with her. Ruby had heard Jesus' teaching about loving your enemies and she was determined to put it into practice. Every day on the way to school she prayed for the people who were being so horrible to her.

Eventually behaviour like Ruby's helped to mend the feeling between the two communities. Ruby is grown up now and she runs an organisation that helps people to live together in peace. Her organisation tries to bring people together who do not get on. This is called reconciliation.

Reflection
Have you ever been a reconciler for your friends?

Prayer (OPTIONAL)
Pupils join, separate and join their hands as the prayer suggests.

> **Almighty God, we sometimes enjoy good friendships and feel close to our friends. At other times we quarrel and separate. Help us to be reconcilers where we can.**

Three circles

You will need

> Three long strips of paper formed into circles of different sizes (see the
> Introduction below and Core material).
> A table and some safe, soft toys.
> Lucy fish.

Introduction

Use Lucy the fish to introduce this assembly (see F1, page 46, Core material).
Place the smallest paper circle on the table. **Today we are thinking about the different
groups of people in our lives. This first circle is for the people close to us. Think about
who you would put in this first circle. We are going to use some soft toys to stand for
friends and family. Who would like to place them? We'll label these toys 'friends and
family'. When we talk about loving others we tend to think of our families and friends.
Today's assembly is about some other people.**

Core material

Add the second larger circle so that you have two concentric circles. **We find it hard
to love those who we don't know well or people who are different from us. Who would
like to add some more soft toys to stand for this second group? We will label these toys
'different and strangers'. The Bible says that the 'stranger' should be welcomed and
cared for** *(Deuteronomy 10:19).*

Add the third and largest circle to make three concentric circles. **It is even harder
to love people we do not like and people we think of as enemies.** Ask someone to
add some more soft toys to this outside circle. **We'll label these toys 'disliked and
enemies'. Jesus asked people to love their enemies. When Jesus used the word 'love'
he was not necessarily talking about feelings. The word 'love' can mean 'behave in a
loving way'.** Remove the two smaller circles but leave the toys and labels. Label the
remaining large circle 'loved'.

**In the Bible Christians read what Jesus said about love: 'If you only love those who
love you, how does that make you different? Most people can do that. But love your
enemies and do good to them.'** *(Luke 6:32–33)*

Reflection

Jesus' teaching is about drawing a circle of love big enough to take in all sorts of people.

Prayer (OPTIONAL)

Ask pupils to draw a circle in the air with a finger.

> **'Lord, you drew your circle of love so wide that it included both friends and
> enemies. Help us to do the same.'**

Running over

You will need
> A packet of rice crispie type cereal.
> A mug and a transparent measuring jug.
> A large mixing bowl.
> Gizela fish.

Introduction
Use Gizela the fish to introduce this assembly (see F1, page 46, Core material). Say that generosity is about giving more than is expected, not just the bare minimum. Ask one pupil to fill the mug full of rice crispies. Level off the top. Tip the crispies from the mug into the measuring jug and read the result. Return the crispies to the box. Now ask another pupil to fill the mug as full as they can. They can press the crispies down and shake or tap the side and pile as much on top as they can until it runs over. Tip these into the jug and measure the result. How much more was fitted in the mug the second time?

Core material
Set up a series of role-plays of situations where people are generous, and give more than is expected.

- **Someone might ask for a donation to charity of 20p and be given 50p. That is generosity with money.**
- **Someone might ask for a few moments of a person's time to play or for help, and be given an hour or more. That is generosity with time.**
- **Someone winning a prize might expect another person to be jealous of their success, but instead they are congratulated. That's generosity of heart. [/BL]**

In the Bible Christians read Jesus' words about generosity. He said: 'Give and you will receive a generous measure, pressed down, shaken and running over' *(Luke 6:38).* Refer to the introductory activity.

Reflection
Listen to the rice crispies as they are poured into the bowl, and think of times when you have been generous or people have been generous to you.

Prayer (OPTIONAL)
Pupils can create actions for key phrases:

> **'Generous God, you give us so many things *pressed down, shaken* and *running over.* Help us to give to others *pressed down, shaken* and *running over.'***

You will need
> Pedro fish.
> An egg timer (large if possible).

Introduction

Use Pedro the fish to introduce this assembly (see F1, page 46, Core material). Enact running out of patience using the egg timer. As the sand runs through get more and more impatient with it, until you get really cross by the time it has all run through. Explain what you were doing and discuss with pupils when they have felt like this. **Today we are looking at patience, which is more than waiting.**

Core material

The following can be role-played.

> ➤ Having to wait to play with a toy, wait in a queue or wait to take turns in a game.
> ➤ Having to do something that is hard or boring that takes a long time.
> ➤ Seeing something wrong happening and not being able to put it right straight away.

Patience helps us cope with situations, but we have to practise patience to stop it running out.

- **Enjoying what you have or are doing now rather than wanting to rush on to the next thing. If you are stuck waiting in a queue, think about something else. There may be things around you that you can enjoy looking at. Turn it into positive time. If you are a person of faith, say a quiet prayer for the people in the queue.**
- **Sticking at something even though it might be hard or boring, because it will be worthwhile in the long run. Think of what you are aiming for.**
- **Being prepared to keep on working towards something even if the situation cannot be changed straight away. Think about the people who will benefit from the change.**

Patience in the Bible is very positive and active; it is not just doing nothing.

> **Run with patience the race of life.** *(Hebrews 12:1)*

> **Difficult times teach us to be patient and keep going.** *(James 1:3)*

Reflection

Think for a moment: what do you really enjoy about being the age you are now?

Prayer (OPTIONAL)

> 'Lord, you are patient with us; teach us to be patient with others.'

The seed

You will need

Gardening items: soil, plant pot, safe seed, plastic spoons, plastic gloves, water. Henry fish.

Introduction

Use Henry the fish to introduce this assembly (see F1, page 46, Core material). **Today we have a made-up story about a plant that we are going to tell together using these gardening items.**

Core material

Long ago in a land far away lived a king who was very old. He knew the time had come to choose someone else to be king after him, so he called all the young people in his kingdom together. He gave each one a seed and told them to go away and plant it, then bring the plant back to him exactly one year later. He would judge the plants and choose someone to be the next king.

Ling was one of the boys who received a seed. He went home and planted it in a pot and watered it each day. Demonstrate. But nothing happened. Weeks and months went by. Ling faithfully watered his pot, but nothing happened. He noticed that the other boys were growing great big plants, and when they asked him about his plant Ling just shrugged his shoulders and looked miserable.

Finally the day came to take the plants to the king. Ling did not want to go but his mother persuaded him. When the other boys saw Ling's pot they laughed. Their pots were full of beautiful flowers and leaves, Ling's was still just a pot of earth. The king entered and looked around the room. Ling hid at the back, but the king saw him and asked him to come forward. The other boys started laughing at Ling again. However, they soon stopped laughing when the king said: 'Here is your new king!' Ling looked as surprised as everyone else. 'Last year,' said the king, 'I gave everyone a seed, but I boiled them first so that they would not grow. All the rest of you must have cheated and planted your own seed. All except Ling; he was honest and brave enough to bring an empty pot.'

Honesty, in all its forms, is important to Christians. Honesty in speaking (not telling lies); honesty in things (not stealing); and honesty in relationships (not deceiving people). In the Bible it says: 'God hates cheating but he delights in honesty.' *(Proverbs 11:1)*

Reflection

Think about a time when you were honest. Did being honest take bravery as well?

Prayer (OPTIONAL)

Place the plant pot as a focus.

'God of truth, help honesty to grow within us as a plant grows from seed.'

The wall

You will need
> Some screwed up scrap paper.
> Some large boxes.
> Simon fish.

Introduction

Use Simon the fish to introduce this assembly (see F1, page 46, Core material).
Invite a member of staff to use the boxes to create a defensive wall. Once it is built,
the teacher or a pupil can sit safe behind the wall. Other pupils can throw some
screwed up paper at the wall.

Core material

Talk with pupils about different sorts of defences: walls, fences, etc. Also talk about
other types of defences, ones that you can wear to protect yourself, like a cycle
helmet or knee and elbow pads . Ask pupils to show these if they have them.

**In Bible times, cities had walls built around the outside as a defence against attack
from enemies. If any attackers were seen coming, the people who lived outside the city
moved inside the walls, so that they would keep safe.** Refer to introductory activity.

**Another, different form of defence is self-control. It protects people from the things
that spoil life, such as greed, selfishness and bad temper. If we have self-control, we
can say 'No' to ourselves when we might want to be greedy, or selfish, or nasty to
someone else. The Bible says that a person who has no self-control is like a city with no
defences** *(Proverbs 25:28).* **A person with no self-control has no defences to stop these
enemies: greed, selfishness and rage.**

Reflection

Pupils can write 'Self-control' on the 'wall'. Situations or types of behaviour that we
need self-control for can be written on pieces of paper, and these can be screwed up
and thrown at the wall.

Prayer (OPTIONAL)

Pupils can suggest prayers to write on the wall, or the prayers below can be used.

> **'Help us, Lord, to say "No" to selfishness.'**
> **'Holy Spirit, when we feel like being nasty, help us to use our self-control.'**
> **'Father, when we want to be greedy and take what belongs to others, help us to say
> "No" to ourselves.'**

The quiz

You will need

A comfortable armchair or office chair.
Some questions to ask staff or pupils (see Introduction below).
Some clean pebbles.
Wendy fish.

Introduction

Use Wendy the fish to introduce this assembly (see F1, page 46, Core material).
Before the assembly organise people to take part in a sort of quiz show. One person
(staff or pupil) should sit in the comfortable chair and be prepared to answer
questions on their chosen subject. A member of staff or pupil can be a quiz-master.
Choose with care who you ask to take part; make sure they are likely to succeed.

Core material

Sometimes, when we watch quiz programmes, we see people who are very clever
at answering questions. They may win a cup, a trophy or some money. Today we are
looking at wisdom and being wise. Wisdom is not the same as being clever. Some clever
people are also wise, but some are not. Being wise is not about being able to answer
hard questions, it is about choosing the right way in life, even if it is not the fastest
way or the most popular. Being wise is about making good decisions every day, for wise
people can spot the right thing to do. Some older people are wise because they have
had time to develop this quality.

Christians use the Bible to help them make good decisions. Jesus told a story about a
wise man and a foolish man.

There were once two men and both wanted to build a house. One built his house
quickly, straight on the sand. The other took ages digging down into the rock, and
then he started to build. When both houses were finished a great storm came. The
house built on sand was washed away, but the house on rock stood firm. Jesus said
that the wise man was like a person who listened to his teachings and tried to put
them into practice. The foolish man heard the teachings but did nothing. *(Matthew
7:24–27)*

Reflection

Think for a moment. Who do you know who is wise? Do you ever ask them for advice?

Prayer (OPTIONAL)

Ask pupils for suggestions of prayers for wisdom. Write them on pieces of paper
and anchor them with pebbles to create a pebble-prayer display. (This can be
removed after the assembly.)

'Heavenly Father, we offer you our prayers and pray for wisdom as we seek to live
out our lives.'

The difficult word

You will need
> A ribbon and a toy archery bow.
> A blindfold.
> Some cushions.
> Fidel fish.

Introduction

Use Fidel the fish to introduce this assembly (see F1, page 46, Core material). Show the ribbon tied in a bow; the toy archery bow; and ask a third pupil to demonstrate giving a bow; each time, ask the pupils what word describes the thing or action, and write it up. What do they notice?

Core material

Some words, like 'bow', can mean different things although it looks the same. Another word like this is 'faith'. Faith can be:

- What people believe (for example, in the Christian faith people believe that God made the world).
- An attitude people have (for example, having faith in other people: 'I have faith that you will do what you say').
- Actions people do (for example, people putting their faith into action).

Faith is what people believe. Christians sometimes say a 'creed', which is a list of beliefs. One part of a creed that many Christians say is: 'I believe in God, the Father almighty, creator of heaven and earth.' (For the full text go to www.creeds.net/ancient/apostles.htm.)

Faith is also an attitude – a way of thinking and feeling about something or someone. If we trust someone we have faith in them. Show the blindfold and arrange the cushions spaced out on the floor, then ask for a volunteer to be blindfolded. We are going to blindfold this person, then ask them to choose a friend that they have faith in. The friend has to lead them safely round the cushions on the floor. Faith for Christians is trusting God.

Faith is also putting beliefs into action. For example, Christians believe that God made everyone and cares for everyone. That belief should affect how Christians treat people. Faith changes actions.

Reflection

Think about one thing you believe that changes how you behave, for the better.

Prayer (OPTIONAL)

As the prayer is said, pupils can touch head, heart and hands.

> 'Lord, help us to believe with our heads, feel trust in our hearts, and act justly with our hands.'

Mark Street

You will need
> Nine sheets of A4 card of different colours
> for doors (see page 95).
> A card street sign saying MARK STREET.
> A Bible.

Note: This first assembly lays out the 'street'. At the beginning of each subsequent assembly a 'door' is opened and a story from Mark's Gospel forms the basis of that assembly. The story or passage from the Bible (Core material) can be photocopied and secured behind the door just before the assembly.

Introduction

Today we are going to make a street. We haven't got room to make the houses, so we are just going to have the doors. There are nine houses in our street. What do you think it is called? Take the pupils' suggestions, then show the street name and explain that it is a story-street. Every house contains a story or a passage or some information. Each of the stories comes from the sacred book of the Christians – the Bible. (You will need to remind pupils of this in each subsequent assembly.) Tape the left-hand edge of each door to the wall and secure the other side of the door. Make sure the doors are at pupil height. Add door numbers, 1 to 9. Pupils can be involved in creating the street with the help of staff. Fix the street name to the wall.

Core material

Now we have our story-street. The stories behind the doors are very special stories for Christians. They come from part of the Bible called Mark's Gospel. Ask an older pupil to find Mark's Gospel in the Bible. There are many different types of stories in our street: stories of boats and heralds; stories about camels and taxes. All these stories were written to help Christians to live their faith in daily life.

Reflection

Ask pupils what areas of daily life they sometimes need help with.

Prayer (OPTIONAL)

Teach pupils to sign the words 'Thank you, God'. (www.britishsignlanguage.com)

> 'Thank you, God, for writers like Mark, who used their skill to help others live their faith. Be with those who translate Mark's Gospel into many languages so that people can read it in their own language.'

Mark the writer

St. Mark

You will need

A larger version of the winged
lion image (see page 86), which
can be downloaded from
www.rmep.co.uk/summer.
A box or container.

Introduction

Show the drawing of the lion. Ask what noise a lion makes. Can pupils roar like
a lion? What might a lion have to do with our assembly? Ask a pupil to knock on
door 1, open it and find the story. Remind them where the story comes from.

Core material

The first story is not a story from Mark's Gospel, but some information about Mark
himself. No one is absolutely sure who wrote Mark's Gospel, as he did not sign it.
However, many people think that Mark was one of the early Christians. He was
probably a friend of Peter's, one of Jesus' special friends called 'disciples'. Mark may
have listened to Peter's stories and written them down. For Mark they were 'good
news' because they told the story of Jesus, who Christians believe is God's Son and
who came to bring God's message of love and hope to people on earth. Mark starts his
Gospel with the words: 'The beginning of the gospel of Jesus Christ the Son of God'.
(Mark 1:1)

Mark was so excited about the story of Jesus that he wanted to share this good news
with everyone. The sign of St Mark is a winged lion, for he is like a lion roaring out the
good news.

Reflection

Think about some good news you have received. Who did you share it with? When you
hear/see the signal, I want you to roar as a reminder of that.

Prayer (OPTIONAL)

Ask pupils to suggest prayers on the theme of good news, which can be written on
pieces of paper and placed in a box. The prayers can be shaken and pulled out one
by one to be used for prayer time. Alternatively use the prayers below:

'Lord, you are a God of good news. Help us to be good news to other people by
what we do and the type of people that we are.'
'God of all joy, teach us to be bringers of your good news in ways that help others.'
'God of the lion and the lamb, help us to roar good news but be as gentle as lambs.'

The herald

You will need
A party trumpet.

Introduction

Arrange to have the pupils all standing up straight and silent for the arrival of the person taking the assembly. If possible play a trumpet fanfare (available online at www.warsource.com/sfx/sfx.htm), or pupils can use the party trumpet. When the person enters, the pupils sit down. Ask what was unusual about the start of the assembly. **The Queen and some other important people have heralds to play a trumpet fanfare when they arrive at somewhere special.**

Explain that today's assembly is about a different sort of herald, called John. He did not blow a trumpet but he did tell people to get ready for the arrival of Jesus. Ask a pupil to knock on door 2, open it and find the story. Remind them where the story comes from. You may need to explain any difficult words.

Core material

This is a story from Mark's Gospel.

> **John lived in the desert. He told people to get ready for the special king who would soon arrive. He said to them: 'Get ready for the one who is coming. He will be so great that I am not good enough even to tie his shoe laces.' Many people listened to John and believed him, and John baptised them in the river.** *(Mark 1:2–8)*

John was like a herald. He did not blow a trumpet, but he did tell people that Jesus was coming, and to get ready for him. That did not mean putting on their best clothes or tidying the house. John asked them to get ready on the inside, by saying sorry for things they had done wrong in the past and by asking God's help to live a better life. Being baptised in the river was an outward sign that people were sorry and wanted a fresh start.

Reflection

If possible, play a trumpet fanfare, while pupils listen and reflect on fresh starts.

Prayer (OPTIONAL)

If possible, play a fanfare, while pupils pray silently. Or use the following prayer:

> **'Father, you know when we are sorry: hear our prayer.**
> **Lord, you are eager to help us start again: hear our prayer.**
> **Holy Spirit, help us in every fresh start: hear our prayer.'**

Catching?

You will need
> Cards showing the names for the game 'tag' in different languages (see
> Introduction below).
> Soft toys on a table.
> Music (see Reflection).

Introduction
Organise a game of 'tag', using the toys. Pupils demonstrate how the toys might
play tag, using the table as a game area. Say that tag is played all around the world.
Pupils can hold up the cards showing the different names for the game. (*Note:*
Some schools no longer allow this game.)

➤ India – 'Parkran purkai'   ➤ Finland – 'Hippa'
➤ Japan – 'Onigokko'   ➤ Iran – 'Sok-sok'
➤ Poland – 'Berek'   ➤ Russia – 'Salki'

In many places the game tag is a reminder of how people used to behave when they
met someone with an infectious (catching) illness such as leprosy. They used to run
away from anyone they might catch an illness from. Leprosy is an illness that we now
know cannot be caught by touching. It can also be cured. (www.leprosymission.org)
Across the world about three million people are still affected by the disease. Reassure
pupils that there is no leprosy in Britain. Ask a pupil to knock on door 3, open it
and find the story. Remind them where the story comes from.

Core material
In Jesus' time people with leprosy had to leave their families because there was no cure
for the illness. They had to go and live in a lonely place so that the disease would not
spread. No one would touch them.

> One day, as Jesus was travelling, a man with leprosy approached him and asked to
> be healed. Jesus was upset to see this man suffering. He was filled with love and
> concern for him. He reached out his hand and touched the man, and his leprosy was
> healed. Jesus told the man to go and show himself to the priest, who also acted as
> the doctor. He told the man not to tell anyone what had happened, but the man was
> so happy that he told everyone he met. *(Mark 1:40–45)*

Reflection
Play some 'lonely' music, such as the Largo from Vivaldi's Concerto in F. Ask the
pupils what it must have meant to the man when Jesus touched him.

Prayer (OPTIONAL)
See the Leprosy Mission website for prayers. Go to 'Getting involved' then 'Prayer'.

> 'Dear God, give skill and care to the doctors and nurses who treat people who
> suffer from leprosy. May they offer not only healing but also love and acceptance,
> as Jesus did.'

The story-man

You will need

A short 'true' story, and a story that teaches a truth, for example a picture book such as *Rainbow Fish* by Marcus Pfister.

Introduction

Tell the two types of story. Ask which one was true. Explain that there are different types of 'truth': there are stories about things that actually happened, and there are stories that are made up to teach something that is true. For example, a moral or spiritual truth such as: 'It's right to care' or 'It's wrong to lie.' Explain the today's assembly is about storytelling. Ask a pupil to knock on door 4, open it and find the story. Remind them where the story comes from.

Core material

Mark tells us that Jesus told lots of stories when he was teaching the ordinary people. In fact, that was how he taught people. Sometimes he made up stories that told a spiritual truth. These are called 'parables'. This is the parable of the Sower.

A man went into a field to sow some seeds. Some fell on the path where the soil was packed hard. The seed did not sink into the ground, it just bounced then laid on top, and birds came and gobbled it up. Some seeds fell on rocks where they had only a little earth to grow in, and there was nowhere to put down roots. Tiny plants grew for a while but when the sun came out the plants just withered in the heat and died. Some seeds fell among the thorns, where they grew but the thorns were stronger and choked the little plants so they too died. Other seeds fell on good soil and sank deep into it. Soon healthy plants grew that produced lots of grain.

Jesus explained this story to his friends. People are like the different seeds. Some people hear God's word but it does not sink in. Instead it is snatched away by the Evil One, and they are like the seed on the path. Some people hear God's word and take it in, and they start to grow in the love of God. But as soon as it gets difficult, they give up because they have no depth. They are like the seed on the rocks. Some people hear God's word but they are so concerned and worried about many other things that God's message gets lost. They are like the seed that fell among the thorns. But some people hear God's word and it sinks in. They grow in goodness and love and they are the healthy plants. *(Mark 4:2–20, 33–34)*

This parable can be enacted, with pupils taking the parts of the seeds, birds, thorns, etc.

Reflection

Do you find it easy to learn through stories?

Prayer (OPTIONAL)

'Thank you, Father, for the power of stories to change the way we think, feel and live.'

Just a carpenter?

You will need
> Images of celebrities from magazines (if possible arrange for pupils to cut these out beforehand).
> A flip-chart.

Introduction
Ask the pupils for the names of the celebrities in the images and what each is famous for. Make a celebrity collage by sticking the images to a flip-chart page, leaving a space in the middle of the page. Ask pupils to imagine growing up with (celebrity's name) living next door. What do you think they were like as a child? Explain that today's story is about people who wanted a celebrity in their home town. Ask a pupil to knock on door 5, open it and find the story. Remind them where the story comes from.

Core material
One day Jesus went to his home town of Nazareth where he had grown up and been to school. He taught the people there, and they were impressed by his teaching. But they were also disappointed because he looked ordinary, just like them. They were so used to seeing the ordinary Jesus they had grown up with, they could not see what was extraordinary about him. Maybe they wanted someone who acted more like a celebrity! They said to each other: 'Where did he get these things and this power from? Isn't he the carpenter? Isn't he Mary's son? We know his brothers and sisters!' *(Mark 6:1–6)*

People were impressed by Jesus but they knew him as a carpenter, the local man who fixed doors and built cupboards. They found it difficult to accept him as a famous teacher because they had known him as the boy next door. They expected 'celebrities' to be different. But most celebrities are ordinary when they are growing up.

Reflection
Do we look at ordinary people and dismiss them? Should we look for the extraordinary in ordinary people?

Prayer (OPTIONAL)
Write 'Jesus – just a carpenter?' in the centre of your celebrity display.

> 'Lord, you grew up as an ordinary child; you went to school and worked as a carpenter. May the ordinary not blind us to what is extraordinary in you and in others.'

Who am I?

You will need
> A series of cards showing statements for the 'Who am I?' game (see
> Introduction below).
> A tray of play sand.

Introduction

Play a game of 'Who am I?' using well-known characters from TV and children's
books. Each card shows four numbered statements describing the character. The
pupil playing the character reads out the first statement and the other pupils
try to guess who they are. If they don't get it right, he or she reads out the other
statements in turn until they guess correctly. This example is Winnie the Pooh:

1 I am brown and cuddly.
2 I like throwing sticks in the river.
3 I like 'Hunny'.
4 My friend is called Christopher Robin.

Say that today's assembly is about when Jesus asked the question 'Who am I?' Ask a
pupil to knock on door 6, open it and find the story. Remind them where the story
comes from.

Core material

> One day Jesus asked his friends, the disciples, what people were saying about him.
> They replied: 'Some say you are John the Baptist. Some say you are the prophet
> Elijah or one of the other prophets.' Jesus turned to Peter and said to him, 'Who am
> I, Peter? Who do you think I am?' Peter replied: 'You are the Christ, the one sent by
> God.' Jesus told them not to tell others of this. *(Mark 8:27–30)*

The Bible says that Jesus did not tell everyone who he was. Everywhere Jesus went,
crowds of people followed – but he wanted quiet to carry on his work.

Reflection

Many celebrities love being in the news, but being in the news is not always easy to
live with.

Prayer (OPTIONAL)

Invite a few pupils to write prayers in the sand and read them aloud. Smooth the
sand after each one. End with:

> 'Lord, we have offered our prayers and now the sand is smooth again. Although the
> prayers cannot be seen, we know you have heard them.'

The eye of the needle

You will need
> A plastic weaving needle.
> A picture of a camel or a soft toy camel.
> Some pieces of cotton thread, wool, string and rope.

Introduction

Show the needle and ask a pupil to select something that could be threaded through the eye of the needle and something that definitely could not. Ask if the camel could go through? Explain that today's assembly is about a camel and a needle. Ask a pupil to knock on door 7, open it and find the story. Remind them where the story comes from.

Core material

Jesus told this story about wealth.

> **As Jesus was walking along one day, a rich young man came up to him and knelt down. 'Good teacher,' he said, 'What must I do to live for ever?'**
> **Jesus replied, 'Obey God's laws.'**
> **'I have kept those since I was a boy,' said the young man.**
> **Jesus looked at the young man and felt for him. 'There is only one thing you need to do. Sell all that you own and give the money to the poor, and follow me. Then you will have treasure in heaven.'**
> **The young man's face fell and he went away, for he was very rich. The disciples were puzzled, so Jesus explained. 'It is very hard for a rich man to enter God's kingdom. In fact it is easier for a camel to go through the eye of a needle! But all things are possible with God.'** *(Mark 10:17–27)*

Jesus was not saying that rich people could not be God's friends. He was saying that for some rich people it is difficult because money sometimes becomes more important than God. He did not say to everyone that they needed to sell everything they had, but he said it to this young man because money was getting in the way of his friendship with God.

Reflection

Show the camel and the needle. **Do money and 'things' sometimes get in the way of ordinary friendships?**

Prayer (OPTIONAL)

Use the camel and the needle as a focus.

> **'Thank you, Lord, for money and possessions. May they never get in the way of our friendships with others and with you.'**

The question

You will need
  Some play money.

Introduction

Ask some pupils to look at a coin and say whose head is on the coin. **In Jesus' time the Roman Emperor's (the king) head was on the coins. He was called 'Caesar'.**

Explain what taxes are. Role-play paying taxes in Jesus' time, when tax collectors went round collecting money from workers. For example:

> **Tax collector: How much have you earned this week?**
> **Worker: 10 pounds.**
> **Tax collector: Then you need to pay 2 pounds in taxes.**

Explain that today's story is about God and taxes. Ask a pupil to knock on door 7, open it and find the story. Remind them where the story comes from.

Core material

At the time Jesus lived, people hated paying taxes. One reason for this was because their taxes paid for the army of the Romans, who had invaded their country.

> **One day, some leaders asked Jesus a question. They said, 'Should people pay their taxes to the Romans?' Inside they were silently laughing; they were trying to get Jesus into trouble. If he said 'no', he would get in trouble with the Romans. If he said 'yes', he would be disliked by the people. Jesus would get into trouble whatever he said.**
> **Jesus sighed and said, 'Show me a coin. Whose head is on this coin?'**
> **'The Roman Emperor, Caesar,' they replied.**
> **'Then give to God what is God's and give to Caesar what belongs to Caesar.'**
> **The leaders were puzzled. They were not sure how he had done it but Jesus had avoided getting into trouble.** *(Mark 12:13–17)*

Christians find this saying hard to understand, but many think that it means that Christians should be good citizens and give to their country, but they should remember that there are some things that they give to God, such as trusting him for how to live.

Reflection

Think about your country. What has it given you? What can people give back?

Prayer (OPTIONAL)

> **'Almighty God, we pray for the rulers of our country. May they make just and fair laws. We pray for its citizens, that they may work together to make it a fair country to live in.'**

A cross and a cave

You will need
   Four strips of paper measuring 15cm x 2cm.
   Two circles of paper each 20cm in diameter.
   An OHP.

Introduction
Please read the note headed 'Pastoral issues' (page 11).

Put the strips of paper on the OHP and ask a few pupils to arrange them into different shapes.

These strips of paper will help tell today's story. Christians read this story at Easter time. Ask a pupil to knock on door 9, open it and find the story. Remind them where the story comes from. Pupils can help make the cross and the cave.

Core material
Jesus was very popular with the ordinary people, but this made some of the leaders jealous. So they decided to get rid of him. Jesus was arrested and put on trial. At the trial people said things about him that were not true and so Jesus was condemned to death on a cross. But even as he was dying he forgave the people who were hurting him. Make a cross with the strips. **It was a very sad day for all Jesus' friends.**

After Jesus died he was buried in a cave. Use four strips to make the cave entrance. **A great stone was laid in front of it.** Place a circle over the cave. **All the next day his friends were sad because they had lost their leader and their friend.** Cut a curved line in the circle to create a sad mouth then replace it over the cave. **On the next morning, which was Sunday, some of the women who had been friends of Jesus went to the cave. But when they got there they were surprised because the great stone had been rolled away and the cave was empty.** Remove the 'sad' circle and place the second circle to the side of the cave. **Then an angel appeared and told the women that Jesus was alive again. At first no one believed the women when they said what had happened, but soon the other followers saw Jesus for themselves and sadness was turned to joy.** Cut a curved line in the second circle to create a smile and place it beside the cave. *(Mark 14–16)*

Easter is a time of celebration for Christians. This is a very special story for them for it tells of Jesus rising from death to be their friend in their lives now. They have special worship with lots of light and flowers, special Easter food, and they may send each other cards.

Reflection
What do you celebrate? How do you celebrate? Does the celebration need to fit what you are celebrating?

Prayer (OPTIONAL)

   'Thank you, Father, for the message of Easter and the hope that it brings.'

The Lavoisiers

You will need

 Metric measuring equipment: rulers, jugs, etc.
 Things that can be measured using the equipment.
 Images from nature that show order and pattern, e.g. snowflakes, shells (search online by 'Patterns in nature') (optional).

Introduction

Use the measuring equipment with the pupils. Then ask them to make up some imaginary measures which they could use to measure things. What would it be like if every town had their own ways of measuring?

Core material

Antoine and Marie-Anne Lavoisier lived and worked in France about 250 years ago. They were a husband and wife team who worked together on many things. Antoine was a scientist working on finding out about the air we breathe and what water is made of. Marie-Anne worked with him, recording the results of his experiments, writing them up and drawing them (she was an artist). Marie-Anne also taught herself English so that she could translate English science books into French for Antoine. Demonstrate translating by giving an example of English into French.

At the time Antoine and Marie-Anne lived in France, people did not all agree on the way measurements were recorded. One part of the country used one system, another part of the country used another. This was no good for scientists; they needed accurate ways of measuring things. Antoine and Marie-Anne needed a way of recording the results of the experiments that was simple and everyone agreed on. To solve the problem, Antoine, along with other scientists, worked out the metric system – the system we use now.

Antoine came from a Christian family who took their faith very seriously, and we know Antoine defended the Bible and the Christian faith. For some scientists faith gives a sense of an ordered world made by God. That order and pattern in the world can be explored and measured by scientists.

Reflection

Look at the images of nature that show order and pattern. For example, snowflakes always have six points or sides. Some shells have a spiral pattern.

Prayer (OPTIONAL)

Show the images while the pupils pray silently. Or use the following prayer:

 'God of the snowflake and the shell, we thank you that our world has order and pattern that we can explore, measure and enjoy.'

Gregor Mendel

You will need
> Cards with plant information in written or picture form (see Introduction below).
> Two vases, with a flower in each, both flowers of the same type but two different
> colours and one taller than the other.

Introduction
Show the two flowers and ask pupils to point out how they are the same and how
they are different.

Bees take pollen (explain) from one plant to another. At the same time they are also
taking little packets of information from one plant to another about making seeds,
which grow to make new plants. These tiny packets of information are called 'genes'.
They are so small that you can only see them with a very powerful microscope. The
plants that receive the information use it when they produce their seeds to make a
baby plant. Two pupils can act as plants. Two other pupils can act as bees carrying
information between the plants.

- Message from plant 1: tall plant.
- Message from plant 2: short plant.
- Message from plant 1: pink flowers *(or appropriate colour)*.
- Message from plant 2: white flowers *(or appropriate colour)*.

When the plant makes its seeds, the new plant that grows from those seeds might
show where it had got messages from. The new plant might be short with pink flowers
or tall with white flowers. We are going to look at the man who discovered that plants
could do this.

Core material
The man who discovered about plant 'genes' was a Christian monk called Gregor Mendel
(1822–84). He lived in a monastery where he did his experiments, and there were many
other people in the monastery also finding out about things. The work that Mendel did on
how plants send messages helped other scientists understand how the human body also
sends messages ('genes'). For Mendel, asking questions and finding out was part of his
Christian faith. His monastery encouraged him in his discoveries, and it was an exciting
place to live, full of people asking questions, finding out things and doing experiments.

Reflection
Encourage pupils to look at the world and ask questions about it.

Prayer (OPTIONAL)
Create a questions board and pin up suggestions of what pupils would like to know
about the world. Add this prayer:

> 'Why is the water wet, God, why is the earth round? Why is the ice cold, God, why
> does a drum sound? Lord, you created our minds to ask questions. Keep us curious.'

Kathleen Lonsdale

You will need
>   Images of crystals (search online) (optional).
>   Sugar and salt crystals, or a precious crystal such as a diamond.
>   Thick card and art materials to make a cross (optional, see Prayer).

Introduction

Show some images of crystals or some sugar crystals and salt. Explain that crystals come in many different shapes. Salt crystals are tiny cubes, sugar crystals are flatter rectangles.

Core material

Kathleen Lonsdale (1903–71) was born into a poor Irish family, who moved to England when she was still a child. Kathleen was good at science and maths subjects, and she went to these classes at the boys' school because in those days the schools that girls went to did not always teach science. Kathleen became a scientist and worked on crystals. All through her life she was excited by crystals and their amazing shapes and patterns.

Kathleen was a Quaker Christian and this meant that she believed in peace, not war and fighting. In 1939, when war broke out, she refused to do any war work because of her beliefs, and she was sent to prison for one month. Kathleen carried on studying while she was in prison; she also helped fellow prisoners and later became a prison visitor. She and her husband also looked after refugees (explain) during the war. She spent much of her life trying to improve prisons; having been in one she knew exactly what they were like.

Kathleen's faith kept her working for peace. For Kathleen, faith and science were similar: both had bits that puzzled her; both demanded a lot of thinking. Kathleen never felt that she had all the answers, either in science or in faith. The Bible has many stories about people who were puzzled by life, and they brought their questions to God. People such as the prophet Jeremiah and King David asked God about things that puzzled them. God did not tell them to stop asking questions.

Reflection

Draw a large question mark. Talk with pupils about the things we don't understand – even as adults. There will always be things we can't explain but that does not stop us thinking and wondering about the world.

Prayer (OPTIONAL)

Make a cross from card. Add question marks in different materials such as felt pen and glitter glue. The cross can be displayed with pupils' questions arranged around it.

>   'Almighty God, you know all the mysteries of life and the universe. We bring to you our questions and our wonderings, knowing that you understand.'

Francis Collins

You will need
    Five plain paper plates.

Introduction
Read the extract from the poem: 'The King's Breakfast' by A. A. Milne, which is about a message being passed. Pupils can take the parts. (You may want to perform the whole poem, which can be found in *When We Were Very Young*.)

The King asked	The Queen asked the Dairymaid,
The Queen, and	The Dairymaid
The Queen asked	Said, 'Certainly,
The Dairymaid:	I'll go and tell the cow
'Could we have some butter for	Now
The Royal slice of bread?'	Before she goes to bed.'

Explain that today's assembly is about messages and sharing.

Core material
Francis Collins is a doctor and a scientist who was born in 1950 in America. When he started as a doctor he did not believe in God, but he noticed that some of the very sick people he met were helped by their faith in God. He began to explore what faith was all about, and as a result Francis Collins became a Christian. Francis, worked with many other scientists to find out about tiny parts of the human body called 'genes' that carry messages (see H2, page 67). Refer to the introductory activity. This project was called 'The Human Genome Project' and Francis was in charge of it.

Francis, along with others, was determined that the information they found out about genes was shared with people all over the world. This meant that every country in the world would have this new knowledge. Hopefully the new knowledge would help in the battle against disease. Francis knew from first-hand experience that this would mean many lives could be saved in some poor countries, for he had worked as a volunteer in a hospital in Africa.

Reflection
Science can be hard work, but it can also be exciting. Francis Collins thought that discovering about genes was so exciting that he said: 'It beats going to the moon.' Encourage pupils to think of something in science that excites them, and suggest endings to the sentence: 'It beats …' For example: 'It beats the water ride at Alton Towers.'

Prayer (OPTIONAL)
Ask five pupils to take one plate each and write these words using pens/crayons, one on each plate: 'Lord, help us to share.' Display the prayer or take a digital photograph.

Jocelyn Bell Burnell

You will need
  A torch.
  Outline of a star (page 86).
  A large sheet of dark blue or black paper.
  Images of stars (optional).

Introduction

Show the star images. Explain that some stars that shine in our sky give off signals of light and energy. Some do this all the time. Ask a pupil to turn on the torch (shining away from pupils' eyes). Others 'blink'. Ask the pupil to turn the torch on and off.

Core material

Ever since she was a young girl, Jocelyn Bell Burnell (born 1943) has been interested in stars. She went to a Christian school where she was encouraged to study science. She studied stars at university and decided that she wanted to spend her life finding out more about them. As part of her work, Jocelyn helped to build a special giant telescope that would be able to track the movements of stars that are far out in space. Jocelyn checked on the telescope daily as it scanned the skies. After a while she noticed that one star was giving a sort of 'blink' at regular intervals. Pupils can show the interval of the 'blink' by clapping the rhythm 'one, two' 'one, two'. Ask pupils to clap their hands on 'one' and tap their legs on 'two'. (The rhythm was actually 1.33 seconds.)

At first no one knew what this strange blinking was, then it was realised that Jocelyn had discovered a special sort of star called a 'pulsar', which blinked because it was spinning round. Jocelyn became famous for this discovery and has been given many prizes for her work. Jocelyn Bell Burnell is an active Christian, and for her, faith is not a barrier to science. In the Bible, people wonder at God's creation of the stars. This appreciation of the beauty of creation is for some people the beginning of an interest in science.

> 'When I look at the skies, at the sun, moon and stars which you made, God, I feel small, yet you care for me.' *(Psalm 8:3–4)*

Reflection

Show images of space and stars. Alternatively, ask pupils to share their experiences of looking at the sky at night.

Prayer (OPTIONAL)

Pupil prayers can be written on star shapes and arranged on a sheet of dark paper.

> 'For the beauty of space, we thank you, God.'
> 'Lord, we feel tiny compared to space, but you still love us.'
> 'Almighty God, maker of the stars, thank you for making us as well.'

Clarks

You will need
   Some shoes (Clarks if possible) and slippers.
   A shop front (see page 93).
   A sheepskin rug (optional).

Introduction
Display the shop front and explain that the next few assemblies will be stories about shops that we find in high streets across the UK. Over the week we will build a mini high street. Show the shoes and ask if anyone can guess the name of the shop. Write the name 'Clarks' on the shop. Ask if any of the pupils know what Clarks sells. Is anyone wearing Clarks shoes?

Core material
Clarks shops have been selling shoes for over 150 years. It all began when a Quaker Christian family began making sheepskin rugs. Young James Clark took home the waste bits of sheepskin that were too small to be made into rugs. He made them into slippers for people who did not have much money. Before long his slippers became very popular and he began to make shoes and boots as well. James Clark began to employ other people to make Clarks shoes and later a factory was set up. Every pair of shoes was checked for quality and each shoe was stamped with the name of the person who made it. James Clark wanted his workers to live good lives and he thought the best way to make that happen was to set an example himself. He did not expect others to do something that he did not do himself. Setting an example is something James would have read about in his Bible: 'Set people an example by what you say and how you live. Set an example in love, in faith and in living rightly.' *(1 Timothy 4:12)*

(Note that Christian origins do not imply that the modern company has a religious affiliation.)

Reflection
We expect other people to behave in a right way, but do we always live up to our own standards?

Prayer (OPTIONAL)
Two pupils can mirror each other's actions as the prayer is said. Pupils can decide on which actions to mirror.

> 'Father, help us to live what we speak. Help us to expect the same standards of ourselves as we expect of others, so that our lives mirror our speech. Forgive us when we say one thing and behave quite differently.'

Dollond and Aitchison

You will need
A pair of glasses.
A shop front (see page 93).
A large sheet of paper.

Introduction
Ask a few members of staff who wear glasses to stand at the front (make sure beforehand that they are happy to do this). Ask the other pupils what they have in common. Show the shop front and ask if anyone can guess what today's shop might be. Write the name 'Dollond and Aitchison' on the shop. Explain that it is an opticians. (www.danda.co.uk/about-us/history/)

Core material
Jean (which is French for John) Dollond was a Huguenot – a French Protestant Christian. The King of France did not like the Huguenots and in 1685 he made a law that took away their right to freedom of religion. Huguenot churches and schools were knocked down and many Huguenots risked their lives escaping to somewhere safe. Many came to England, and that was what happened to Jean and his wife. The Huguenots brought with them their working skills, and also a new word which was added to our language: 'refugee'. Jean and his wife settled in the East End of London, with many other French Huguenots. Their first child, John, was born in 1706.

As John Dollond grew up, he became very interested in all sorts of glasses, and he started to make them: glasses that people used to see better, glasses used in telescopes and in instruments that sailors used at sea. As the business grew he opened a shop where he and his sons and eventually his grandsons experimented to improve and make better glasses and telescopes. Captain Cook and Lord Nelson were two of their customers. James Aitchison was an optician in the nineteenth century. He was concerned that opticians should be properly trained to test people's eyes. As part of his business he made cheap glasses that most people could afford. Dollond and Aitchison joined together as one company in 1927 and we now have a chain of opticians called Dollond and Aitchison, or D&A, all over the UK. It all started with a French refugee who left his country to find freedom of worship.

(Note that the Christian background of the founder's family does not imply that the modern company has a religious affiliation.)

Reflection
We take glasses for granted but in some countries they are a luxury, and are too expensive for most people.

Prayer (OPTIONAL)
In an outline of a pair of glasses, pupils can write the following prayer:

'Thank you, God – for glasses to see your world.'

Boots the Chemist

You will need
Some safe chemist's items such as plasters, bandage and soap.
A hand bell.
A shop front (see page 93).

Introduction
Go through the items and ask the pupils to guess what sort of shop today's assembly
is about. Show the shop front and ask if anyone can guess the name of today's shop.
Write the name 'Boots the Chemist' on the shop. (www.boots-the-chemists.co.uk)

Core material
Jesse Boot was born into a poor family in 1850. His father was a farm worker but he
became ill and had to give up his job, and he became interested in helping local people
who were very poor. Medicines were expensive, and Jesse's father and mother learned
to make simple, safe medicines, often using herbs, for themselves and other people.
The family went to the local Methodist chapel and some friends from the chapel helped
Jesse's family to open a small shop where they could sell their medicines and other
items such as soap. Jesse helped his parents in the shop and spent all his spare time
learning how to make medicines.

Jesse thought that it was unfair that medicines were so expensive; he wanted to make
medicines available to the poor. In 1877, when he was 27, Jesse took over the shop and
continued the family's work. The medicines he sold were cheap enough for ordinary
people to afford. To make sure that people knew about this he used a bell-ringer to
go around the town telling people about his prices. In 1886 Jesse met and married
Florence Rowe. Florence joined him in the shop. She knew that people who were ill
were often bored – there were no televisions in those days – and so she set up a
lending library in the shop.

Jesse and Florence Boot were very successful in their business. They made enough
money to be able to give away over £2 million. As a Christian Jesse would have read in
his Bible about caring for the sick. St Paul said: 'It must have been hard for you when
I was ill but instead of rejecting me because I was sick, you treated me like angel.'
(Galatians 4:14)

(Note that Christian origins do not imply that the modern company has a religious
affiliation.)

Reflection
As a pupil rings the bell, others think about their attitudes to those who are ill.

Prayer (OPTIONAL)
After each ring of the bell, pupils can say a 'thank you' prayer for a specific
medicine, e.g. cough medicine.

Thomas Cook

You will need
> Thomas Cook holiday brochures (optional).
> Some holiday items (optional).
> A shop front (see page 93).

Introduction
Go through the holiday items or brochures and ask pupils to guess what sort of shop today's assembly is about. Show the shop front and ask if anyone can guess the name of today's shop. Write the name 'Thomas Cook' on the shop. (www.thomascook.com)

Core material
The young Thomas Cook (1808–92) was a Christian and a Baptist preacher. He travelled round the country giving talks and trying to persuade people to give up drinking alcohol. At that time many people drank too much alcohol and it was causing a lot of problems. You may need to explain the temperance movement. It aimed to reduce how much alcohol people drank because of the many problems it caused. Alcohol abuse particularly affected women and children – money needed for food and housing was often spent on alcohol instead.

In 1841 Thomas arranged a trip for people to travel by train from Leicester to a temperance meeting in Loughborough. The trip from Leicester to Loughborough cost one shilling (5p) and included travel, food and entertainment. Train travel was new: the railways were newly built and exciting. Thomas went on to organise more trips and soon he decided to make it his main job. Thomas Cook's travel business was born.

Thomas was keen to give people something better to do than drink. He did not want to stop others having fun, but he wanted them to have fun in a way that did not spoil life. His company allowed ordinary people to get out into the country and see the beauty of nature. It meant that ordinary people could enjoy travelling and seeing new places.

(Note that Christian origins do not imply that the modern company has a religious affiliation.)

Reflection
How can we be good travellers and make life easier for drivers and other passengers? Various scenarios can be role-played to give pupils something to think about.

Prayer (OPTIONAL)
> 'O Lord, long ago you led the people of Israel across the desert.
> Guide us as we travel by foot and bicycle, by car, train and bus.
> Bring us safe to where we want to go.
> Help us to be good travellers, patient and considerate, helping others on the way.
> As we travel, may we feel you close, travelling with us.
> Lord, our lives are a journey that we travel together.
> May we help each other along life's road.'

Lloyds

You will need
- Some money and valuables (e.g. cheap jewellery).
- Some goods to buy and sell.
- A shop front (page 93).
- A paper speech bubble, laminated if possible, or draw one on a wipe-clean board.

Introduction
Go through the items and ask the pupils to guess what sort of shop today's assembly is about. Show the shop front and ask if anyone can guess the name of today's shop. Write the name 'Lloyds Bank' on the shop.

Core material
Before 1640, the money and valuables of the businessmen of London were looked after by the king. However, in 1640 King Charles I took some of their money for himself, which made the businessmen very angry. After that they gave their money to the goldsmiths of London to look after, who they trusted to keep it safe for them. The goldsmiths had a good idea. The businessmen left lots of money with the goldsmiths, and only needed a small amount of it at a time to run their businesses. The rest of their money just sat there being kept safe. The goldsmiths thought, why not use the rest of the money to lend to other people? This is how banks started and it's what they do now.

Barclays was one of these goldsmiths that became a bank. From the early days of banks, Quaker Christians became bankers; people trusted them with their money, because Quakers had a reputation for strict honesty. Banks depend on trust. Lloyds and Barclays were both Quaker banks originally.

The Bible stresses honesty that builds up trust. 'Do what is right and honest before God and before other people.' *(2 Corinthians 8:21)*

(Note that Christian origins do not imply that the modern company has a religious affiliation.)

Reflection
A reputation is what other people think about us. We often create our reputations by the way we behave. We need to think about the reputation we are creating, but also remember that reputations can be changed. Write some types of reputations on the speech bubble, then wipe them out and write something different. We need to take care of our reputation. We should also take care of other people's reputations, because sometimes a person's reputation can be destroyed by someone spreading untrue stories.

Prayer (OPTIONAL)
Ask pupils to hold their hands as if cupping water.

'Lord, we hold other people's reputations in our hands. Help us not to destroy them by gossip.'

Dr Kim Tan

You will need
> Drinks cartons.
> A bag made from recycled drinks cartons, or an online image of one (optional).

Introduction

Show the drinks cartons and ask pupils what they might be able to make from them. Show the bag made from cartons, or the image. **Imagine Dorcas, who is a young woman from Kenya who is good at designing bags and other items that can be made from recycled drinks cartons. How could she start a business to make and sell her bags? What will she need?** Below are some suggestions, if pupils get stuck. They can be written on cards and held up by pupils.

- **The materials to make the bags.**
- **People to help make the bags.**
- **Some machinery such as sewing machines.**
- **Somewhere to make the bags.**
- **Advice on how to run a business.**
- **Money to buy everything needed to make the bags.**
- **A way of letting people know that she has bags for sale.**
- **Somewhere to sell the bags: shop or website.**

Core material

Kim Tan is a scientist and businessman. His family came from Malaysia to Britain. Early in his life Kim discovered he had a talent for business, and he has been very successful, but he uses the money he has made in an unusual way: it is business with a difference. As a scientist Kim was struck by the beauty he saw in nature. As a Christian he believed that this beauty came from the creativity of God *(Genesis 1:31)*. Kim wanted to help people to develop their God-given creativity to the full, through business. Often people have creativity but do not succeed in business because they don't have the money to get started, or they lack the experience of running a business.

Kim helps people like Dorcas, by lending her money to get started in business, and by sharing his time and business skills. If the business works, he gets his money back and he then uses that money to help someone else get started. He chooses to help businesses in places where people need the work and where the business will benefit the community. As a Christian he believes in following the example of Jesus, who said that he came to serve others *(Mark 10:45)*. He believes that business can be used in Christian service.

Reflection

Think about yourself. How do you use your creativity?

Prayer (OPTIONAL)

> 'Father, we thank you for the way you have created us. We pray that we may use the creativity you have put inside us to the full and help others to do the same.'

Changing communities

You will need
> Some toy money.
> A £5 note.

Introduction
Role-play the journey that money (coins and notes) can go on. One person buys something at a shop, the shopkeeper uses the money to pay a member of staff, who uses it to buy food, so the shopkeeper has more money to pay other staff.

Core material
Most business people give money to start a business hoping to get much more money back. Kim Tan and others (see J1, page 76) set up a network of business people who are willing to use their time, experience and money for businesses where they do not get as much back as they would in other projects, but what they see is changed lives and communities. People in the Transformational Business Network (www.tbnetwork. org) put their money and skills into businesses in areas where there is little work for local people, in places like Africa and India. The businesses are sometimes risky, and they don't all succeed, but what comes back is more than money. This is a description of how people's lives can be changed. Pupils can role-play the parts using toy money.

- I help Dorcas by giving her advice on starting a business and by investing (lending her) some money.
- I work for Dorcas making bags. I use the money I am paid to buy things for my family.
- I work for Dorcas supplying some of the things she needs to make her bags. Now that I earn more, I can spend more in local shops.
- I'm a local shopkeeper. Now that more people have work, they are spending more money in my shop. I need to take on more people to work in my shop.
- I have learned to sew bags by working for Dorcas. Now that I have a new skill, I will find it easier to get another job.
- I have learned about business by working for Dorcas. I am going to start a business of my own. This will give more people work.
- I sell the bags and help Dorcas make money. Soon she will pay back the loan.

Kim Tan believes that wealth is not meant to stay in the hands of a few rich people. In the Bible it says that wealth is for sharing *(Luke 3:11)*. For Kim Tan, business is a way of sharing wealth. But it is not charity. The money is not given away, it is on loan. People have the pride of running their own business, earning money and helping others to earn. This can change whole communities.

Reflection
Look at the £5 note. Think about the way money can change communities.

Prayer (OPTIONAL)

> 'Father, we thank you for business people who help to change whole communities.'

Kuzuko game park

You will need
    Animal drawings (see pages 96).

Introduction

We need five people to hold up some pictures of animals. Can anyone name the animals? These animals need freedom but they also need protecting and today's assembly is about a project that benefits animals and people. Images of the Addo elephant, black rhino, buffalo, leopard and lion can also be found online.

Core material

Read the following account and be prepared to explain any difficult words. More information and images can be found at http://cybercapetown.com/KuzukoLodge/, www.legacyhotels.co.za (go to 'Bush lodges' then 'Kuzuko') and www.springhilluk.com (go to 'Social venture capital' then 'Investee companies').

In parts of South Africa only three people in every ten have jobs. Kim Tan (see J1, page 76) had the idea of building a game park in an area where tourists would have the chance to see African animals in the wild and where local people needed work. A hotel was built, and land was bought to turn into a game park. Slowly a collection of animals was brought and released into the park, including rare animals such as the Addo elephant and the black rhino. Buffaloes, leopards and lions were added. This makes the 'big five': the animals that tourists want to see and that need care and protection. Some local men were given lots of work building fences around the edge of the park, to stop the animals getting out. Once the fences were built, these men were helped to start their own fencing business. Other local people were trained as builders to help build the hotel and the staff buildings. These new skills will help them get other jobs. The people who work at Kuzuko get paid wages that are higher than usual, and they have good staff housing and health care. When tourists come to the area they spend money locally, and this creates more jobs. Local businesses are expected to grow as they supply what the park and hotel needs.

For Christians, sharing money by backing projects such as Kuzuko is a response to what they feel God has given them: 'God gives people lots of things to enjoy, so if you are rich, do good with your money and share what you have.' *(1 Timothy 6:17–18)*

Reflection

Think about this: if you had helped to get this project started, how would you be feeling now?

Prayer (OPTIONAL)

    'Father, we pray for those involved in business. We pray for wisdom so that they know where to put their money and how to use their skills and time.'

Success and significance

You will need

A long ribbon with labels fixed at each end: 'Success' and 'Significance'.

Introduction

Ask two pupils to hold the ribbon taut, showing the label at each end. Pupils can suggest ways in which people can be successful; other pupils can adopt the roles and stand by the Success label. Some suggestions:

- A successful football player may scores lots of goals.
- A successful music star may become famous by selling lots of CDs.
- A successful business person may make lots of money.
- A successful shop assistant may sell lots of clothes or jewellery or food.

Core material

Some successful people do not think just about being successful. They also ask the question, 'Am I significant?' Significance is a big word that means 'important', and 'worthwhile'. Some people want to feel that they have not only been successful, but have done something worthwhile with their life; they want to have made a difference, to have done something to make life better for others – family, friends, or the wider community. What could our successful people do to be significant? As you suggest ideas, our successful people can move along the line to the Significance label.

- The footballer could set a good example, using some of his money to provide sports activities for children who have little chance to play football.
- The music star could sing about things that really mattered.
- The business person could use their business skills to help others start businesses.
- The shop assistant could encourage the selling of Fairtrade goods, or adopt a local charity.

For Christians, success is to be enjoyed, but it is not enough on its own. The Bible reminds Christians that success must be achieved fairly and according to God's standards *(Joshua 1:8)*. Jesus summed up God's standards as loving God and loving your neighbour as yourself. Success does not have to be in terms of fame and money; we can be successful in relationships and other areas of life.

Reflection

We can be both successful and significant, it is not an 'either/or' choice.

Prayer (OPTIONAL)

Look at the Success label. Think about times when you have been successful. Thank God for those. Now look at the Significance label. Think of ways in which you can make life better for others.

Lord Chan

You will need
   Four pieces of card, A4 size.

Introduction

Invite the pupils to think of one friend, and find two positive words to describe that friend. For example, 'fun' and 'helpful'. Stand four pupils in a row, each holding a card. Other pupils can suggest pairs of words that describe them. (Choose pupils sensitively.) Write the words on the cards. **Today we are learning about a doctor who was described as 'gentle and fair'. What does that mean? Both his gentleness and his fairness helped him to change situations.**

Core material

Michael Chew Koon Chan was born in Singapore in 1940, and came to England to train as a doctor at Guy's Hospital. Dr Chan returned to Singapore, where he developed an interest in tropical medicine and working with children. Dr Chan then came back to London to continue to work with children at Great Ormond Street Hospital. He was a committed Christian and he had a reputation for gentleness, and for working tirelessly for justice (fairness), to make sure that everyone had good health care. Dr Chan's combination of gentleness and fairness stemmed from his Christian faith. The Bible encourages people to be both gentle and just (fair).

> **Let your gentleness be known to everyone.** *(Philippians 4:5)*

> **Put on love, kindness, humility, patience and gentleness like clothes.** *(Colossians 3:12)*

> **Hate evil and love good, and bring justice into everyday life.** *(Amos 5:15)*

Dr Chan worked to change situations for the better. His work was recognised in 2001 when he was made a people's peer. He became known as Baron Chan of Oxton. His advice on living well was: 'Honesty and hard work, respect for the elderly and the vulnerable. Treat others as you want to be treated.'

Reflection

Think about yourself. What two positive words would be used to describe you?

Prayer (OPTIONAL)

Ask pupils for words that could be used to describe God. Put these words together in pairs to form prayers:

> **'God of gentleness and fairness, teach us to be gentle and fair.'**
> **'Spirit of love and truth, teach us to be loving and truthful.'**

The hill of crosses

You will need
    Some crosses.
    Some strips of firm card to make small crosses.
    A pot of play sand.

Introduction
Show the crosses and ask pupils where they might see them. Talk with the pupils about what the cross stands for. **Today we are going to find out about a hill of crosses. For Christians the cross is a symbol of suffering, because Jesus died on a cross, but it is also a sign of hope, because they believe Jesus rose from the dead.**

Core material
Lithuania is a small country between Poland and Russia. For hundreds of years it was ruled by Russia and the people of Lithuania were very unhappy. Twice they tried to get their freedom but both times they failed and many people died as a result. To remember those who had died trying to get their freedom, some crosses were placed on a hill. The hill became a symbol of the people's faith and hope. In the year 1900 there were 130 crosses; by 1938 there were 400. The numbers continued to grow until there were thousands of crosses. The Russian rulers didn't like the crosses, and several times they destroyed them, but the crosses were always replaced and more added. Then the rulers tried to block the roads to the hill of crosses, and guarded it with soldiers, but still crosses would appear overnight. Placing crosses on the hill was the people's way of keeping their hope alive. In 1990 Lithuania became a free country. By that time there were 55,000 crosses!

The hill of crosses is still an important place for the people of Lithuania. It has become a place where people visit. When life gets hard they go there to pray and worship. There they see the thousands of crosses, the Christian symbol of hope. Each cross tells its own story: some were put there with prayers of thanks, others were put there after a sad event. Today the hill of crosses is visited by people from all over the world who go to pray and worship. What was once a symbol of suffering and hope for one country has become a symbol of hope for many.

Reflection
What symbol would you use if you wanted to remind people to hope?

Prayer (OPTIONAL)
Make a card cross and cut the bottom into a point. Ask pupils for a prayer to write on the cross. Plant it in the sand. Some pupils might like to make their own prayer-cross to add.

> **'Lord of all hope, give us hope in difficult times and comfort those who mourn and suffer.'**

Iona

You will need

Some means of marking four or five places around the hall.

Introduction

Ask one or two pupils to walk around the hall, making sure that they touch each of your markers on their way. Explain that we could turn this into a 'thinking journey' by adding something to think about at each marker. Ask pupils for suggestions and add them to the markers. Explain that today's assembly is about a special journey where people think and pray.

Core material

Iona is a small island off Scotland. It is a place of pilgrimage. A pilgrimage is a journey to a religious or spiritual place. The Celtic saint Columba came from Ireland to Iona in 563ce to spread the Christian message. St Columba originally came from Ireland but he left his home and sailed to Iona. What Columba did was to sail round the island of Iona and land at the first place where he could no longer see Ireland. He thought that if he could still see his homeland he would always be looking backwards and never forward.

Iona became a centre for Christian faith and learning. It was on Iona that Oswald learned about the Christian faith (A5, page 19). Oswald then invited monks from Iona to bring the Christian faith to his own country of Northumbria (northern England). From Iona the Christian faith spread across Scotland and England.

For over 1,000 years people have come on pilgrimages to Iona. The pilgrims walk around the island, stopping at twelve special places and saying prayers. They start at St Martin's cross. Before they begin their walk they say this prayer:

Bless to us, O God, the earth beneath our feet,
Bless to us, O God, the path whereon we go,
Bless to us, O God, the people who we meet,
Evermore and evermore, be with us on our way. *(From the Carmina Gadelica)*

One of the prayer-stops is the bay where Columba landed. There people pray about new beginnings in their own lives: new jobs, new schools, new friendships. (See also www. request.org.uk/main/dowhat/pilgrimage/iona/iona05.htm.)

Reflection

Do you have a special place where you go to think?

Prayer (OPTIONAL)

Create a 'prayer journey' by adding prayers to the markers. A few pupils can walk the journey and read out the prayers. Prayers from different parts of this book could be used, depending on the theme you want for the journey.

The Black Madonna

You will need

A small birthday candle in a tray of damp play sand.
Matches and oven gloves (teacher only).
Ways of putting out the candle (see Introduction below).
A lapel pin.

Introduction

Light the candle and ask the pupils to suggest different ways of putting it out. After each suggestion relight it. Make sure this is done safely. Leave the water suggestion until the end.

➤ Blow it out.
➤ Snuff it out.
➤ Starve it of air (using a heatproof container).
➤ Put it out with water.

Core material

The Black Madonna of Czestochowa (Chestohova) in Poland is a sacred painting of Mary and the baby Jesus in the monastery of Jasna Gora. Unlike many paintings of Mary, her face is dark, so she is called the Black Madonna. No one knows why Mary was painted with a dark face: some people think that candles and time have darkened the wood and paint; others think she was painted that way and the real Mary may have been dark-skinned as she came from Israel. Through all the ups and downs of the history of the Polish people, this sacred painting of Mary has inspired them to resist bad rulers. It was as if the faith of the people was like a flame and the painting helped to keep the flame alight. Refer to the introductory activity.

In the twentieth century, when the Germans and later the Russians invaded Poland, the people continued to go to Jasna Gora to pray in front of the painting, and the flame of faith was kept alive. In the 1980s a Christian called Lech Walesa, who worked as an electrician in a shipyard, started a movement to free Poland. Lech Walesa used to wear a lapel pin showing the Black Madonna, which everyone knew was a sign that they must not give up. Show the lapel pin. The movement spread and a peaceful rebellion happened. By 1990 Lech Walesa was president of a free Poland. If you visit a Catholic church in Poland today, you are likely to see a copy of this painting.

Reflection

Why do you think the painting helped the people of Poland?

Prayer (OPTIONAL)

Light the candle.

'Lord, we pray for all those who live in difficult conditions. We pray for justice and for change. Be with those who work for change. Keep them safe. Keep the flame of faith alive.'

Walsingham

You will need
> Pictures of different types of house (optional).
> Duplo.
> Some shoe boxes.

Introduction

Ask some pupils to create different types of houses using Duplo. Ask other pupils to list different types of houses, for example, semi-detached, flats, terraced, caravans, etc. Explain that today's assembly is about a special house.

Core material

Nazareth is a town in the country called Israel. It is the town where Jesus grew up. Jesus was brought up in a simple workman's house, nothing like the types of houses we know. In the 2,000 years since Jesus lived, people have always wanted to go to Israel to visit the place where he grew up. For most people until recently, it was much too far away and travel was hard, and most people could not afford it. About 1,000 years ago, in 1061, a wealthy lady called Richeldis had a dream which gave her the idea of building a simple house, in Walsingham in Norfolk. She hoped that the house would remind Christians that Jesus grew up in an ordinary home and knew what ordinary family life was like. The house became known as the 'English Nazareth' or the 'holy house'. This simple house became a place where Christians would go to talk to Jesus (pray). They believe that he listens to them and understands.

Because the house was in England more people could go to visit it, and Walsingham became a place of pilgrimage – a special religious journey. People would travel from where they lived to Norfolk to pray at the 'holy house'. In 1938 on Pentecost Sunday a national pilgrimage took place and 6,000 people walked together from the parish church in Walsingham to the 'holy house'. Since then this Pentecost pilgrimage has happened almost every year.

Reflection

Think about it. Do you find it easier to talk to people when they know what your life is like?

Prayer (OPTIONAL)

Write some prayers suggested by pupils on shoe boxes, or use the ones below. Build the boxes into a house (just a rectangle of boxes). You can complete the house if you wish by adding folded card to make a roof and pieces of paper for a door and windows.

> 'Bless those who share their homes with other people, inviting others in to share in food and fun.'
> 'Lord, you lived in an ordinary house that was made special by the people who lived there. Help us to make our homes special by the love and care we show to the people who live there.'

Bardsey Island

You will need
> Travel brochures.
> Images of Bardsey Island (optional).

Introduction

Ask some pupils to look through the travel brochures and suggest where they would like to go. How would they get there: by train, plane, car or boat? Why would they go there? What would be their reason for travelling? Explain that today's assembly is about a journey to an island.

Core material

Bardsey Island (Ynys Enlli) is a small island that lies off the tip of North Wales. Pilgrims have been travelling to this rocky island for nearly 1,500 years. There is little on the island: a few ruins, a couple of farms and lots of birds and seals. It is not easy to get to Bardsey, you can only get there by boat and the sea is very rough round the island. Why do people still want to come? Some come for the wildlife; the island is a bird sanctuary. Others come for a different reason. Bardsey's other name is 'the island of 20,000 saints'. About 600 years after Jesus lived, a Celtic saint from Brittany (northern France) called Cadfan came to the island and founded a monastery there. It is thought that each monk had their own little 'cell' that was shaped like a beehive, and the cells were built round a central church (see images at www.worldheritagesite.org/sites/ skelligmichael.html).

From that time onwards, many thousands of Christians have come to Bardsey over the years, and have found it quiet and peaceful. People can be alone with God. The island became a 'people sanctuary' as well as a bird sanctuary. Long ago some of these Christian visitors stayed there and died and were buried on the island. That is how it got its name: 'the island of 20,000 saints'. The 'saints' were probably the many pilgrims who are buried there. People coming to Bardsey today pray in places where Christians have prayed for nearly 1,500 years. Celtic Christians (C1, page 25) were very aware of all the people who had lived before them and all the Christians around the world. They did not feel 'alone', even when they were on an island like Bardsey.

Reflection

What would your 'people sanctuary' look like? Would it be an island?

Prayer (OPTIONAL)

Close your eyes and imagine people like you but from earlier times. Try to imagine the different clothes and hairstyles. For thousands of years Christians have been worshipping and praying. This is a prayer that Christians sometimes say to remind them of that.

> 'Therefore with angels and archangels, and all the company of heaven, we proclaim your great and glorious name.'

Appendix

The illustrations in the Appendix are photocopiable. They can also be downloaded free as a PDF file for printing from RMEP's website: www.rmep.co.uk/summer.

Making the jigsaws for Summer saints assemblies (A4–A5, pages 18–19)

Jigsaws can be made during the assembly or drawn and cut out beforehand – it is up to the teacher.

➤ Take a large piece of thick paper or card.
➤ Draw a four-piece jigsaw on it.
➤ Cut out the jigsaw.
➤ Enlarge the relevant illustrations.
➤ Glue one illustration to each piece of jigsaw.

Star outline for Jocelyn Bell Burnett (H5, page 70)

Enlarge and photocopy onto lightweight card.

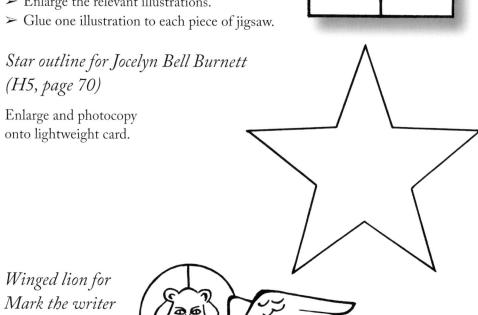

Winged lion for Mark the writer (G2, page 57)

Extract from the prayer of St Patrick for The caim (C1, page 25)

Christ beside me, Christ before me,
Christ behind me, Christ within me,
Christ beneath me, Christ above me,
Christ at my right, Christ at my left.

A modern Caim prayer for The caim (C1, page 25)

Circle us Lord, keep lies out, keep truth within.
Circle us Lord, keep worry out, keep peace within.
Circle us Lord, keep danger out, keep us safe within.

Celtic prayers and blessings for A prayer basket (C4, page 28)

A school blessing
The peace of God be on this school:
On the bricks and roof,
On the windows and doors,
On all who are inside it.
May God the Father protect all the people here,
May Jesus guide them in the way,
May the gentle Spirit be always present.
The blessing of the Friendly Three be on each one.

A journey blessing
May God's hand hold yours as you journey.
May God's sunshine brighten your road.
May God's rainbow paint hope in your heart.
And may God walk beside you all the way.

A work blessing
May God bless my work today:
Bless my hand as it writes,
And my mind as it thinks.
Bless my pen and my computer,
Bless me heart and soul.

Pachelbel's Canon for Creativity (C2, page 26)

This can be sung in unison with more pupils joining in each line until the whole school sings the last line. Add an 'Amen' to finish the song.

Canon in D

Johann Pachelbel

Extra information for Tearfund assemblies (D1–D10, pages 31–40)

D1 and D2 (Climate change/recycle): The Tearfund website has climate change pentathlon games to play that includes a recycle game. www.tearfund.org/ Campaigning/Climate+change+and+disasters/Pentathlon.htm See also http:// actionpack.tearfund.org/fact_climate.htm. Search the site by 'Climate change partners' to find out some local initiatives.

A global warming mug can be purchased. As the mug warms up, the map on the outside changes showing areas affected by global warming. http://youth.tearfund. org/campaigning/climate+change/goodgoods_cc.htm

D3 (Food): Go to www.tearfund.org and search by 'Nutrition' for adult information. Go to http://actionpack.tearfund.org/fun.htm for fun games such as 'Potato invaders'. The packs 'Glorious food' and 'Bite back' have lots of images, recipes, activities and information.

D4 (Micro credit): More information is available on the Tearfund website www. tearfund.org. Search by 'Heed' or see the schools' pack. The pack 'Get cracking' has lots of activities and images.

D5 and D6 (toilets and water): Go to www.tearfund.org and search by 'Sanitation' or 'Water'. See also the schools' pack.

D7 (Responding): For ideas go to http://actionpack.tearfund.org. Look at 'Faith' and 'Feedback'. See also the children's pack.

D8 (TB): Go to www.tearfund.org and search by 'Killer TB' or 'TB' for adult information.

D9 (Child-parents) Go to www.tearfund.org and search by 'Bring childhood back to life' for adult information. A pack of that name is available, which is about HIV/AIDS, so choose material sensitively. However, the issue of child-parents can be dealt with without mentioning AIDS, using some of the information from the pack. Go to http://actionpack.tearfund.org/fact.htm for 'Rachel's story'.

D10 (Trade injustice): See children's pack and search the whole site by 'Trade justice' or 'Fair trade' for adult information. http://actionpack.tearfund.org/fair-trade.htm

What £5 can do for Be an angel (D7, page 37)

This section describes how small amounts of money can be used by Tearfund. Other aid agencies do similar things – see the websites on page 30. An older pupil can keep a running total as the statements are read and add them up at the end to make £5. The statements can be read by different people.

Note: The small amounts indicate a proportion of salaries, etc. Many people are volunteers, others are full-time workers.

My name is Marcella; I use £1.80 to help homeless teenagers in Bolivia, South America.

My name is Dan; I use £2.20 to provide safe water and toilets for refugees in Sudan.

My name is Andy; I use 25p to talk to the prime minister about climate change.

My name is Rose; I spend some of my time checking wooden bowls made by people with disabilities in Thailand. People sell them to create an income. That costs 10p.

My name is Mark; I visit a youth group to talk about changing the way we live. That costs 25p.

My name is Ian; I write to people about supporting those who work to stop disease. That costs 35p.

My name is Richard; I use just 5p from every £5 to make sure that the money is being spent properly.

The five senses for The five-stringed harp (C3, page 27)

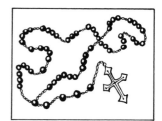

This shop front can be enlarged and photocopied onto different coloured paper.

Photocopy, enlarge and cut mouth, nose and eye holes. A strip of card can be added to enable children to hold the mask in front of their face. A larger version can be downloaded from the RMEP website: www.rmep.co.uk/summer.

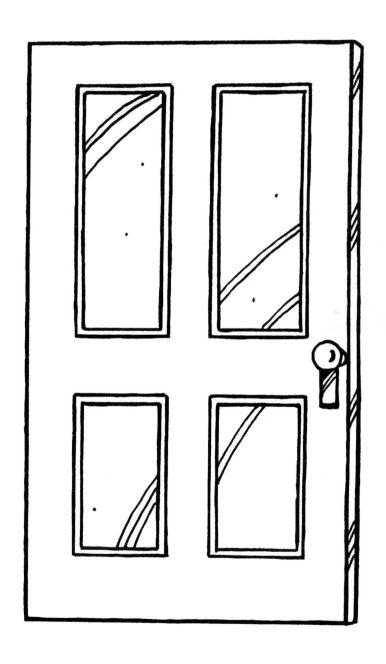

Larger versions of these pictures can be downloaded from the RMEP website: www.rmep.co.uk/summer.

Make a **winning** decision.

Your choice of marine electronics is one of the most important decisions you will have to make as a boat owner, next to choosing the boat itself of course. Thousands of sailors head to the water everyday, confident in the performance and accuracy of their chosen Raymarine equipment.

When you buy Raymarine equipment, you are buying into world-class performance, top-notch integration, and the latest proven design technologies. Years of research and development, and customer feedback have resulted in the 'simple-on-the-outside, sophisticated-on-the-inside' design philosophy that is behind all our intuitive easy-to-use equipment.

Worldwide support and warranty

That's why Raymarine has a worldwide network of product-trained distributors and service dealers and offers a comprehensive warranty to handle the unexpected… wherever you decide to go.

Every change in direction. Every shift in the wind. Every change in depth. Every port you pass. Every ship on your ocean. Every fish in your sea…

2009/Mg98/v

www.raymarine.co.uk

Raymarine®

… with you every degree of the way.

SOUTH EAST ENGLAND - Selsey Bill to North Foreland

Key to Marina Plans symbols

🔥 Bottled gas		P Parking	
Chandler		Pub/Restaurant	
Disabled facilities		Pump out	
Electrical supply		Rigging service	
Electrical repairs		Sail repairs	
Engine repairs		Shipwright	
First Aid		Shop/Supermarket	
Fresh Water		Showers	
Fuel - Diesel		Slipway	
Fuel - Petrol		WC Toilets	
Hardstanding/boatyard		Telephone	
@ Internet Café		Trolleys	
Laundry facilities		V Visitors berths	
Lift-out facilities		Wi-Fi	

3

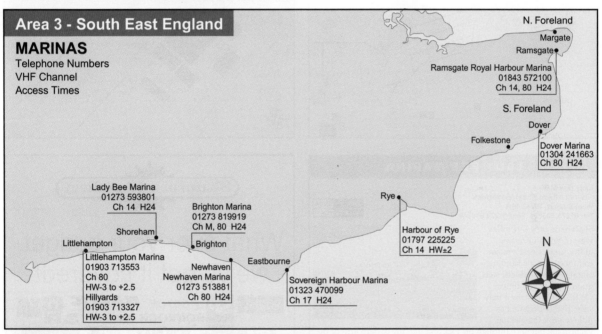

Area 3 - South East England

MARINAS
Telephone Numbers
VHF Channel
Access Times

N. Foreland

Margate

Ramsgate

Ramsgate Royal Harbour Marina
01843 572100
Ch 14, 80 H24

S. Foreland

Dover

Folkestone

Dover Marina
01304 241663
Ch 80 H24

Lady Bee Marina
01273 593801
Ch 14 H24

Brighton Marina
01273 819919
Ch M, 80 H24

Rye

Shoreham

Littlehampton

Brighton

Harbour of Rye
01797 225225
Ch 14 HW±2

Littlehampton Marina
01903 713553
Ch 80
HW-3 to +2.5
Hillyards
01903 713327
HW-3 to +2.5

Newhaven
Newhaven Marina
01273 513881
Ch 80 H24

Eastbourne

Sovereign Harbour Marina
01323 470099
Ch 17 H24

N

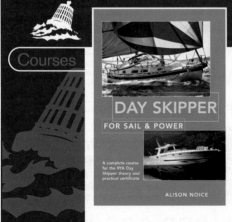

LITTLEHAMPTON MARINA

Littlehampton Marina
Ferry Road, Littlehampton, W Sussex
Tel: 01903 713553 Fax: 01903 732264
Email: sales@littlehamptonmarina.co.uk

VHF Ch 80
ACCESS HW-3 to +2.5

A typical English seaside town with funfair, promenade and fine sandy beaches, Littlehampton lies roughly midway between Brighton and Chichester at the mouth of the River Arun. It affords a convenient stopover for yachts either east or west bound, providing you have the right tidal conditions to cross the entrance bar with its charted depth of 0.7m. The marina lies about three cables above Town Quay and Fisherman's Quay, both of which are on the starboard side of the River Arun, and is accessed via a retractable footbridge that opens on request to the HM (note that you should contact him by 1630 the day before you require entry).

FACILITIES AT A GLANCE

Key
a Marina offices
b Cafe

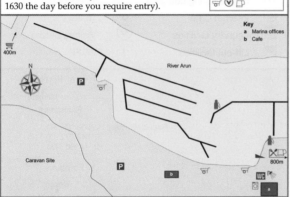

HILLYARDS

Hillyards
Rope Walk, Littlehampton, West Sussex, BN17 5DG
Tel: 01903 713327 Fax: 01903 722787
www.hillyards.co.uk Email: info@hillyards.co.uk

VHF
ACCESS HW-3 to +2.5

Established for more than 100 years Hillyards is a full service boatyard with moorings and storage for up to 50 boats. Based on the south coast within easy reach of London and the main yachting centres of the UK and Europe, Hillyards provides a comprehensive range of marine services.

The buildings of the boatyard are on the River Arun, a short distance from the English Channel. They provide the ideal conditions to accommodate and service craft up to 36m in length and with a maximum draft 3.5m. There is also craning services for craft up to 40 tons and the facilities to slip vessels up to 27m. In addition there are secure facilities to accommodate vessels up to 54m in dry dock.

FACILITIES AT A GLANCE

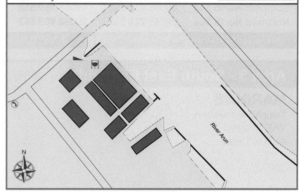

LADY BEE MARINA

Lady Bee Marina
138-140 Albion Street, Southwick
West Sussex, BN42 4EG
Tel: 01273 593801 Fax: 01273 870349

VHF Ch 14
ACCESS H24

Shoreham, only five miles west of Brighton, is one of the South Coast's major commercial ports handling, among other products, steel, grain, tarmac and timber. On first impressions it may seem that Shoreham has little to offer the visiting yachtsman, but once through the lock and into the eastern arm of the River Adur, the quiet Lady Bee Marina, with its Spanish waterside restaurant, can make this harbour an interesting alternative to the lively atmosphere of Brighton Marina. Run by the Harbour Office, the marina meets all the usual requirements, although fuel is available in cans from Southwick garage or from Corral's diesel pump situated in the western arm.

FACILITIES AT A GLANCE

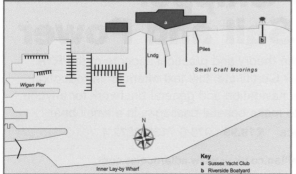

Key
a Sussex Yacht Club
b Riverside Boatyard

3

BRIGHTON MARINA

Brighton Marina
West Jetty, Brighton, East Sussex, BN2 5UP
Tel: 01273 819919 Fax: 01273 675082
Email: brighton@premiermarinas.com
www.premiermarinas.com

VHF	Ch M, 80
ACCESS	H24

Brighton Marina is the largest marina in the country and with its extensive range of shops, restaurants and facilities, is a popular and convenient stop-over for east and west-going passagemakers. Note, however, that it is not advisable to attempt entry in strong S to SE winds.

Only half a mile from the marina is the historic city of Brighton itself, renowned for being a cultural centre with a cosmopolitan atmosphere. Among its numerous attractions are the exotic Royal Pavilion, built for King George IV in the 1800s, and the Lanes, with its multitude of antiques shops.

FACILITIES AT A GLANCE

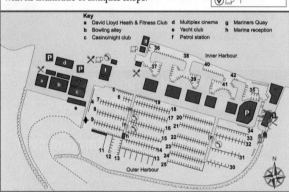

Key
a David Lloyd Heath & Fitness Club
b Bowling alley
c Casino/night club
d Multiplex cinema
e Yacht club
f Petrol station
g Mariners Quay
h Marina reception

NEWHAVEN MARINA

Newhaven Marina
The Yacht Harbour, Fort Road, Newhaven
East Sussex, BN9 9BY
Tel: 01273 513881 Fax: 01273 510493
Email: john.stirling@seacontainers.com

| VHF | Ch 80 |
| ACCESS | H24 |

Some seven miles from Brighton, Newhaven lies at the mouth of the River Ouse. With its large fishing fleet and regular ferry services to Dieppe, the harbour has over the years become progressively commercial, therefore care is needed to keep clear of large vessels under manoeuvre. The marina lies approximately quarter of a mile from the harbour entrance on the west bank and was recently dredged to allow full tidal access except on LWS.

FACILITIES AT A GLANCE

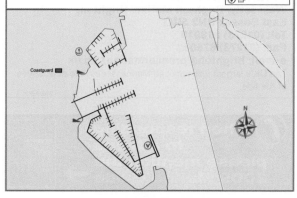

Coastguard

3

SOVEREIGN HARBOUR MARINA

Sovereign Harbour Marina Ltd
Pacific Drive, Eastbourne, East Sussex, BN23 5BJ
Tel: 01323 470099 Fax: 01323 470077
Email: taylor.janet@carillianplc.com
www.sovereignharbour.co.uk

VHF Ch 17
ACCESS H24

Opened in 1993, Sovereign Harbour is situated a few miles NE of Eastbourne and is accessible at all states of the tide and weather except for in strong NE to SE'ly winds. Entered via a lock at all times of the day or night, the marina is part of one of the largest waterfront complexes in Britain, enjoying close proximity to shops, restaurants and a multiplex cinema. A short bus or taxi ride takes you to Eastbourne, where again you will find an array of shops and eating places to suit all tastes and budgets.

FACILITIES AT A GLANCE

Key
a The Waterfront, shops, restaurants, pubs and offices
b Harbour office - weather information and visitor's information
c Cinema
d Retail park - supermarket and post office
e Restaurant
f Toilets, showers, telephone, launderette and disabled facilities
g 24 hr fuel pontoon (diesel, petrol and holding tank pump out)
h Recycling centre
i Boatyard, boatpark, marine engineers, riggers and electricians

HARBOUR OF RYE

Harbour of Rye
New Lydd Road, Camber, E Sussex, TN31 7QS
Tel: 01797 225225 Fax: 01797 227429
Email: rye.harbour@environment-agency.gov.uk
www.environment-agency.gov.uk/harbourofrye

VHF Ch 14
ACCESS HW±2

The Strand Quay moorings are located in the centre of the historic town of Rye with all of its amenities a short walk away. The town caters for a wide variety of interests with the nearby Rye Harbour Nature Reserve, a museum, numerous antique shops and plentiful pubs, bars and restaurants. Vessels, up to a length of 15 metres, wishing to berth in the soft mud in or near the town of Rye should time their arrival at the entrance for not later than one hour after high water. Larger vessels should make prior arrangements with the Harbour Master. Fresh water, electricity, shower and toilet facilities are available.

FACILITIES AT A GLANCE

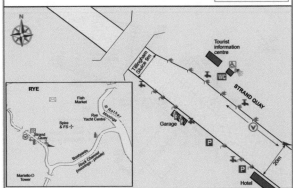

2009/MG2/v

DOVER MARINA

Dover Harbour Board
Harbour House, Dover, Kent, CT17 9TF
Tel: 01304 241663 Fax: 01304 242549
Email: marina@doverport.co.uk

| VHF | Ch 80 |
| ACCESS | H24 |

Nestling under the famous White Cliffs, Dover sits between South Foreland to the NE and Folkestone to the SW. Boasting a maritime history stretching back as far as the Bronze Age, Dover is today one of Britain's busiest commercial ports, with a continuous stream of ferries and cruise liners plying to and from their European destinations. However, over the past years the harbour has made itself more attractive to the cruising yachtsman, with the marina, set well away from the busy ferry terminal, offering three sheltered berthing options in the Tidal Harbour, Granville Dock and Wellington Dock.

FACILITIES AT A GLANCE

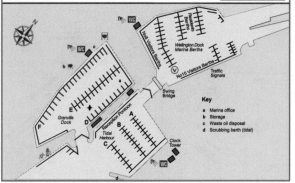

Key
a Marina office
b Storage
c Waste oil disposal
d Scrubbing berth (tidal)

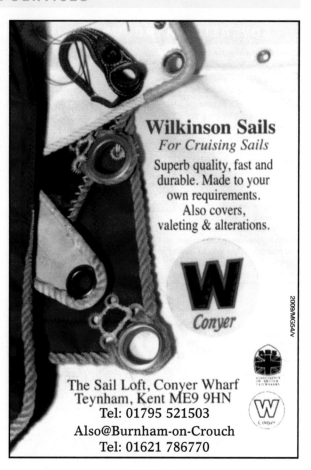
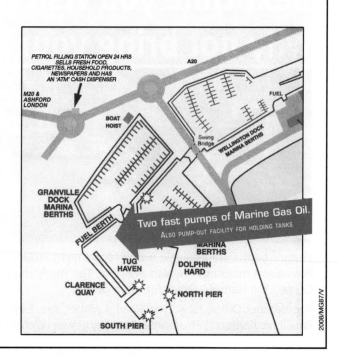

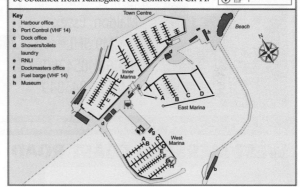

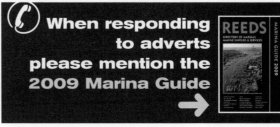

Widely regarded as the finest marina facility on the River Crouch, Fambridge Yacht Haven is nestled within our surrounding salt marsh's providing naturally sheltered swinging moorings, pontoon berths and extensive hard standing. Visitors are always welcome, whether staying over night afloat or wintering ashore.

Undercover & Indoor Boat Storage Units

• New indoor boat storage facilities available for long or short term hire. These secure, well lit units are suitable for vessels up to 16m LOA and 5m beam. The units can be hired for painting, GRP repairs, welding, osmosis treatment and new builds.

• Valet Berthing, with just a few hours notice we will collect your boat from its river mooring and place it alongside our new visitor pontoon, you can then just step aboard and go sailing. On return you leave your boat alongside the pontoon and we will return it to its river mooring.

• Secure 'Bosuns Lockers' available to rent for the storage of general boat maintenance equipment, outboards, sails etc

• Long term & project boat storage in secure compound at reduced rates

• Modern boat handling and lifting equipment

2009/MG28/r

• 120 deep-water swinging moorings
• 180 berth marina with 24 hours access
• Thames and Dutch barges welcome any time of year on fully serviceable mud berths
• Extensive hardstanding for long and short term storage, visitors welcome
• WISE 25 ton slipway hoist

• Mobile crane and pressure washing
• 24 hour CCTV
• 120 meter, deep water visitors' pontoon
• Valet berthing service, contact us for further information
• 2 x concrete slipways

Fambridge Yacht Haven
Church Road, North Fambridge, Essex, CM3 6LR
Telephone 01621 740370

www.yachthavens.com
email: fambridge@yachthavens.com

THE wildlife TRUSTS
ESSEX Wildlife Trust
Corporate Members

EAST ENGLAND - North Foreland to Great Yarmouth

Key to Marina Plans symbols

Bottled gas		Parking
Chandler		Pub/Restaurant
Disabled facilities		Pump out
Electrical supply		Rigging service
Electrical repairs		Sail repairs
Engine repairs		Shipwright
First Aid		Shop/Supermarket
Fresh Water		Showers
Fuel - Diesel		Slipway
Fuel - Petrol		Toilets
Hardstanding/boatyard		Telephone
Internet Café		Trolleys
Laundry facilities		Visitors berths
Lift-out facilities		Wi-Fi

4

Area 4 - East England

MARINAS
Telephone Numbers
VHF Channel
Access Times

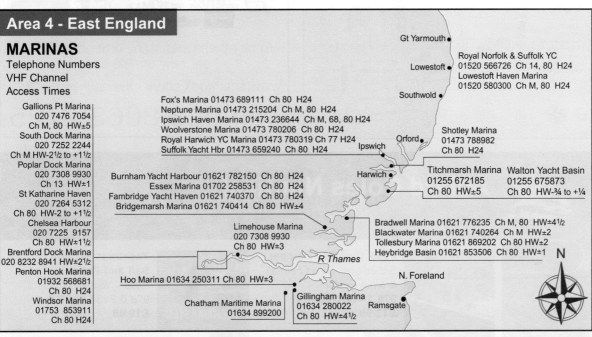

Gallions Pt Marina
020 7476 7054
Ch M, 80 HW±5
South Dock Marina
020 7252 2244
Ch M HW-2½ to +1½
Poplar Dock Marina
020 7308 9930
Ch 13 HW±1
St Katharine Haven
020 7264 5312
Ch 80 HW-2 to +1½
Chelsea Harbour
020 7225 9157
Ch 80 HW±1½
Brentford Dock Marina
020 8232 8941 HW±2½
Penton Hook Marina
01932 568681
Ch 80 H24
Windsor Marina
01753 853911
Ch 80 H24

Fox's Marina 01473 689111 Ch 80 H24
Neptune Marina 01473 215204 Ch M, 80 H24
Ipswich Haven Marina 01473 236644 Ch M, 68, 80 H24
Woolverstone Marina 01473 780206 Ch 80 H24
Royal Harwich YC Marina 01473 780319 Ch 77 H24
Suffolk Yacht Hbr 01473 659240 Ch 80 H24

Burnham Yacht Harbour 01621 782150 Ch 80 H24
Essex Marina 01702 258531 Ch 80 H24
Fambridge Yacht Haven 01621 740370 Ch 80 H24
Bridgemarsh Marina 01621 740414 Ch 80 HW±4

Limehouse Marina
020 7308 9930
Ch 80 HW±3

Hoo Marina 01634 250311 Ch 80 HW±3

Chatham Maritime Marina
01634 899200

Gillingham Marina
01634 280022
Ch 80 HW±4½

Gt Yarmouth

Royal Norfolk & Suffolk YC
01520 566726 Ch 14, 80 H24
Lowestoft Haven Marina
01520 580300 Ch M, 80 H24

Lowestoft

Southwold

Orford

Ipswich

Shotley Marina
01473 788982
Ch 80 H24

Harwich

Titchmarsh Marina
01255 672185
Ch 80 HW±5

Walton Yacht Basin
01255 675873
Ch 80 HW-¾ to +¼

Bradwell Marina 01621 776235 Ch M, 80 HW±4½
Blackwater Marina 01621 740264 Ch M HW±2
Tollesbury Marina 01621 869202 Ch 80 HW±2
Heybridge Basin 01621 853506 Ch 80 HW±1

R Thames

N. Foreland

Ramsgate

N

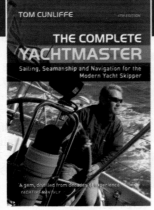

GILLINGHAM MARINA

Gillingham Marina
173 Pier Road, Gillingham, Kent, ME7 1UB
Tel: 01634 280022 Fax: 01634 280164
Email: berthing@gillingham-marina.co.uk
www.gillingham-marina.co.uk

VHF	Ch 80
ACCESS	HW±4.5

Gillingham Marina comprises a locked basin, accessible four and a half hours either side of high water, and a tidal basin upstream which can be entered approximately two hours either side of high water. Deep water moorings in the river cater for yachts arriving at other times.

Visiting yachts are usually accommodated in the locked basin, although it is best to contact the marina ahead of time. Lying on the south bank of the River Medway, the marina is approximately eight miles from Sheerness, at the mouth of the river, and five miles downstream of Rochester Bridge. Facilities include a well-stocked chandlery, brokerage and an extensive workshop.

FACILITIES AT A GLANCE

Key
a Workshop
b Showers & toilets
c Shop
d Laundry
e Play area
f Reception & club
g Tender storage
h Lead in pontoon
i Petrol & diesel
j Leisure centre

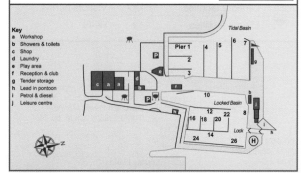

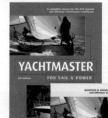

HOO MARINA

Hoo Marina
Vicarage Lane, Hoo, Rochester, Kent, ME3 9LE
Tel: 01634 250311 Fax: 01634 251761
Email: jcmarine@btconnect.com

VHF	Ch 80
ACCESS	HW±3

Hoo is a small village on the Isle of Grain, situated on a drying creek on the north bank of the River Medway approximately eight miles inland from Sheerness. Its marina was the first to be constructed on the East Coast and comprises finger berths supplied by all the usual services. It can be approached either straight across the mudflats near HW or, for a 1.5m draught, three hours either side of HW via a creek known locally as Orinoco. The entrance to this creek, which is marked by posts that must be left to port, is located a mile NW of Hoo Ness. Note that the final mark comprises a small, yellow buoy which you should pass close to starboard just before crossing the marina's sill.

Grocery stores can be found either in the adjacent chalet park or else in Hoo Village, while the Hoo Ness Yacht Club welcomes visitors to its bar and restaurant. There are also frequent bus services to the nearby town of Rochester.

FACILITIES AT A GLANCE

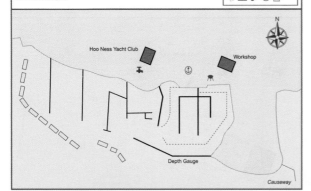

CHATHAM MARITIME MARINA

MDL, The Lock Building, Chatham Maritime Marina
Leviathan Way, Chatham Maritime, Chatham, Medway, ME4 4LP
Tel: 01634 899200 Fax: 01634 899201
Email: chatham@mdlmarinas.co.uk www.marinas.co.uk

VHF	Ch 80
ACCESS	H24

Chatham Maritime Marina is situated on the banks of the River Medway in Kent, providing an ideal location from which to explore the surrounding area. There are plenty of secluded anchorages in the lower reaches of the Medway Estuary, while the river is navigable for some 13 miles from its mouth at Sheerness right up to Rochester, and even beyond for those yachts drawing less than 2m. Only 45 minutes from London by road, the marina is part of a multi-million pound leisure and retail development, currently accommodating 300 yachts.

FACILITIES AT A GLANCE

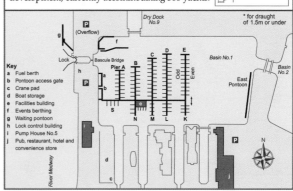

4

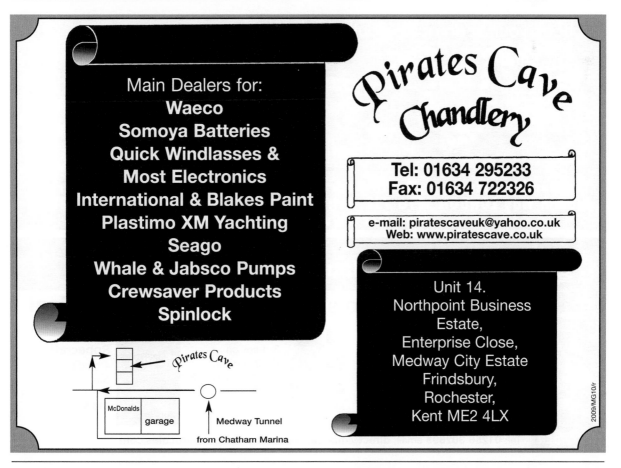

GALLIONS POINT MARINA

Gallions Point Marina, Gate 14, Royal Albert Basin
Woolwich Manor Way, North Woolwich
London, E16 2QY. Tel: 020 7476 7054 Fax: 020 7474 7056
Email: info@gallionspointmarina.co.uk
www.gallionspointmarina.co.uk

VHF	Ch M, 80
ACCESS	HW±5

Gallions Point Marina lies about 500 metres downstream of the Woolwich Ferry on the north side of Gallions Reach. Accessed via a lock at the entrance to the Royal Albert Basin, the marina offers deep water pontoon berths as well as hard standing. Future plans to improve facilities include the development of a bar/restaurant, a chandlery and an RYA tuition school.

FACILITIES AT A GLANCE

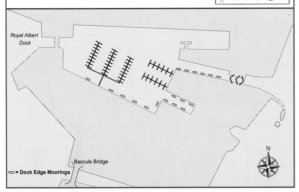

Royal Albert Dock

Bascule Bridge

◁ = Dock Edge Moorings

N

SOUTH DOCK MARINA

South Dock Marina
Rope Street, Off Plough Way
London, SE16 7SZ
Tel: 020 7252 2244 Fax: 020 7237 3806
Email: gary.bettesworth@southwark.gov.uk

VHF	Ch M
ACCESS	HW-2.5 to +1.5

South Dock Marina is housed in part of the old Surrey Dock complex on the south bank of the River Thames. Its locked entrance is immediately downstream of Greenland Pier, just a few miles down river of Tower Bridge. For yachts with a 2m draught, the lock can be entered HW-2½ to HW+1½ London Bridge, although if you arrive early there is a holding pontoon on the pier. The marina can be easily identified by the conspicuous arched rooftops of Baltic Quay, a luxury waterside apartment block. Once inside this secure, 200-berth marina, you can take full advantage of all its facilities as well as enjoy a range of restaurants and bars close by or visit historic maritime Greenwich.

FACILITIES AT A GLANCE

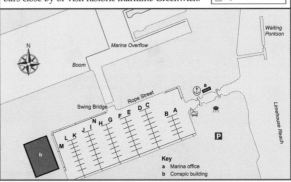

Waiting Pontoon

Marina Overflow

Boom

N

Swing Bridge

Rope Street

Limehouse Reach

L K J I N H G F E D C B A

M

b

P

Key
a   Marina office
b   Conspic building

POPLAR DOCK MARINA

Poplar Dock Marina
c/o Harbourmaster's Office
Limehouse Marina
46 Goodhart Place, London, E14 8EG
Tel: 020 7308 9930 Fax: 020 7363 0428
www.bwml.co.uk

VHF	Ch 13
ACCESS	HW±1 0700-1700

Poplar Dock was originally designed and constructed to maintain the water level in the West India Docks. Nowadays, with Canary Wharf lying to the west and the Millennium Dome to the east, it has been converted into London's newest marina and was officially opened by the Queen in June 1999. Canary Wharf, boasting as many as 90 shops, bars and restaurants, is just a five minute walk away, while slightly further north of this is West India Quay, where Grade I listed warehouses have been converted into waterside eating places, a 12-screen cinema and fitness centre.

FACILITIES AT A GLANCE

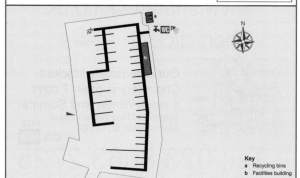

Key
a   Recycling bins
b   Facilities building

LIMEHOUSE MARINA

Limehouse Marina
46 Goodhart Place, London, E14 8EG
Tel: 020 7308 9930 Fax: 020 7363 0428
www.bwml.co.uk

VHF	Ch 80
ACCESS	HW±3

Limehouse Marina, situated where the canal system meets the Thames, is now considered the 'Jewel in the Crown' of the British inland waterways network. With complete access to 2,000 miles of inland waterway systems and with access to the Thames at most stages of the tide except around low water, the marina provides a superb location for river, canal and sea-going pleasure craft alike. Boasting a wide range of facilities and up to 90 berths, Limehouse Marina is housed in the old Regent's Canal Dock.

FACILITIES AT A GLANCE

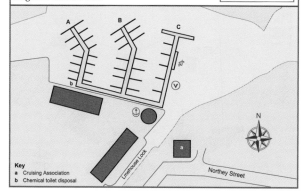

Key
a   Cruising Association
b   Chemical toilet disposal

ST KATHARINE HAVEN

St Katharine's Marina Ltd
50 St Katharine's Way, London, E1W 1LA
Tel: 020 7264 5312 Fax: 020 7702 2252
Email: haven.reception@skdocks.co.uk
www.skdocks.co.uk

VHF	Ch 80
ACCESS	HW -2 to +1.5

St Katharine Docks has played a significant role in worldwide trade and commerce for over 1,000 years. Formerly a working dock, today it is an attractive waterside development housing a mixture of shops, restaurants, luxury flats and offices as well as a state-of-the-art marina. St Katharine Haven is ideally situated for exploring central London and taking full advantage of the West End's theatres and cinemas. Within easy walking distance are Tower Bridge, the Tower of London and the historic warship HMS *Belfast*. No stay at the docks is complete without a visit to the famous Dickens Inn, an impressive three storey timber building incorporating a pizza bar and stylish restaurant.

FACILITIES AT A GLANCE

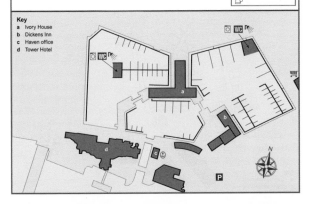

Key
a Ivory House
b Dickens Inn
c Haven office
d Tower Hotel

CHELSEA HARBOUR MARINA

Chelsea Harbour Marina
Estate Managements Office
C2-3 The Chambers, London, SW10 0XF
Tel: 07770 542783 Fax: 020 7352 7868
Email: harbourmaster@chelsea-harbour.co.uk

VHF	
ACCESS	HW±1.5

Chelsea Harbour is now widely thought of as one of London's most significant maritime sites. It is located in the heart of South West London, therefore enjoying easy access to the amenities of Chelsea and the West End. On site is the Chelsea Harbour Design Centre, where 80 showrooms exhibit the best in British and International interior design, while offering superb waterside views along with excellent cuisine is the Conrad Hotel.

The harbour lies approximately 48 miles up river from Sea Reach No 1 buoy in the Thames Estuary and is accessed via the Thames Flood Barrier in Woolwich Reach. With its basin gate operating one and a half hours either side of HW (+ 20 minutes at London Bridge), the marina welcomes visiting yachtsmen.

FACILITIES AT A GLANCE

Key
a Belvedere Tower
b Harbour Yard
c Conrad Hotel
d Kings Quay
e Chelsea Crescent
f Thames Quay
 Showers, toilets & laundry

Sailing Information

Location and Access:
From the sea, Chelsea Harbour is 48 nautical miles upriver from Sea Reach No: 1 Buoy in the Thames Estuary. For vessels entering or leaving the Thames, the recommended overnight mooring, if required, is at Queenbough at the river entrance to the River Medway. Vessels bound for Chelsea Harbour will pass through the Thames Floor Barrier located in Woolwich Reach. Traffic is controlled by Woolwich Radio (VHF Ch 14), and vessels equipped with VHF are required to call up Barrier Control on passing Margaret Ness when proceeding upstream, or on passing Blackwall Point when heading downstream. There is a speed limit of 8 knots on the tideway above Wandsworth Bridge.

Visitors:
Visitor yachtsmen from home and abroad are most welcome to Chelsea Harbour Marina, and are able to make prior arrangements by telephoning the Harbour Master's office on +44 (0) 7770 542783

Basin Gate Operation:
Approximately 1? hours either side of high water +20 minutes at London Bridge. With spring tide it may be necessary to close the outer gates around high water to control marina level.

Marina Lock Dimensions (Maximum for Craft):
Beam 5.5m (18')
Draught 2.5m (8')

Recommended Charts and Publications:
Admiralty: 1183, 2151 2484, 3319
Imray: C1, C2.

Cruising Opportunities:
Chelsea Harbour is ideally located for day, weekend or longer trips either upstream to Kew, Richmond, Hampton Court, or downstream to Rochester.

2009/MG89/v

BRENTFORD DOCK MARINA

Brentford Dock Marina
2 Justine Close, Brentford, Middlesex, TW8 8QE
Tel: 020 8232 8941 Fax: 020 8560 5486 Mob: 07920 143 987
E-mail: sam.langton@brentford-dock.co.uk

VHF
ACCESS HW±2.5

Brentford Dock Marina is situated on the River Thames at the junction with the Grand Union Canal. Its hydraulic lock is accessible for up to two and a half hours either side of high water, although boats over 9.5m LOA enter on high water by prior arrangement. There is a Spar grocery store on site. The main attractions within the area are the Royal Botanic Gardens at Kew and the Kew Bridge Steam Museum at Brentford.

FACILITIES AT A GLANCE

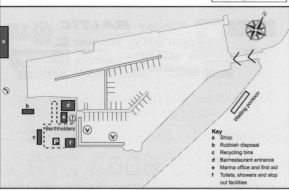

Key
a Shop
b Rubbish disposal
c Recycling bins
d Bar/restaurant entrance
e Marina office and first aid
f Toilets, showers and slop out facilities

PENTON HOOK MARINA

Penton Hook
Staines Road, Chertsey, Surrey, KT16 8PY
Tel: 01932 568681 Fax: 01932 567423
Email: pentonhook@mdlmarinas.co.uk
www.marinas.co.uk

VHF Ch 80
ACCESS H24

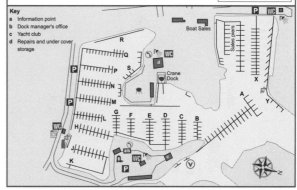

Penton Hook Marina is situated on what is considered to be one of the most attractive reaches of the River Thames, close to Chertsey and about a mile downstream of Runnymede. Providing unrestricted access to the River Thames through a deep water channel below Penton Hook Lock, the marina can accommodate ocean-going craft of up to 21m LOA and is ideally placed for a visit to Thorpe Park, reputedly one of Europe's most popular family leisure attractions.

FACILITIES AT A GLANCE

Key
a Information point
b Dock manager's office
c Yacht club
d Repairs and under cover storage

WINDSOR MARINA

Windsor Marina
Maidenhead Road, Windsor
Berkshire, SL4 5TZ
Tel: 01753 853911 Fax: 01753 868195
Email: windsor@mdlmarinas.co.uk www.marinas.co.uk

VHF Ch 80
ACCESS H24

Situated on the outskirts of Windsor town on the south bank of the River Thames, Windsor Marina enjoys a peaceful garden setting. On site are the Windsor Yacht Club as well as boat lifting and repair facilities, a chandlery and brokerage.

A trip to the town of Windsor, comprising beautiful Georgian and Victorian buildings, would not be complete without a visit to Windsor Castle. With its construction inaugurated over 900 years ago by William the Conqueror, it is the oldest inhabited castle in the world and accommodates a priceless art and furniture collection.

FACILITIES AT A GLANCE

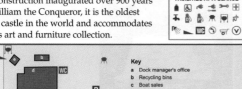

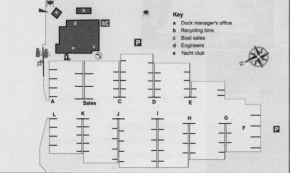

Key
a Dock manager's office
b Recycling bins
c Boat sales
d Engineers
e Yacht club

BRAY MARINA

Bray Marina
Monkey Island Lane, Bray
Berkshire, SL6 2EB
Tel: 01628 623654 Fax: 01628 773485
Email: bray@mdlmarinas.co.uk www.marinas.co.uk

VHF Ch 80
ACCESS H24

Bray Marina is situated in a country park setting among shady trees, providing berth holders with a delightfully tranquil mooring. From the marina there is direct access to the Thames and there are extensive well-maintained facilities available for all boat owners. Also on site is the highly acclaimed Riverside Brasserie. Twice winner of the AA rosette award for culinary excellence and short-listed for the Tatler best country restaurant, the Brasserie is especially popular with Club Outlook members who enjoy a 15% discount. The 400-berth marina boasts an active club, which holds social functions as well as boat training lessons and handling competitions, a chandlery and engineering services.

FACILITIES AT A GLANCE

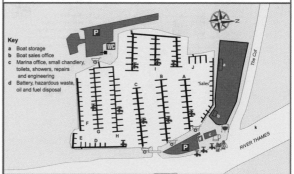

Key
a Boat storage
b Boat sales office
c Marina office, small chandlery, toilets, showers, repairs and engineering
d Battery, hazardous waste, oil and fuel disposal

BURNHAM YACHT HARBOUR MARINA

Burnham Yacht Harbour Marina Ltd
Burnham-on-Crouch, Essex, CM0 8BL
Tel: 01621 782150 Fax: 01621 785848
Email: admin@burnhamyachtharbour.co.uk

VHF	Ch 80
ACCESS	H24

Boasting four major yacht clubs, each with comprehensive racing programmes, Burnham-on-Crouch has come to be regarded by some as 'the Cowes of the East Coast'. At the western end of the town lies Burnham Yacht Harbour, dredged 2.2m below datum. Offering a variety of on site facilities, its entrance can be easily identified by a yellow pillar buoy with an 'X' topmark.

The historic town, with its 'weatherboard' and early brick buildings, elegant quayside and scenic riverside walks, exudes plenty of charm. Among its attractions are a sports centre, a railway museum and a two-screen cinema.

FACILITIES AT A GLANCE

Key
a Workshop
b Yacht sales
c Marina office
d Shower block
e The Swallowtail
f RNLI shore station
g Country park

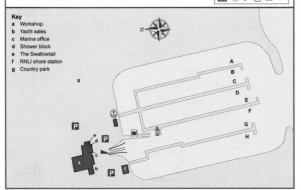

FAMBRIDGE YACHT HAVEN

Fambridge Yacht Haven
Church Road, North Fambridge, Essex, CM3 6LR
Tel: 01621 740370 Fax: 01621 742359
Email: fambridge@yachthavens.com

VHF	Ch 80
ACCESS	H24

Just under a mile upstream of North Fambridge, Stow Creek branches off to the north of the River Crouch. The creek, marked with occasional starboard hand buoys and leading lights, leads to the entrance to Fambridge Yacht Haven, which enjoys an unspoilt, tranquil setting between saltings and farmland. Home to West Wick Yacht Club, the marina has 180 berths and can accommodate vessels up to 17m LOA.

The nearby village of North Fambridge features the Ferryboat Inn, a favourite haunt with the boating fraternity. Only six miles down river lies Burnham-on-Crouch, while the Essex and Kent coasts are within easy sailing distance.

FACILITIES AT A GLANCE

Key
a Marina reception
b Waste
c West Wick YC
d Boat Shed Essex
e Marina maintenance, workshop & stores
f Under cover storage

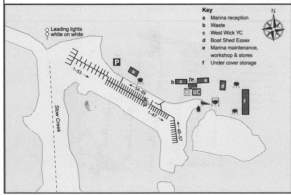

ESSEX MARINA

Essex Marina
Wallasea Island, Essex, SS4 2HF
Tel: 01702 258531 Fax: 01702 258227
Email: info@essexmarina.co.uk
www.essexmarina.co.uk

VHF Ch 80
ACCESS H24

Surrounded by beautiful countryside in an area of Special Scientific Interest, Essex Marina is situated in Wallasea Bay, about half a mile up river of Burnham on Crouch. Boasting 500 deep water berths, including 50 swinging moorings, the marina can be accessed at all states of the tide. On site are a 70 ton boat hoist, a chandlery and brokerage service as well as the Essex Marina Yacht Club.

Buses run frequently to Southend-on-Sea, just seven miles away, while a ferry service takes passengers across the river on weekends to Burnham, where you will find numerous shops and restaurants. Benefiting from its close proximity to London (just under an hour's drive away) and Rochford Airport (approximately four miles away), the marina provides a suitable location for crew changeovers.

FACILITIES AT A GLANCE

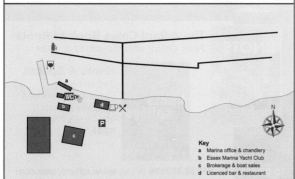

Key
a   Marina office & chandlery
b   Essex Marina Yacht Club
c   Brokerage & boat sales
d   Licenced bar & restaurant

BRIDGEMARSH MARINA

Bridge Marsh Marine
Fairholme, Bridge Marsh Lane, Althorne, Essex
Tel: 01621 740414 Mobile: 07968 696815 Fax: 01621 740414

VHF Ch 80
ACCESS HW±4

On the north side of Bridgemarsh Island, just beyond Essex Marina on the River Crouch, lies Althorne Creek. Here Bridgemarsh Marine accommodates over 100 boats berthed alongside pontoons supplied with water and electricity. A red beacon marks the entrance to the creek, with red can buoys identifying the approach channel into the marina. Accessible four hours either side of high water, the marina has an on site yard with two docks, a slipway and crane. The village of Althorne is just a short walk away, from where there are direct train services (taking approximately one hour) to London.

FACILITIES AT A GLANCE

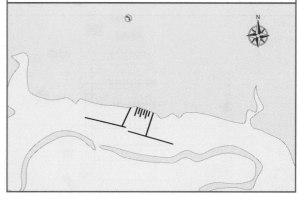

4

BRADWELL MARINA

Bradwell Marina, Port Flair Ltd, Waterside
Bradwell-on-Sea, Essex, CM0 7RB
Tel: 01621 776235 Fax: 01621 776393
Email: info@bradwellmarina.com
www.bradwellmarina.com

VHF	Ch M, 80
ACCESS	HW±4.5

Opened in 1984, Bradwell is a privately-owned marina situated in the mouth of the River Blackwater, serving as a convenient base from which to explore the Essex coastline or as a departure point for cruising further afield to Holland and Belgium. The yacht basin can be accessed four and a half hours either side of HW and offers plenty of protection from all wind directions. With a total of 300 fully serviced berths, generous space has been allocated for manoeuvring between pontoons. Overlooking the marina is Bradwell Club House, incorporating a bar, restaurant, launderette and ablution facilities.

FACILITIES AT A GLANCE

Key
a Clubhouse
b Tower office

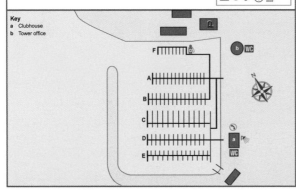

BLACKWATER MARINA

Blackwater Marina
Marine Parade, Maylandsea, Essex
Tel: 01621 740264 Tel: 01621 742122
Email: info@blackwater-marina.co.uk

VHF	Ch M
ACCESS	HW±2

Blackwater Marina is a place where families in day boats mix with Smack owners and yacht crews; here seals, avocets and porpoises roam beneath the big, sheltering East Coast skies and here the area's rich heritage of working Thames Barges and Smacks remains part of daily life today. But it isn't just classic sailing boats that thrive on the Blackwater. An eclectic mix of motor cruisers, open boats and modern yachts enjoy the advantages of a marina sheltered by its natural habitat, where the absence of harbour walls allows uninterrupted views of some of Britain's rarest wildlife and where the 21st century shoreside facilities are looked after by experienced professionals, who are often found sailing on their days off.

FACILITIES AT A GLANCE

Key
a Maylandsea Bay YC
b Harlow (Blackwater) Sailing Club
c Main office

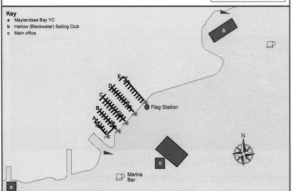

Flag Station

Marina Bar

TOLLESBURY MARINA

Tollesbury Marina
The Yacht Harbour, Tollesbury, Essex, CM9 8SE
Tel: 01621 869202 Fax: 01621 868489
email: marina@woodrolfe.com

VHF | Ch M, 80
ACCESS | HW±2

Tollesbury Marina lies at the mouth of the River Blackwater in the heart of the Essex countryside. Within easy access from London and the Home Counties, it has been designed as a leisure centre for the whole family, with on-site activities comprising tennis courts and a covered heated swimming pool as well as a convivial bar and restaurant. Accommodating over 240 boats, the marina can be accessed two hours either side of HW and is ideally situated for those wishing to explore the River Crouch to the south and the Rivers Colne, Orwell and Deben to the north.

FACILITIES AT A GLANCE

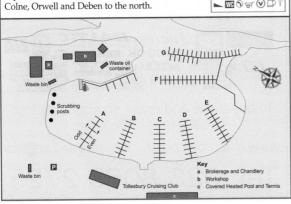

Key
a Brokerage and Chandlery
b Workshop
c Covered Heated Pool and Tennis

HEYBRIDGE BASIN

Heybridge Basin
Lock Hill, Heybridge Basin, Maldon, Essex, CM9 4RX
Tel: 01621 853506 Fax: 01621 859689
Email: colinandmargeret@lockkeepers.fsnet.co.uk
www.cbn.co.uk

VHF | Ch 80
ACCESS | HW±1

Towards the head of the River Blackwater, not far from Maldon, lies Heybridge Basin. Situated at the lower end of the 14–mile long Chelmer and Blackwater Navigation Canal, it can be reached via a lock about one hour either side of HW for a yacht drawing around 2m. If you arrive too early, there is good holding ground in the river just outside the lock. Incorporating as many as 200 berths, the basin has a range of facilities, including shower and laundry amenities. It is strongly recommendedthat you book 24 hours in advance for summer weekends.

FACILITIES AT A GLANCE

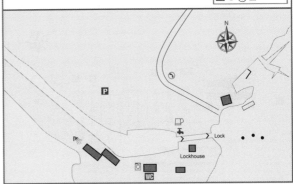

Lock
Lockhouse

TITCHMARSH MARINA

Titchmarsh Marina Ltd
Coles Lane, Walton on the Naze, Essex, CO14 8SL
Tel: 01255 672185 Fax: 01255 851901
Email: info@titchmarshmarina.co.uk
www.titchmarshmarina.co.uk

VHF | Ch 80
ACCESS | HW±5

Titchmarsh Marina sits on the south side of The Twizzle in the heart of the Walton Backwaters. As the area is designated as a 'wetland of international importance', the marina has been designed and developed to function as a natural harbour. The 420 berths are well sheltered by the high-grassed clay banks, offering good protection in all conditions. Access to Titchmarsh is over a sill, which has a depth of about 1m at LWS, but once inside the basin, the depth increases to around 2m. Among the excellent facilities are an on site chandlery as well as the Harbour Lights Restaurant & Bar serving breakfasts, lunch and dinners.

FACILITIES AT A GLANCE

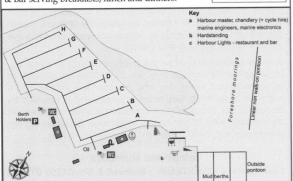

Key
a Harbour master, chandlery (+ cycle hire) marine engineers, marine electronics
b Hardstanding
c Harbour Lights - restaurant and bar

SHOTLEY MARINA

Shotley Marina Ltd
Shotley Gate, Ipswich, Suffolk, IP9 1QJ
Tel: 01473 788982 Fax: 01473 788868
Email: sales@shotleymarina.co.uk
www.shotleymarina.co.uk

VHF Ch 80
ACCESS H24

Based in the well protected Harwich Harbour where the River Stour joins the River Orwell, Shotley Marina is only eight miles from the county town of Ipswich. Entered via a lock at all states of the tide, its first class facilities include extensive boat repair and maintenance services as well as a well-stocked chandlery and on site bar and restaurant. The marina is strategically placed for sailing up the Stour to Manningtree, up the Orwell to Pin Mill or exploring the Rivers Deben, Crouch and Blackwater as well as the Walton Backwaters.

FACILITIES AT A GLANCE

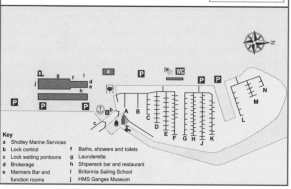

Key
a Shotley Marine Services
b Lock control
c Lock waiting pontoons
d Brokerage
e Mariners Bar and function rooms
f Baths, showers and toilets
g Launderette
h Shipwreck bar and restaurant
i Britannia Sailing School
j HMS Ganges Museum

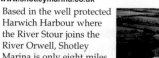

WALTON YACHT BASIN

Walton and Frinton Yacht Trust
Mill Lane, Walton on the Naze, CO14 8PF
Managed by Bedwell & Co Tel: 01255 675873
Fax: 01255 677405 After hours Tel: 01255 672655

VHF
ACCESS HW-0.75,HW+0.25

Walton Yacht Basin lies at the head of Walton Creek, an area made famous in Arthur Ransome's *Swallows & Amazons* and *Secret Waters*. The creek can only be navigated two hours either side of HW, although yachts heading for the Yacht Basin should arrive on a rising tide as the entrance gate is kept shut once the tide turns in order to retain the water inside. Before entering the gate, moor up against the Club Quay to enquire about berthing availability.

A short walk away is the popular seaside town of Walton, full of shops, pubs and restaurants. Its focal point is the pier which, overlooking superb sandy beaches, offers various attractions including a ten-pin bowling alley. Slightly further out of town, the Naze affords pleasant coastal walks with striking panoramic views.

FACILITIES AT A GLANCE

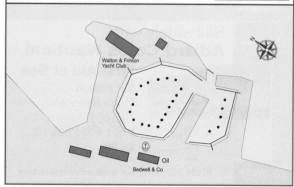

Walton & Frinton Yacht Club

Oil
Bedwell & Co

FOX'S MARINA

Fox's Marina Ipswich Ltd
The Strand, Wherstead, Ipswich, Suffolk, IP2 8SA
Tel: 01473 689111 Fax: 01473 601737
Email: foxs@foxsmarina.com

VHF | Ch 80
ACCESS | H24

One of five marinas on the River Orwell, Fox's provides good shelter in all conditions and, dredged to 2m below chart datum, benefits from full tidal access from Ostrich Creek. Accommodating yachts up to 21m LOA, it has enough storage ashore for over 200 vessels and offers a comprehensive refit, repair and maintenance service. Since becoming part of the Oyster Group of Companies, Fox's facilities have further improved with ongoing investment. Besides several workshops, other services on hand include an osmosis centre, a spray centre, engineering, rigging and electronic specialists as well as one of the largest chandleries on the East Coast. In addition there are regular bus services to Ipswich, which is only about one to two miles away.

FACILITIES AT A GLANCE

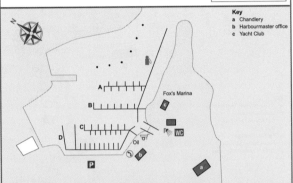

Key
a　Chandlery
b　Harbourmaster office
c　Yacht Club

NEPTUNE MARINA

Neptune Marina Ltd
Neptune Quay, Ipswich, IP4 1AX
Tel: 01473 215204 Fax: 01473 215206
Email: enquiries@neptune-marina.com

VHF | Ch M, 80
ACCESS | H±2.5

The Wet Dock at Ipswich, which was opened in 1850, became the largest in Europe and was in use right up until the 1930s. Now the dock incorporates Neptune Marina, situated at Neptune Quay on the Historic Waterfront, and ever increasing shoreside developments. This 26-acre dock is accessible through a 24-hr lock gate, with a waiting pontoon outside. The town centre is a 10 minute walk away, while Cardinal Park, a relatively new complex housing an 11-screen cinema and several eating places, is nearby. There are also a number of other excellent restaurants along the quayside and adjacent to the Marina. The new Neptune Marina building occupies an imposing position in the NE corner of the dock with quality coffee shop and associated retail units.

FACILITIES AT A GLANCE

Key
a　Old Custom House
b　Conference centre
c　Floating French restaurant
d　Bistro
e　Bellway apartments
f　Neptune Marina office & facilities
g　Marina storage yard

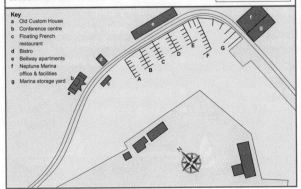

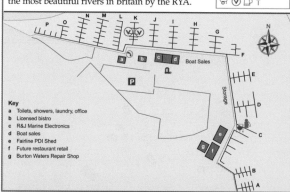

4

LOWESTOFT HAVEN MARINA

Lowestoft Haven Marina
School Road, Lowestoft, Suffolk, NR33 9NB
Tel: 01502 580300 Fax: 01502 581851
Email: lowestofhaven@abports.co.uk

VHF	Ch M, 80
ACCESS	H24

Lowestoft HavenLowestoft Haven Marina is phase 1 of a new marina complex for Lowestoft and is based on Lake Lothing and offering easy access to both the open sea and the Norfolk Broads. The town centres of both Lowestoft and Oulton Broad are within a short distance of the marina. The marina's 140 berths can accommodate vessels from 7-20m. Offering a full range of modern facilities the marina welcomes all visitors.

FACILITIES AT A GLANCE

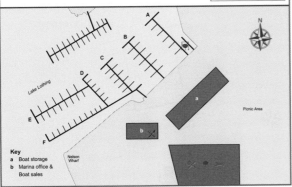

Key
a Boat storage
b Marina office & Boat sales

Lake Lothing
Picnic Area
Nelson Wharf

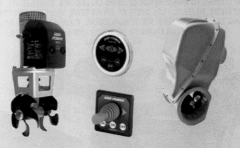

WOOLVERSTONE MARINA

Woolverstone Marina
Woolverstone, Ipswich, Suffolk, IP9 1AS
Tel: 01473 780206 Fax: 01473 780273
Email: t.barnes@mdlmarinas.co.uk www.marinas.co.uk

VHF | Ch 80
ACCESS | H24

Set in 22 acres of parkland, within close proximity to the Royal Harwich Yacht Club, Woolverstone Marina boasts 210 pontoon berths as well as 120 swinging moorings, all of which are served by a water taxi. Besides boat repair services, an on site chandlery and excellent ablution facilities, the marina also incorporates a sailing school and yacht brokerage.

Woolverstone's location on the scenic River Orwell makes it ideally placed for exploring the various cruising grounds along the East Coast, including the adjacent River Stour, the Colne and Blackwater estuaries to the south and the River Deben to the north.

FACILITIES AT A GLANCE

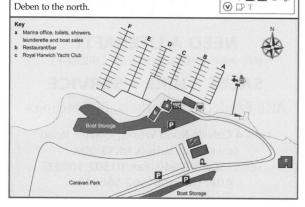

Key
a Marina office, toilets, showers, launderette and boat sales
b Restaurant/bar
c Royal Harwich Yacht Club

Boat Storage
Caravan Park
Boat Storage

ROYAL HARWICH YACHT CLUB MARINA

Royal Harwich Yacht Club Marina
Marina Road, Woolverstone, Suffolk, IP9 1BA
Tel: 01473 780319 Fax: 01473 780919
www.rhyc.demon.co.uk
Email: secretary@rhyc.demon.co.uk

VHF | Ch 77
ACCESS | H24

This 54 berth marina is ideally situated at a mid point on the Orwell between Levington and Ipswich. The facility is owned and run by the Royal Harwich Yacht Club and enjoys a full catering and bar service in the Clubhouse. The marina benefits from full tidal access, and can accommodate yachts up to 4.5m on the hammerhead. Within the immediate surrounds, there are boat repair services, and a well stocked chandlery. The marina is situated a mile's walk from the world famous Pin Mill and is a favoured destination with visitors from Holland, Belgium and Germany. The marina welcomes racing yachts and cruisers, and is able to accommodate multiple bookings.

FACILITIES AT A GLANCE

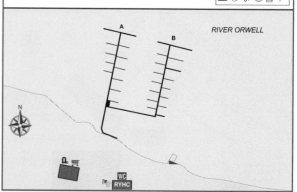

RIVER ORWELL

A B

WC
RYHC

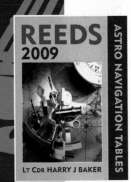
SUFFOLK YACHT HARBOUR

Suffolk Yacht Harbour Ltd
Levington, Ipswich, Suffolk, IP10 0LN
Tel: 01473 659240 Fax: 01473 659632
Email: enquiries@syharbour.co.uk
www.syharbour.co.uk

| VHF | Ch 80 |
| ACCESS | H24 |

A friendly, independently-run marina on the East Coast of England, Suffolk Yacht Harbour enjoys a beautiful rural setting on the River Orwell, yet is within easy access of Ipswich, Woodbridge and Felixstowe. With approximately 500 berths, the marina offers extensive facilities while the Haven Ports Yacht Club provides a bar and restaurant.

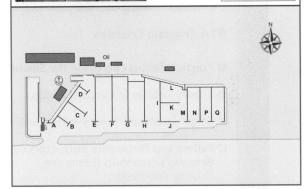

ROYAL NORFOLK & SUFFOLK YACHT CLUB

Royal Norfolk and Suffolk Yacht Club
Royal Plain, Lowestoft, Suffolk, NR33 0AQ
Tel: 01502 566726 Fax: 01502 517981
Email: marinaoffice@rnsyc.org.uk

| VHF | Ch 14, 80 |
| ACCESS | H24 |

With its entrance at the inner end of the South Pier, opposite the Trawl Basin on the north bank, the Royal Norfolk and Suffolk Yacht Club marina occupies a sheltered position in Lowestoft Harbour. Lowestoft has always been an appealing destination to yachtsmen due to the fact that it can be accessed at any state of the tide, 24 hours a day. Note, however, that conditions just outside the entrance can get pretty lively when the wind is against tide. The clubhouse is enclosed in an impressive Grade 2 listed building overlooking the marina and its facilities include a bar and restaurant as well as a formal dining room with a full *à la carte* menu.

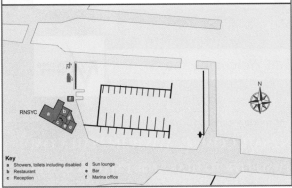

Key
a   Showers, toilets including disabled   d   Sun lounge
b   Restaurant   e   Bar
c   Reception   f   Marina office

Experience the fine art of sailing with In2Sail

"Seriously Good Sail Training On-Board Quality Yachts with Friendly Professional Skippers, Served with Good Food and Fun."

RYA Training Courses

- Practical Sailing Courses in the Solent.
- Theory Courses in Central London.
- Solent Combined Theory & Practical.
- Patient and Personable Instructors to help you Learn Skills & Improve Existing Knowledge.
- Personalised for Families & Couples.

Blue Water & Long Distance

- Fun Long Weekend Trips to Cherbourg & St Vaast.
- Discover UK & Irish Sailing Waters.
- Normandy & Brittany Coastlines.
- Adventure Sailing to Spain & Portugal.
- Customised Skippered Charter to Locations of your Choice.

Specialist Courses

- Racing Yacht Training and Race Participation.
- Specialised Boat Handling and Technical Sailing Courses.
- Yacht Maintenance Programme.
- Fast Track Yachtmaster.

Racing Events

- Fastnet Yacht Race 2009.
- Round the Island 2008.
- Cowes Week 2008.
- Cork Week.
- Spring and Winter Series.

"New or Experienced - In2Sail Welcomes You."

+44 (0) 1983 615557 | INFO@IN2SAIL.COM | WWW.IN2SAIL.COM

ONLINE BOOKING | SUBSCRIBE TO E- NEWSLETTER TO HEAR ABOUT SPECIAL OFFERS

2009/mg171/v

NORTH EAST ENGLAND - Great Yarmouth to Berwick-upon-Tweed

ADLARD COLES NAUTICAL
WEATHER FORECASTS
BY FAX & TELEPHONE

Coastal/Inshore	2-day by Fax	5-day by Phone
Anglia	09065 222 345	09068 969 645
East	09065 222 344	09068 969 644
North East	09065 222 343	09068 969 643
Scotland East	09065 222 342	09068 969 642
National (3-5 day)	09065 222 340	09068 969 640

Offshore	2-5 day by Fax	2-5 day by Phone
English Channel	09065 222 357	09068 969 657
Southern North Sea	09065 222 358	09068 969 658
Northern North Sea	09065 222 362	09068 969 662
North West Scotland	09065 222 361	09068 969 661

09068 CALLS COST 60P PER MIN. 09065 CALLS COST £1.50 PER MIN.

Key to Marina Plans symbols

Bottled gas		Parking	
Chandler		Pub/Restaurant	
Disabled facilities		Pump out	
Electrical supply		Rigging service	
Electrical repairs		Sail repairs	
Engine repairs		Shipwright	
First Aid		Shop/Supermarket	
Fresh Water		Showers	
Fuel - Diesel		Slipway	
Fuel - Petrol		Toilets	
Hardstanding/boatyard		Telephone	
Internet Café		Trolleys	
Laundry facilities		Visitors berths	
Lift-out facilities		Wi-Fi	

5

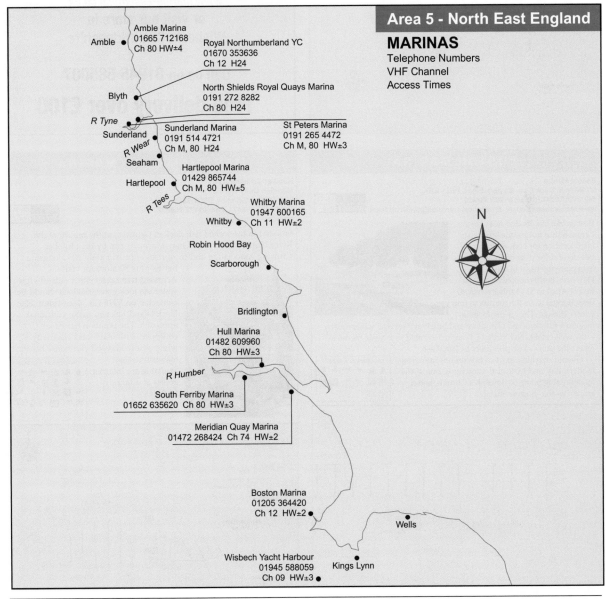

Area 5 - North East England

MARINAS
Telephone Numbers
VHF Channel
Access Times

Amble
Amble Marina
01665 712168
Ch 80 HW±4

Royal Northumberland YC
01670 353636
Ch 12 H24

North Shields Royal Quays Marina
0191 272 8282
Ch 80 H24

Blyth

R Tyne

Sunderland Marina
0191 514 4721
Ch M, 80 H24

St Peters Marina
0191 265 4472
Ch M, 80 HW±3

Sunderland

R Wear

Seaham

Hartlepool Marina
01429 865744
Ch M, 80 HW±5

Hartlepool

R Tees

Whitby Marina
01947 600165
Ch 11 HW±2

Whitby

Robin Hood Bay

Scarborough

Bridlington

Hull Marina
01482 609960
Ch 80 HW±3

R Humber

South Ferriby Marina
01652 635620 Ch 80 HW±3

Meridian Quay Marina
01472 268424 Ch 74 HW±2

Boston Marina
01205 364420
Ch 12 HW±2

Wells

Wisbech Yacht Harbour
01945 588059
Ch 09 HW±3

Kings Lynn

N

WISBECH YACHT HARBOUR

Wisbech Yacht Harbour
Harbour Master, Harbour Office, Dock Cottage
Wisbech, Cambridgeshire PE13 3JJ
Tel: 01945 588059 Fax: 01945 580589
Email: torbeau@btinternet.com www.fenland.gov.uk

VHF	Ch 9
ACCESS	HW±3

Regarded as the capital of the
English Fens, Wisbech is situated
about 25 miles north east of
Peterborough and is a market
town of considerable character
and historical significance. Rows
of elegant houses line the banks
of the River Nene, with the North
and South Brink still deemed two
of the finest Georgian streets in England.

Wisbech Yacht Harbour, linking Cambridgeshire with the sea,
is proving increasingly popular as a haven for small
craft, despite the busy commercial shipping. In
recent years the facilities have been developed and
improved upon and the HM is always on hand to
help with passage planning both up or downstream.

FACILITIES AT A GLANCE

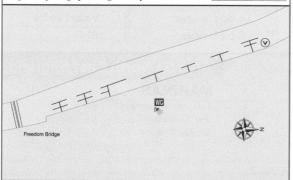

Freedom Bridge

BOSTON MARINA

Boston Marina
5/7 Witham Bank East, Boston, Lincs, PE21 9JU
Tel: 01205 364420 Fax: 01205 364420
www.bostonmarina.co.uk Email: bostonmarina@5witham.fsnet

VHF	Ch 12
ACCESS	H±2

Boston Marina, located near Boston
Grand Sluice in Lincolnshire, is an
ideal location for both seagoing
vessels and for river boats wanting
to explore the heart of the Fens.
However, berths are only available
from 1 April to 31 October when all
vessels must leave the marina to find
winter storage. The on site facilities

include a fully-stocked chandlery and brokerage service, while nearby
is the well-established Witham Tavern, decorated in a rustic theme to
reflect the pub's close proximity to The Wash.

The old maritime port of Boston has numerous
modern-day and historical attractions, one of the
most notable being St Botolph's Church, better
known as the 'Boston Stump'.

FACILITIES AT A GLANCE

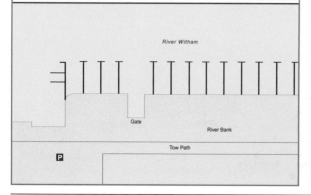

River Witham

Gate

River Bank

Tow Path

MERIDIAN QUAY MARINA

Humber Cruising Assn
Meridian Quay Marina
Fish Docks, Grimsby, DN31 3SD
Tel: 01472 268424 Fax: 01472 269832
www.hcagrimsby.co.uk

VHF	Ch 74
ACCESS	HW±2

Situated in the locked fish dock of Grimsby, at the mouth of the
River Humber, Meridian Quay Marina is run by the Humber
Cruising Association and comprises approximately 200 alongside
berths plus 30 more for visitors.
Accessed two hours either side of high
water via lock gates, the lock should be
contacted on VHF Ch 74 (call sign 'Fish
Dock Island') as you make your final
approach. The pontoon berths are
equipped with water and electricity,
while a fully licensed clubhouse boasts a
television. Also
available are internet
access and laundry
facilities.

FACILITIES AT A GLANCE

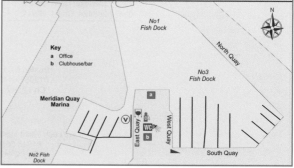

No1
Fish Dock

North Quay

Key
a Office
b Clubhouse/bar

No3
Fish Dock

Meridian Quay
Marina

West Quay

South Quay

No2 Fish
Dock

East Quay

SOUTH FERRIBY MARINA

South Ferriby Marina
Barton on Humber, Lincolnshire, DN18 6JH
Tel: 01652 635620 (Lock 635219) Fax: 01652 660517
www.clapsons.co.uk Email: marina@clapsons.co.uk

VHF Ch 80
ACCESS HW±3

South Ferriby Marina is run by Clapson & Sons, an established company founded in 1912. The marina site was developed in 1967 and today offers a comprehensive range of services, including heated workshops for osmosis repairs, general boat repairs and ample storage space. Its well stocked on site chandlery is open until 1700 seven days a week.

Situated at Barton upon Humber, the marina lies on the south bank of the River Humber at the southern crossing of the Humber Bridge, approximately eight miles south west of Kingston upon Hull. Good public transport links to nearby towns and villages include train services to Cleethorpes and Grimsby, and bus connections to Scunthorpe and Hull.

FACILITIES AT A GLANCE

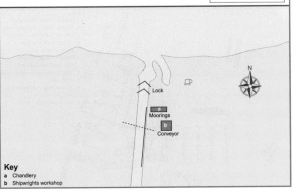

Key
a Chandlery
b Shipwrights workshop

HULL MARINA

Hull Marina
Railway Street, Hull, HU1 2DQ
Tel: 01482 609960 Fax: 01482 224148
www.britishwaterways.co.uk
Email: hullmarina@bwml.co.uk

VHF Ch 80
ACCESS HW±3

Situated on the River Humber, Hull Marina is literally a stone's throw from the bustling city centre with its array of arts and entertainments. Besides the numerous historic bars and cafés surrounding the marina itself, there are plenty of traditional taverns to be sampled in the Old Town, while also found here is the Street Life Museum, vividly depicting the history of the city.

Yachtsmen enter the marina via a tidal lock, operating HW±3, and should try to give 15 minutes' notice of arrival via VHF Ch 80. Hull is perfectly positioned for exploring the Trent, Ouse and the Yorkshire coast as well as across the North Sea to Holland or Belgium.

FACILITIES AT A GLANCE

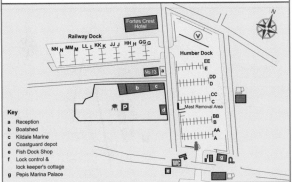

Key
a Reception
b Boatshed
c Kildale Marine
d Coastguard depot
e Fish Dock Shop
f Lock control &
   lock keeper's cottage
g Pepis Marina Palace

5

WHITBY MARINA

Whitby Marina
Whitby Harbour Office, Endeavour Wharf
Whitby, North Yorkshire YO21 1DN
Harbour Office: 01947 602354 Marina: 01947 600165
Email: lesley.dale@scarborough.gov.uk

VHF	Ch 11, 16
ACCESS	HW±2

The only natural harbour between the Tees and the Humber, Whitby lies some 20 miles north of Scarborough on the River Esk. The historic town is said to date back as far as the Roman times, although it is better known for its abbey, which was founded over 1,300 years ago by King Oswy of Northumberland. Another place of interest is the Captain Cook Memorial Museum, a tribute to Whitby's greatest seaman.

A swing bridge divides the harbour into upper and lower sections, with the marina being in the Upper Harbour. The bridge opens on request (VHF Ch 11) each half hour for two hours either side of high water.

FACILITIES AT A GLANCE

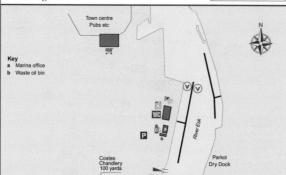

Key
a Marina office
b Waste oil bin

HARTLEPOOL MARINA

Hartlepool Marina
Lock Office, Slake Terrace, Hartlepool, TS24 0UR
Tel: 01429 865744 Fax: 01429 865947
Email: allan@hartlepool-marina.com

VHF	Ch M, 80
ACCESS	HW±5

Hartlepool Marina is a major boating facility on the North East coast with over 500 fully serviced berths surrounded by a cosmopolitan mix of bars restaurants and hotels. The Historic Quay is nearby with the 17th Century warship, Trincomelee. A tourist town with shopping centre is an easy walk away. Beautiful crusing water north and south access channel dredged to chart datum.

The marina can be accessed five hours either side of high water via a lock: note that yachtsmen wishing to enter should contact the marina on VHF Ch 80 about 15 minutes before arrival.

FACILITIES AT A GLANCE

Key
a Brittania House - amenity/cafe
b Neptune House - restaurant & bar
c Lock office and marina reception
d 220m complex with retail, restaurants and cafes
e Hartlepool Diving Club and HMS Abdiel sea cadet unit
f Fisherman's stores & landing area
g Office units
h Old West Quay Pub, restaurant and travel inn
i Trincomalee visitors centre

SUNDERLAND MARINA

The Marine Activities Centre
Sunderland Marina, Sunderland, SR6 0PW
Tel: 0191 514 4721 Fax: 0191 514 1847
Email: mervyn.templeton@marineactivitiescentre.co.uk

VHF Ch M, 80
ACCESS H24

Sunderland Marina sits on the north bank of the River Wear and is easily accessible through the outer breakwater at all states of the tide. Among the extensive range of facilities on site are a newsagent, café, hairdresser and top quality Italian restaurant. Other pubs, restaurants, hotels and cafés are located nearby on the waterfront. Both the Wear Boating Association and the Sunderland Yacht Club are also located in the vicinity and welcome yachtsmen to their respective bars and lounges.

FACILITIES AT A GLANCE

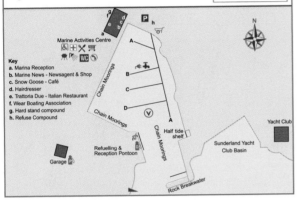

Key
a. Marina Reception
b. Marine News - Newsagent & Shop
c. Snow Goose - Café
d. Hairdresser
e. Trattoria Due - Italian Restaurant
f. Wear Boating Association
g. Hard stand compound
h. Refuse Compound

NORTH SHIELDS ROYAL QUAYS MARINA

North Shields Royal Quays Marina
Coble Dene Road, North Shields, NE29 6DU
Tel: 0191 272 8282 Fax: 0191 272 8288
www.quaymarinas.com
Email: royalquaysmarina@quaymarinas.com

VHF Ch 80
ACCESS H24

North Shields Royal Quays Marina enjoys close proximity to the entrance to the River Tyne, allowing easy access to and from the open sea as well as being ideally placed for cruising further up the Tyne. Just over an hour's motoring upstream brings you to the heart of the city of Newcastle, where you can tie up on a security controlled visitors' pontoon right outside the Pitcher and Piano Bar.

With a reputation for a high standard of service, the marina accommodates 300 pontoon berths, all of which are fully serviced. It is accessed via double sector lock gates which operate at all states

FACILITIES AT A GLANCE

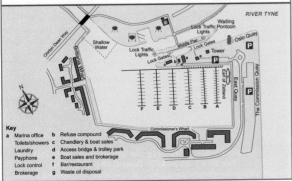

Key
a Marina office
   Toilets/showers
   Laundry
   Payphone
   Lock control
   Brokerage
b Refuse compound
c Chandlery & boat sales
d Access bridge & trolley park
e Boat sales and brokerage
f Bar/restaurant
g Waste oil disposal

ST PETERS MARINA

**St Peters Marina, St Peters Basin
Newcastle upon Tyne, NE6 1HX
Tel: 0191 2654472 Fax: 0191 2762618
Email: info@stpetersmarina.co.uk
www.stpetersmarina.co.uk**

VHF	Ch 80, M
ACCESS	HW±3

Nestling on the north bank of the River Tyne, some eight miles upstream of the river entrance, St Peters Marina is a fully serviced, 150-berth marina with the capacity to accommodate large vessels of up to 37m LOA. Situated on site is the Bascule Bar and Bistro, while a few minutes away is the centre of Newcastle. This city, along with its surrounding area, offers an array of interesting sites, among which are Hadrian's Wall, the award winning Gateshead Millennium Bridge and the Baltic Art Centre.

FACILITIES AT A GLANCE

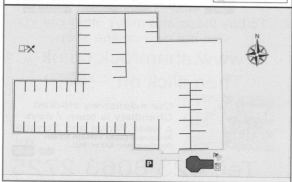

ROYAL NORTHUMBERLAND YACHT CLUB

**Royal Northumberland Yacht Club
South Harbour, Blyth, Northumberland, NE24 3PB
Tel: 01670 353636**

VHF	Ch 12
ACCESS	H24

The Royal Northumberland Yacht Club is based at Blyth, a well-sheltered port that is accessible at all states of the tide and in all weathers except for when there is a combination of low water and strong south-easterly winds. The yacht club is a private club with some 75 pontoon berths and a further 20 fore and aft moorings.

Visitors usually berth on the north side of the most northerly pontoon and are welcome to use the clubship, HY *Tyne* – a wooden lightship built in 1880 which incorporates a bar, showers and toilet facilities. The club also controls its own boatyard, providing under cover and outside storage space plus a 20 ton boat hoist.

FACILITIES AT A GLANCE

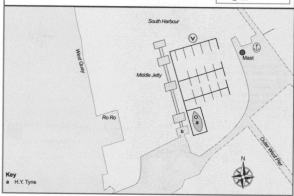

Key
a H.Y. Tyne

AMBLE MARINA

**Amble Marina Ltd
Amble, Northumberland, NE65 0YP
Tel: 01665 712168 Fax:01665 713363
Email: marina@amble.co.uk www.amble.co.uk**

VHF	Ch 80
ACCESS	HW±4

Amble Marina is a small family run business offering peace, security and a countryside setting at the heart of the small town of Amble. It is located on the banks of the beautiful River Coquet and at the start of the Northumberland coast's area of outstanding natural beauty. Amble Marina has 250 fully serviced berths for residential and visiting yachts. Cafes, bars, restaurants and shops are all within a short walk. From your berth watch the sun rise at the entrance to the harbour and set behind Warkworth Castle or walk on wide empty beaches. There is so much to do or if you prefer simply enjoy the peace, tranquillity and friendliness at Amble Marina.

FACILITIES AT A GLANCE

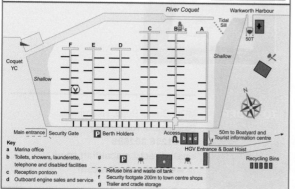

Key
a Marina office
b Toilets, showers, launderette, telephone and disabled facilities
c Reception pontoon
d Outboard engine sales and service
e Refuse bins and waste oil tank
f Security footgate 200m to town centre shops
g Trailer and cradle storage

What ever your budget, we've got it covered!

To buy these and many other brands
visit our new on-line shop

www.shamrock.co.uk
Then click on

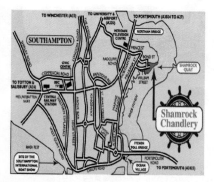

Our extensively stocked
Chandlery is open 7 days
a week Winter and Summer
Shamrock Quay William Street
Southampton SO14 5QL

VISA
Maestro MasterCard

Tel: 023 8063 2725

ADLARD COLES NAUTICAL
WEATHER FORECASTS
BY FAX & TELEPHONE

Coastal/Inshore	2-day by Fax	5-day by Phone
East	09065 222 344	09068 969 644
North East	09065 222 343	09068 969 643
Scotland East	09065 222 342	09068 969 642
Scotland North	09065 222 341	09068 969 641
National (3-5 day)	09065 222 340	09068 969 640

Offshore	2-5 day by Fax	2-5 day by Phone
English Channel	09065 222 357	09068 969 657
Southern North Sea	09065 222 358	09068 969 658
Northern North Sea	09065 222 362	09068 969 662
North West Scotland	09065 222 361	09068 969 661

09068 CALLS COST 60P PER MIN. 09065 CALLS COST £1.50 PER MIN.

Key to Marina Plans symbols

🔵	Bottled gas	P	Parking
	Chandler	✕	Pub/Restaurant
♿	Disabled facilities		Pump out
	Electrical supply		Rigging service
	Electrical repairs		Sail repairs
	Engine repairs		Shipwright
✚	First Aid		Shop/Supermarket
	Fresh Water		Showers
D	Fuel - Diesel		Slipway
P	Fuel - Petrol	WC	Toilets
	Hardstanding/boatyard		Telephone
@	Internet Café		Trolleys
	Laundry facilities	V	Visitors berths
	Lift-out facilities		Wi-Fi

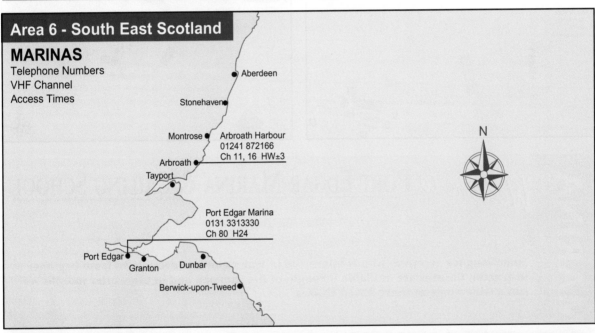

Area 6 - South East Scotland

MARINAS
Telephone Numbers
VHF Channel
Access Times

Aberdeen

Stonehaven

Montrose   Arbroath Harbour
            01241 872166
            Ch 11, 16 HW±3
Arbroath

Tayport

Port Edgar Marina
0131 3313330
Ch 80 H24

Port Edgar
    Granton   Dunbar

Berwick-upon-Tweed

N

6

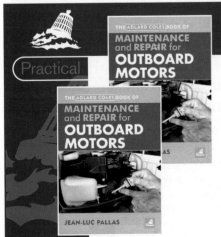

Adlard Coles Nautical
THE BEST SAILING BOOKS

The Adlard Coles Book of Maintenance and Repair for Diesel Engines
Jean-Luc Pallas
£22.99   978 0 7136 7614 3

The Adlard Coles Book of Maintenance and Repair for Outboard Motors
Jean-Luc Pallas
£19.99   978 0 7136 7615 0

TO ORDER   Tel: **01256 302699** email: **direct@macmillan.co.uk** or **www.adlardcoles.com**

PORT EDGAR MARINA

Port Edgar Marina
Shore Road, South Queensferry
West Lothian, EH3 9SX
Tel: 0131 331 3330 Fax: 0131 331 4878
Email: admin.pe@edinburghleisure.co.uk

VHF	Ch 80
ACCESS	H24

Port Edgar is a large watersports centre and marina found on the south bank of the sheltered Firth of Forth. Situated in the village of South Queensferry, just west of the Forth Road Bridge, it is managed by Edinburgh Leisure on behalf of the City of Edinburgh Council and is reached via a deep water channel just west of the suspension bridge.

The nearby village offers a sufficient range of shops and restaurants, while Port Edgar is only a 20-minute walk from Dalmeny Station from where trains run regularly to Edinburgh.

FACILITIES AT A GLANCE

Key
a   Changing rooms and toilets
b   Landing and trolleys
c   Port Edgar Yacht Club
d   Sail loft
e   Cafe
f   Marina office
g   Ferry Marine
h   Blue V
i   Bosuns Locker

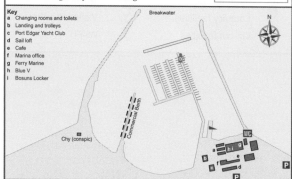

ARBROATH HARBOUR

Arbroath Harbour
Harbour Office, Arbroath, DD11 1PD
Tel: 01241 872166 Fax: 01241 878472
Email: harbourmaster@arbroathharbour.sol.co.uk

VHF	Ch 11, 16
ACCESS	HW±3

Arbroath harbour has 59 floating pontoon berths with security entrance which are serviced with electricity and fresh water to accommodate all types of leisure craft. Half height dock gates with walkway are located between the inner and outer harbours, which open and close at half tide, maintaining a minimum of 2.5m of water in the inner harbour.

The town of Arbroath offers a variety of social and sporting amenities to visiting crews and a number of quality pubs, restaurants, the famous twelfth century Abbey and Signal Tower Museum are located close to the harbour. Railway and bus stations are only 1km from the harbour with direct north and south connections.

FACILITIES AT A GLANCE

Key
a   Signal Tower Museum
b   Tourist Information
c   RNLI
d   Harbourmaster
e   Harbour gates & walkway

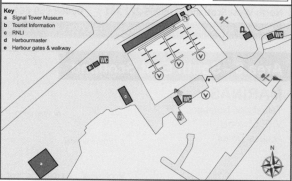

NORTH EAST SCOTLAND - Peterhead to Cape Wrath & Orkney & Shetland Is

ADLARD COLES NAUTICAL
WEATHER FORECASTS
BY FAX & TELEPHONE

Coastal/Inshore	2-day by Fax	5-day by Phone
North East	09065 222 343	09068 969 643
Scotland East	09065 222 342	09068 969 642
Scotland North	09065 222 341	09068 969 641
Minch	09065 222 354	09068 969 654
National (3-5 day)	09065 222 340	09068 969 640

Offshore	2-5 day by Fax	2-5 day by Phone
Southern North Sea	09065 222 358	09068 969 658
Northern North Sea	09065 222 362	09068 969 662
North West Scotland	09065 222 361	09068 969 661
Irish Sea	09065 222 359	09068 969 659

09068 CALLS COST 60P PER MIN. 09065 CALLS COST £1.50 PER MIN.

Key to Marina Plans symbols

	Bottled gas	P	Parking
	Chandler	✕	Pub/Restaurant
	Disabled facilities		Pump out
	Electrical supply		Rigging service
	Electrical repairs		Sail repairs
	Engine repairs		Shipwright
	First Aid		Shop/Supermarket
	Fresh Water		Showers
	Fuel - Diesel		Slipway
	Fuel - Petrol	WC	Toilets
	Hardstanding/boatyard		Telephone
@	Internet Café		Trolleys
	Laundry facilities	Ⓥ	Visitors berths
	Lift-out facilities		Wi-Fi

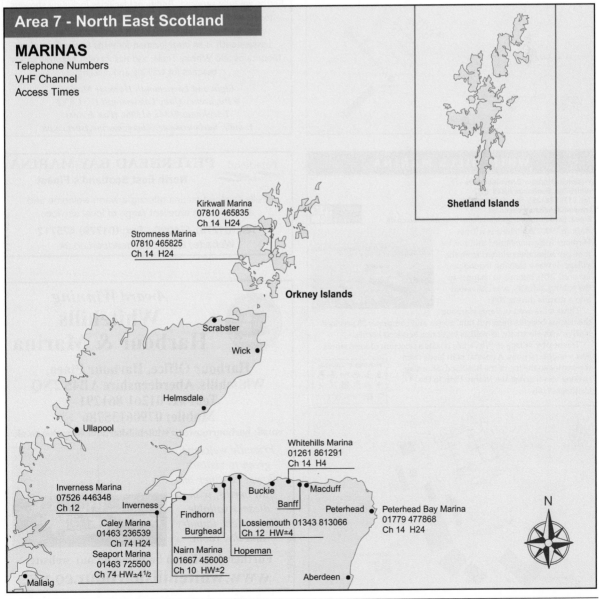

Area 7 - North East Scotland

MARINAS
Telephone Numbers
VHF Channel
Access Times

Shetland Islands

Kirkwall Marina
07810 465835
Ch 14 H24

Stromness Marina
07810 465825
Ch 14 H24

Orkney Islands

Scrabster

Wick

Helmsdale

Ullapool

Whitehills Marina
01261 861291
Ch 14 H4

Inverness Marina
07526 446348
Ch 12

Inverness

Buckie

Banff

Macduff

Peterhead

Peterhead Bay Marina
01779 477868
Ch 14 H24

Findhorn

Caley Marina
01463 236539
Ch 74 H24

Burghead

Lossiemouth 01343 813066
Ch 12 HW±4

Seaport Marina
01463 725500
Ch 74 HW±4½

Nairn Marina
01667 456008
Ch 10 HW±2

Hopeman

Mallaig

Aberdeen

N

PETERHEAD BAY MARINA

Peterhead Port Authority
Harbour Office, West Pier, Peterhead, AB42 1DW
Tel: 01779 477868 Fax: 01779 478397
Email: info@peterheadport.co.uk
www.peterheadport.co.uk

VHF | Ch 14
ACCESS | H24

Based in the south west corner of Peterhead Bay Harbour, the marina provides one of the finest marine leisure facilities in the east of Scotland. In addition to the services on site, there are plenty of nautical businesses in the vicinity, ranging from ship chandlers and electrical servicing to boat repairs and surveying.

Due to its easterly location, Peterhead affords an ideal stopover for those yachts heading to or from Scandinavia as well as for vessels making for the Caledonian Canal.

FACILITIES AT A GLANCE

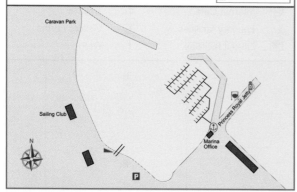

WHITEHILLS MARINA

Whitehills Harbour Commissioners
Whitehills, Banffshire AB45 2NQ
Tel: 01261 861291 Fax: 01261 861291
www.whitehillsharbour.co.uk
Email: harbourmaster@whitehillsharbour.wanadoo.co.uk

VHF | Ch 14
ACCESS | H24

Built in 1900, Whitehills is a Trust Harbour fully maintained and run by nine commissioners elected from the village. It was a thriving fishing port up until 1999, but due to changes in the fishing industry, was converted into a marina during 2000.

Three miles west of Banff Harbour the marina benefits from full tidal access and comprises 38 serviced berths, with electricity, as well as eight non-serviced berths.

The nearby village of Whitehills boasts a selection of local stores and a couple of pubs. A coastal path leads from the marina to the top of the headland, affording striking views across the Moray Firth to the Caithness Hills.

FACILITIES AT A GLANCE

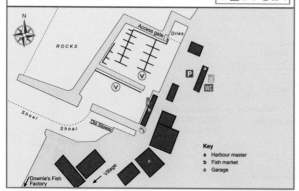

Key
a Harbour master
b Fish market
c Garage

NAIRN MARINA

Nairn Marina
Nairn Harbour, Nairnshire, Scotland
Tel: 01667 456008
Email: nairn.harbourmaster@virgin.net

VHF Ch 10
ACCESS HW±2

Nairn is a small town on the coast of the Moray Firth. Formerly renowned both as a fishing port and as a holiday resort dating back to Victorian times, it boasts miles of award-winning, sandy beaches, famous castles such as Cawdor, Brodie and Castle Stuart, and two championship golf courses. Other recreational activities include horse riding or walking through spectacular countryside.

The marina lies at the mouth of the River Nairn, entry to which should be avoided in strong N to NE winds. The approach is made from the NW at or around high water as the entrance is badly silted and dries out.

FACILITIES AT A GLANCE

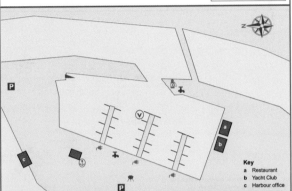

Key
a Restaurant
b Yacht Club
c Harbour office

LOSSIEMOUTH MARINA

The Harbour Office
Lossiemouth, Moray, IV31 6NT
Tel: 01343 813066 Fax: 01343 813066
Email: harbourmaster@lossiemarina.fsnet.co.uk

VHF Ch 12
ACCESS HW±4

Situated on the beautiful Moray Firth coastline, Lossiemouth Marina provides 47 berths in its East Basin and 25 berths for larger vessels in its West Basin. Although the berths are primarily taken up by residential yachts, during the summer months a certain number are allocated to visitors who can benefit from the friendly, efficient service. The marina lies within easy walking distance of the town, which has a good range of shops and restaurants and boasts an array of leisure facilities, two golf courses and acres of sandy beaches. Lossiemouth is also a great starting off point for Scotland's whisky trail.

FACILITIES AT A GLANCE

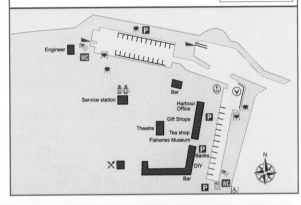

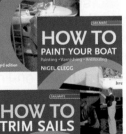
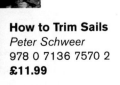

CALEY MARINA

Caley Marina
Canal Road, Inverness, IV3 8NF
Tel: 01463 236539 Fax: 01463 238323
Email: info@caleymarina.com
www.caleymarina.com

VHF   Ch 74
ACCESS   H24

Caley Marina is a family run business based near Inverness. With the four flight Muirtown locks and the Kessock Bridge providing a dramatic backdrop, the marina runs alongside the Caledonian Canal which, opened in 1822, is regarded as one of the most spectacular waterways in Europe. Built as a short cut between the North Sea and the Atlantic Ocean, thus avoiding the potentially dangerous Pentland Firth on the north coast of Scotland, the canal is around 60 miles long and takes about three days to cruise from east to west. With the prevailing winds behind you, it takes slightly less time to cruise in the other direction.

FACILITIES AT A GLANCE

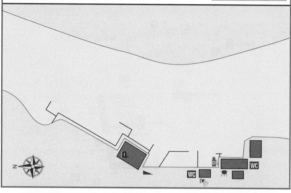

SEAPORT MARINA

Seaport Marina
Muirtown Wharf, Inverness, IV3 5LE
Tel: 01463 725500 Fax: 01463 710942
Email: enquiries.scotland@britishwaterways.co.uk
www.scottishcanals.co.uk

VHF   Ch 74
ACCESS   HW±4

Seaport Marina is situated at Inverness at the head of the Caledonian Canal. Although it only incorporates 80 berths, it proves a popular location for long and short term berthing and is accessible four hours either side of HW. The centre of Inverness is just a 15-minute walk away, where you will find a full range of shops, pubs and restaurants, while entertainment venues include a theatre, bowling alley and multiplex cinema.

As the capital of the Highlands, Inverness attracts thousands of visitors each year, providing the ideal base from which to explore the surrounding area by road, coach or train. In addition, Inverness airport is only 20 minutes by taxi from the marina.

FACILITIES AT A GLANCE

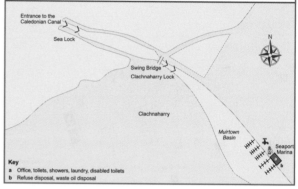

Key
a Office, toilets, showers, laundry, disabled toilets
b Refuse disposal, waste oil disposal

INVERNESS MARINA

Inverness Marina
Longman Drive, Inverness, IV1 1SU
Tel: 07526 446348 Fax: 01463 238323
Email: info@invernessmarina.co.uk
www.invernessmarina.com

VHF   Ch 12
ACCESS   H24

Inverness Marina is a brand new marina (October 2008) situated in the Inverness firth just 1 mile (1.6km) from Inverness city centre and half a mile (0.8km) from the entrance to the Caledonian Canal. The marina has a minimum depth of 2.5m, 24hr access and 150 fully serviced berths. On site are a chandlery and access to full repair services including rigging, engineering, electronics and boat repair.

Inverness is the capital of the highlands with transport networks that link including bus, train, and flights to the rest of the UK and continental Europe, Inverness Airport is less than 7 miles (11km) from the marina and within easy walking distance is the city centre which contains many hotels, restaurants, pubs and excellent shopping. Inverness is the gateway to the Highlands with best possible location as a base for touring with golf courses, historic sites and the Whisky Trail all within easy reach.

FACILITIES AT A GLANCE

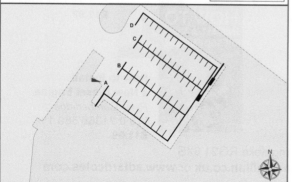

KIRKWALL MARINA

Kirkwall Marina
Harbour Street, Kirkwall, Orkney, KW15
Tel: 07810 465835 Fax: 01856 871313
Email: info@orkneymarinas.co.uk www.orkneymarinas.co.uk

VHF Ch 14
ACCESS H24

The Orkney Isles, comprising 70 islands in total, provides some of the finest cruising grounds in Northern Europe. The Main Island, incorporating the ancient port of Kirkwall, is the largest, although 16 others have lively communities and are rich in archaeological sites as well as spectacular scenery and wildlife.

Kirkwall Marina offers excellent facilities along with 24hr access and good shelter. The marina is very close to the historic Kirkwall, whose original town is one of the best preserved examples of an ancient Norse dwelling.

FACILITIES AT A GLANCE

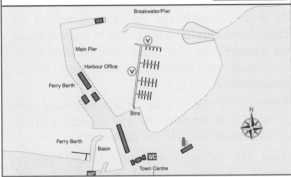

STROMNESS MARINA

Stromness Marina
Stromness, Orkney, KW16
Tel: 07810 465825 Fax: 01856 871313
Email: info@orkneymarinas.co.uk
www.orkneymarinas.co.uk

VHF Ch 14
ACCESS H24

Just 16 miles to the west of Kirkwall, Stromness lies on the south-western tip of the Orkney Isles' Mainland. Sitting beneath the rocky ridge known as Brinkie's Brae, it is considered one of Orkney's major seaports, with sailors first attracted to the fine anchorage provided by the bay of Hamnavoe.

Stromness, like Kirkwall, is a brand new marina, offering comprehensive facilities including a chandlery and repair services. Also on hand are an internet café, a fitness suite and swimming pool as well as car and bike hire.

FACILITIES AT A GLANCE

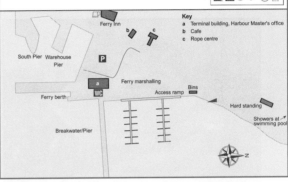

Key
a Terminal building, Harbour Master's office
b Cafe
c Rope centre

7

Sail Orkney

Orkney Marinas
126 Victoria Street
Stromness
Orkney KW16 3BU
Tel/Fax 018856 852888   www.orkneymarinas.co.uk   info@orkneymarinas.co.uk

**Tel:
01631 566555
Fax:
01631 571044**

**Dunstaffnage
Marina Ltd,
Dunbeg,
Oban Argyll,
PA37 1PX**

Email: info@dunstaffnagemarina.com • Website: www.dunstaffnagemarina.com

Whether you are a first time visitor or regular customer, we hope you enjoy our recently expanded facilities and the magnificent environment in which we are located.

Dunstaffnage Marina is located on the shores of Dunstaffnage Bay overlooking Dunstaffnage Castle at the entrance to Loch Etive.

Just 3 miles from Oban, the gateway to the Western Isles, Dunstaffnage is easily accessible by road, rail and ferry, or by air from Oban Airport at Connel just 2 miles away.

The Marina has excellent facilities with 150 fully serviced berths able to accommodate yachts or motor vessels up to 25 metres loa.

Operating in tandem with the renowned Wide Mouthed Frog, the Marina provides a unique range of services. The Frog is the social hub of the Marina and includes the acclaimed seafood restaurant, a family bistro,a friendly bar and 9 en-suite rooms.

To enter Dunstaffnage Bay from the Firth of Lorne leave Dunstaffnage Castle to starboard and the island Eilean Mor to port. Navigation Lights are fixed on both the Castle and island foreshores.

Entrance to the marina is by following the fairway in a direction of 150 degrees leaving green marker buoys to the starboard.

After the second buoy, the Marina Fairway should become apparent on a course of 270 degrees.

Strong currents exist in the bay due to the effect of tidal flow in Loch Etive. The prevailing current follows the shores of the Bay in an anti-clockwise direction.

Please do not attempt to cut through the Moorings on your approach to the Marina.

Please show consideration to other users by not exceeding 4 knots within the anchorage and bay.

2009/MG32/v

666

ADLARD COLES NAUTICAL
WEATHER FORECASTS
BY FAX & TELEPHONE

Coastal/Inshore	2-day by Fax	5-day by Phone
Scotland North	09065 222 341	09068 969 641
Minch	09065 222 354	09068 969 654
Caledonia	09065 222 353	09068 969 653
Clyde	09065 222 352	09068 969 652
National (3-5 day)	09065 222 340	09068 969 640

Offshore	2-5 day by Fax	2-5 day by Phone
Southern North Sea	09065 222 358	09068 969 658
Northern North Sea	09065 222 362	09068 969 662
North West Scotland	09065 222 361	09068 969 661
Irish Sea	09065 222 359	09068 969 659

09068 CALLS COST 60P PER MIN. 09065 CALLS COST £1.50 PER MIN.

Key to Marina Plans symbols

- Bottled gas
- Chandler
- Disabled facilities
- Electrical supply
- Electrical repairs
- Engine repairs
- First Aid
- Fresh Water
- Fuel - Diesel
- Fuel - Petrol
- Hardstanding/boatyard
- Internet Café
- Laundry facilities
- Lift-out facilities
- P Parking
- Pub/Restaurant
- Pump out
- Rigging service
- Sail repairs
- Shipwright
- Shop/Supermarket
- Showers
- Slipway
- WC Toilets
- Telephone
- Trolleys
- V Visitors berths
- Wi-Fi

Area 8 - North West Scotland

MARINAS
Telephone Numbers
VHF Channel
Access Times

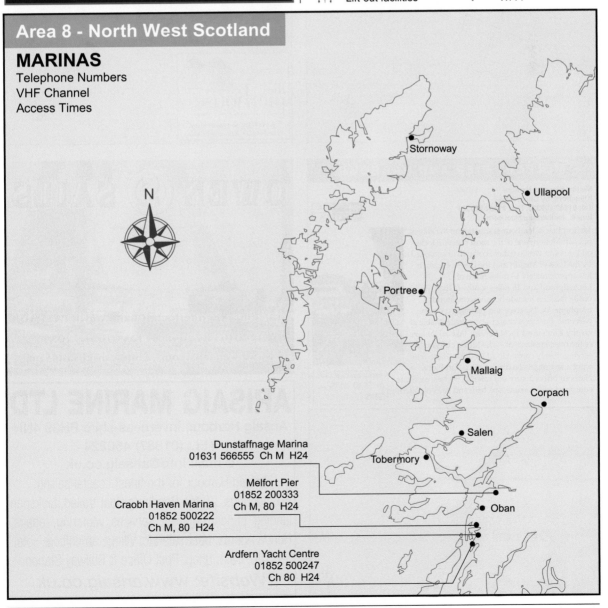

Stornoway
Ullapool
Portree
Mallaig
Corpach
Salen
Tobermory
Oban

Dunstaffnage Marina
01631 566555 Ch M H24

Melfort Pier
01852 200333
Ch M, 80 H24

Craobh Haven Marina
01852 500222
Ch M, 80 H24

Ardfern Yacht Centre
01852 500247
Ch 80 H24

DUNSTAFFNAGE MARINA

Dunstaffnage Marina Ltd
Dunbeg, by Oban, Argyll, PA37 1PX
Tel: 01631 566555 Fax: 01631 571044
Email: lizzy@dunstaffnage.sol.co.uk

VHF	Ch M
ACCESS	H24

Located just two to three miles north of Oban, Dunstaffnage Marina has recently been renovated to include an additional 36 fully serviced berths, a new breakwater providing shelter from NE'ly to E'ly winds and an increased amount of hard standing. Also on site is the Wide Mouthed Frog, offering a convivial bar, restaurant and accomodation with spectacular views of the 13th century Dunstaffnage Castle.

The marina is perfectly placed to explore Scotland's stunning west coast and Hebridean Islands. Only 10 miles NE up Loch Linnhe is Port Appin, while sailing 15 miles S, down the Firth of Lorne, brings you to Puldohran where you can walk to an ancient hostelry situated next to the C18 Bridge Over the Atlantic.

FACILITIES AT A GLANCE

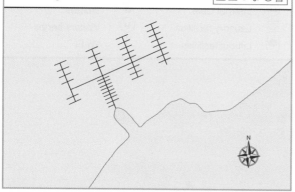

THE PIERHOUSE HOTEL MOORINGS

The Pierhouse Hotel
Port Appin, by Oban, Argyll, PA34 5UL
Tel: 01631 730302 Fax: 01631 730400
Email: reservations@pierhousehotel.co.uk

VHF	
ACCESS	H24

Situated in one of Argyll's most spectacular destinations on Loch Linnhe, just 10 miles by sea (20 miles by road) north of Oban, The 10 new Pierhouse Hotel Moorings (max. capacity 20 tonnes) offer 5 inner & 5 outer lines at 3 metres & 5 metres depth respectively at low water.

A concrete ferry jetty co-located alongside is available for private boat use, providing shelter for landing on the northern side. Marine facilities include sauna, showers/ washing facilities. The Pierhouse Hotel is renowned for its award-winning restaurant serving fresh local seafood, meat & game. Daily lunch and bar dinner menus, home baking and teas/coffees.

FACILITIES AT A GLANCE

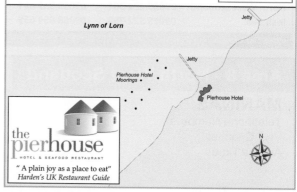

Lynn of Lorn

Jetty

Jetty

Pierhouse Hotel Moorings

Pierhouse Hotel

the **pierhouse**
HOTEL & SEAFOOD RESTAURANT
" A plain joy as a place to eat"
Harden's UK Restaurant Guide

MELFORT PIER AND HARBOUR

Melfort Pier and Harbour
Kilmelford, by Oban, Argyll
Tel: 01852 200333 Fax: 01852 200329
Email: melharbour@aol.com

VHF	M, 80
ACCESS	H24

Melfort Pier & Harbour is situated on the shores of Loch Melfort, one of the most peaceful lochs on the south west coast of Scotland. Overlooked by the Pass of Melfort and the Braes of Lorn, it lies approximately 18 miles north of Lochgilphead and 16 miles south of Oban. Its onsite facilities include hot showers, laundry, telephone, Wi-Fi access and parking – pets are welcome. Fuel, power and water are available at nearby Kilmelford Yacht Haven. Take advantage of the onsite restaurant – The Melfort Mermaid serving freshly cooked local food. For those who want a few nights on dry land, Melfort Pier & Harbour offers luxury self catering houses, each one equipped with a sauna, spa bath and balcony offering

FACILITIES AT A GLANCE

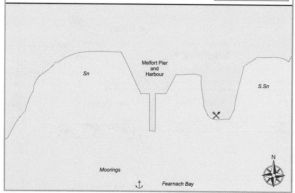

Melfort Pier and Harbour

Sn

S.Sn

Moorings

Fearnach Bay

CRAOBH HAVEN MARINA

Craobh Haven Marina
By Lochgilphead, Argyll, Scotland, PA31 8UA
Tel: 01852 500222 Fax: 01852 500252
Email: info@craobhmarina.co.uk
www.craobhmarina.co.uk

| VHF | Ch M, 80 |
| ACCESS | H24 |

Craobh Marina is idyllically situated in the heart of Scotland's most sought after cruising grounds. Not only does Craobh offer ready access to a wonderful choice of scenic cruising throughout the western isles, the marina is conveniently close to Glasgow and its international transport hub.

Craobh Marina has been developed from a near perfect natural harbour, offering secure and sheltered berthing for up to 250 vessels to 22m LOA and with a draft of 4m. With an unusually deep and wide entrance Craobh Marina provides shelter and a warm welcome for all types of craft.

FACILITIES AT A GLANCE

Key
a Holiday cottages
b Village store
c Bar
d Gift shop
e Waste oil
f Boat shed
g Marina office

ARDFERN YACHT CENTRE

Ardfern Yacht Centre
Ardfern, by Lochgilphead, Argyll, PA31 8QN
Tel: 01852 500247 Fax: 01852 500624
www.ardfernyacht.co.uk Email: office@ardfernyacht.co.uk

| VHF | Ch 80 |
| ACCESS | H24 |

Developed around an old pier once frequented by steamers, Ardfern Yacht Centre lies at the head of Loch Craignish, one of Scotland's most sheltered and picturesque sea lochs. With several islands and protected anchorages nearby, Ardfern is an ideal place from which to cruise the west coast of Scotland and the Outer Hebrides.

The Yacht Centre comprises pontoon berths and swinging moorings as well as a workshop, boat storage and well-stocked chandlery, while a grocery store and eating places can be found in the village. Among the onshore activities available locally are horse riding, cycling, and walking.

FACILITIES AT A GLANCE

Key
a Workshop
b Showers, toilets and launderette
c Chandlery and office

Village (300m)
Waste Oil
Hard Standing

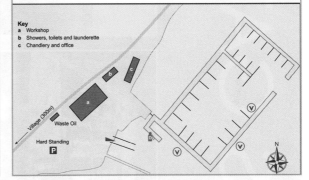

8

Key to Marina Plans symbols

Bottled gas		P	Parking
Chandler			Pub/Restaurant
Disabled facilities			Pump out
Electrical supply			Rigging service
Electrical repairs			Sail repairs
Engine repairs			Shipwright
First Aid			Shop/Supermarket
Fresh Water			Showers
Fuel - Diesel			Slipway
Fuel - Petrol		WC	Toilets
Hardstanding/boatyard			Telephone
Internet Café	@		Trolleys
Laundry facilities		V	Visitors berths
Lift-out facilities			Wi-Fi

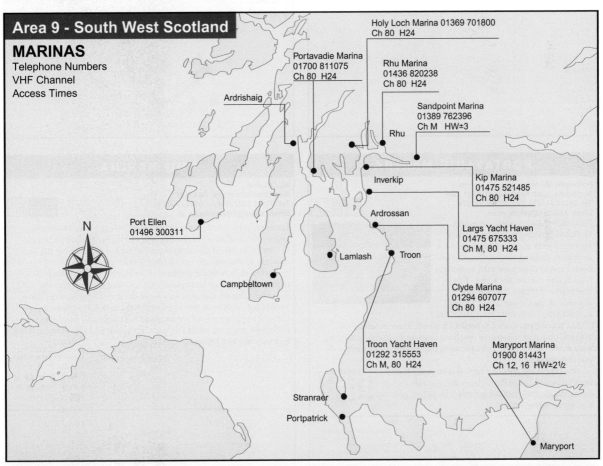

Area 9 - South West Scotland

MARINAS
Telephone Numbers
VHF Channel
Access Times

Holy Loch Marina 01369 701800
Ch 80 H24

Portavadie Marina
01700 811075
Ch 80 H24

Rhu Marina
01436 820238
Ch 80 H24

Sandpoint Marina
01389 762396
Ch M HW±3

Ardrishaig

Rhu

Inverkip

Kip Marina
01475 521485
Ch 80 H24

Ardrossan

Largs Yacht Haven
01475 675333
Ch M, 80 H24

Port Ellen
01496 300311

Lamlash

Troon

Clyde Marina
01294 607077
Ch 80 H24

Campbeltown

Troon Yacht Haven
01292 315553
Ch M, 80 H24

Maryport Marina
01900 814431
Ch 12, 16 HW±2½

Stranraer

Portpatrick

Maryport

9

PORT ELLEN MARINA

Port Ellen Marina
Port Ellen, Islay, Argyll, PA42 7DB
Tel: 01496 300301 Fax: 01496 300302
www.portellenmarina.com

VHF
ACCESS H24

A safe and relaxed marina for visitors to the *Malt Whisky Island*. There are seven classic distilleries and yet another still (private) to start production soon. If you are planning a cruise to the north then superb sailing will take you onward via Craighouse on Jura. Meeting guests or short term storage is trouble free with the excellent air and ferry services connecting to Glasgow. Once on Islay you will be tempted to extend your stay so be warned, check www.portellenmarina.com for the many reasons to visit, from golf to music.

FACILITIES AT A GLANCE

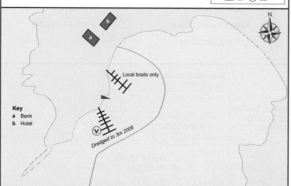

Key
a Bank
b Hotel

Local boats only

Dredged to 3m 2006

HOLY LOCH MARINA

Holy Loch Marina
Rankin's Brae, Sandbank, Dunoon, PA23 8FE
Tel: 01369 701800 Fax: 01369 704749
Email: info@holylochmarina.co.uk

VHF Ch 80
ACCESS H24

Holy Loch Marina, the marine gateway to Loch Lomond and the Trossachs National Park, lies on the south shore of the loch, roughly half a mile west of Lazaretto Point. Holy Loch is among the Clyde's most beautiful natural harbours and, besides being a peaceful location, offers an abundance of wildlife, places of local historical interest as well as excellent walking and cycling through the Argyll Forest Park. The marina can be entered in all weather conditions and is within easy sailing distance of Loch Long and Upper Firth.

FACILITIES AT A GLANCE

Key
a Office/Harbourmaster
b Boat storage
c Holy Loch Sailing Club
d Pier

Sandbank Village

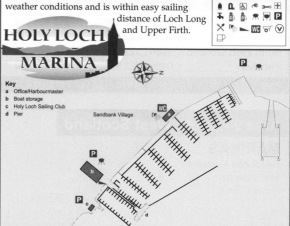

PORTAVADIE MARINA

Portavadie Marina
Portavadie, Loch Fyne, Argyll, PA21 2DA
Tel: 01700 811075 Fax: 01700 811074
Email: r.kitchin@yahoo.co.uk

VHF Ch 80
ACCESS H24

Portavadie Marina offers deep and sheltered berthing to residential and visiting yachts in an area renowned for its superb cruising waters. Situated on Loch Fyne in close proximity to several islands and the famous Kyles of Bute, Portavadie is within easy sailing distance of the Crinan Canal, giving access to the Inner and Outer Hebrides.

The marina provides 230 berths, of which 50 are reserved for visitors, plus comprehensive on-shore facilities including a bar and restaurant. Self-catering cottages, with free berthing for small craft, are also available.

This unspoiled area of Argyll is less than 2 hours from Glasgow. In nearby villages there are shops, eating places and outdoor activities including golf and horse-riding.

FACILITIES AT A GLANCE

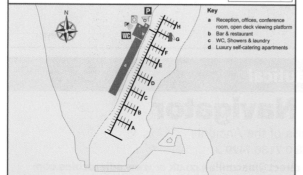

Key
a Reception, offices, conference room, open deck viewing platform
b Bar & restaurant
c WC, Showers & laundry
d Luxury self-catering apartments

RHU MARINA

Rhu Marina
Rhu, Dunbartonshire, G84 8LH
Tel: 01436 820238 Fax: 01436 821039
Email: sales@rhumarina.co.uk

VHF Ch 80
ACCESS H24

Located on the north shore of the Clyde Estuary, Rhu Marina is accessible at all states of the tide and can accommodate yachts up to 18m in length. It also operates 60 swinging moorings in the bay adjacent to the marina, with a ferry service provided.

Within easy walking distance of the marina is Rhu village, a conservation village incorporating a few shops, a pub and the beautiful Glenarn Gardens as well as the Royal Northern & Clyde Yacht Club. A mile or two to the east lies the holiday town of Helensburgh, renowned for its attractive architecture and elegant parks and gardens, while Glasgow city is just 40 miles away and can be easily reached by train.

FACILITIES AT A GLANCE

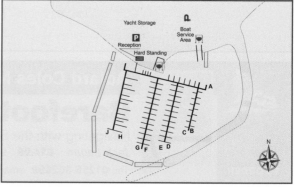

Yacht Storage
Boat Service Area
Reception
Hard Standing

SANDPOINT MARINA

Sandpoint Marina Ltd
Sandpoint, Woodyard Road, Dumbarton, G82 4BG
Tel: 01389 762396 Fax: 01389 732605
Email: sales@sandpoint-marina.co.uk
www.sandpoint-marina.co.uk

VHF CH M
ACCESS HW±3

Lying on the north bank of the Clyde estuary on the opposite side of the River Leven from Dumbarton Castle, Sandpoint Marina provides easy access to some of the most stunning cruising grounds in the United Kingdom. It is an independently run marina, offering a professional yet personal service to every boat owner. Among the facilities to hand are an on site chandlery, storage areas, a 40 ton travel hoist and 20 individual workshop units.

Within a 20-minute drive of Glasgow city centre, the marina is situated close to the shores of Loch Lomond, the largest fresh water loch in Britain.

FACILITIES AT A GLANCE

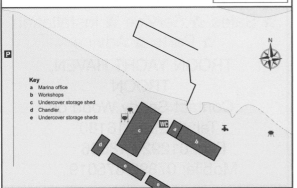

Key
a Marina office
b Workshops
c Undercover storage shed
d Chandler
e Undercover storage sheds

KIP MARINA

Kip Marina, The Yacht Harbour
Inverkip, Renfrewshire, Scotland, PA16 0AS
Tel: 01475 521485 Fax: 01475 521298
www.kipmarina.co.uk Email: enquire@kipmarina.co.uk

VHF Ch 80
ACCESS H24

Inverkip is a small village which lies on the south shores of the River Kip as it enters the Firth of Clyde. Once established for fishing, smuggling and, in the 17th century, witch-hunts, it became a seaside resort in the 1860s as a result of the installation of the railway. Today it is a yachting centre, boasting a state-of-the-art marina with over 600 berths and full boatyard facilities. With the capacity to accommodate yachts of up to 23m LOA, Kip Marina offers direct road and rail access to Glasgow and its international airport, therefore making it an ideal location for either a winter lay up or crew changeover.

FACILITIES AT A GLANCE

Key
a Boat sales, chandlery and reception
b Workshop and contractors
c Chartroom and superloos

LARGS YACHT HAVEN

Largs Yacht Haven Ltd
Irvine Road, Largs, Ayrshire, KA30 8EZ
Tel: 01475 675333 Fax: 01475 672245
www.yachthavens.com   Email: largs@yachthavens.com

VHF | Ch M, 80
ACCESS | H24

Largs Yacht Haven offers a superb location among lochs and islands, with numerous fishing villages and harbours nearby. Sheltered cruising can be enjoyed in the inner Clyde, while the west coast and Ireland are only a day's sail away. With a stunning backdrop of the Scottish mountains, Largs incorporates 700 fully serviced berths and provides a range of on site facilities including chandlers, sailmakers, divers, engineers, shops, restaurants and club.

A 20-minute coastal walk brings you to the town of Largs, which has all the usual amenities as well as good road and rail connections to Glasgow.

FACILITIES AT A GLANCE

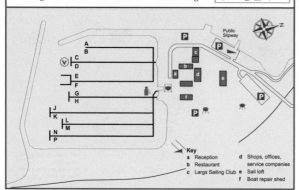

Key
a Reception
b Restaurant
c Largs Sailing Club
d Shops, offices, service companies
e Sail loft
f Boat repair shed

CLYDE MARINA

Clyde Marina Ltd
The Harbour, Ardrossan, Ayrshire, KA22 8DB
Tel: 01294 607077 Fax: 01294 607076
www.clydemarina.com   Email: info@clydemarina.com

VHF | Ch 80
ACCESS | H24

CLYDE MARINA

Situated on the Clyde Coast between Irvine and Largs, Clyde Marina is a modern bustling yacht harbour with boatyard, 50 Tonne hoist and active boat sales, set in a landscaped environment. A deep draft marina accommodating vessels up to 30m LOA, draft up to 5m. Recent arrivals include tall ships and Whitbread 60s plus a variety of sail and power craft. Fully serviced pontoons plus all the yard facilities you would expect from a leading marina including boatyard and boatshed for repairs or storage. Good road and rail connections and only 30 minutes from Glasgow and Prestwick airports.

FACILITIES AT A GLANCE
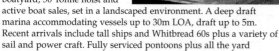

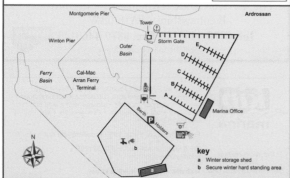

key
a Winter storage shed
b Secure winter hard standing area

TROON YACHT HAVEN

Troon Yacht Haven Ltd
The Harbour, Troon, Ayrshire, KA10 6DJ
Tel: 01292 315553 Fax: 01292 312836
Email: troon@yachthavens.com
www.yachthavens.com

VHF | Ch 80, M
ACCESS | H24

Troon Yacht Haven, situated on the Southern Clyde Estuary, benefits from deep water at all states of the tide. Tucked away in the harbour of Troon, it is well sheltered and within easy access of the town centre. There are plenty of cruising opportunities to be had from here, whether it be hopping across to the Isle of Arran, with its peaceful anchorages and mountain walks, sailing round the Mull or through the Crinan Canal to the Western Isles, or heading for the sheltered waters of the Clyde.

FACILITIES AT A GLANCE

Key
a Main building
   Toilets
   Showers
   Baths
   Laundry
b Marina office

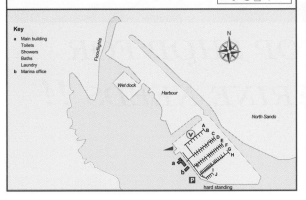

MARYPORT MARINA

Maryport Development Ltd
Marine Road, Maryport, Cumbria, CA15 8AY
Tel: 01900 814431 Fax: 01900 810212
www.maryportmarina.com
Email: enquires@maryportmarina.com

VHF | Ch 12, 16
ACCESS | HW±2.5

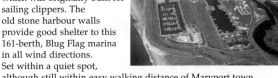

Maryport Marina lies in the historic Senhouse Dock, which was originally built for sailing clippers. The old stone harbour walls provide good shelter to this 161-berth, Blug Flag marina in all wind directions. Set within a quiet spot, although still within easy walking distance of Maryport town centre, it affords a perfect location from which to explore the west coast of Scotland as well as the Isle of Man and the Galloway Coast. For those who wish to venture inland, then the Lake District is only seven miles away.

FACILITIES AT A GLANCE

Key
a Marina Office
b Boat repair facility
c Coastguard building
d Fish handling building
e Wet fish shop
f Aquarium, cafe
g Play area
h Admin/accounts office

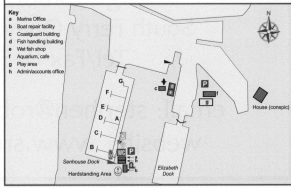

9

S. ROBERTS MARINE LIMITED
at

Liverpool Marina

*YOUR ONE STOP SHOP FOR
ALL YOUR MARINE NEEDS !!*

✔ **Boatbuilding**
✔ **Repairs**
✔ **Surveying**
✔ **Consultancy**
✔ **Chandlery**
✔ **Rigging** up to 12mm

Barge Turbot, Coburg Wharf,
South Ferry Quay, Liverpool L3 4BP
Tel/Fax 0151 707 8300

email: stephen@robmar.freeserve.co.uk
website: www.srobertsmarine.com

2009/MG78/e

ADLARD COLES NAUTICAL
WEATHER FORECASTS
BY FAX & TELEPHONE

Coastal/Inshore	2-day by Fax	5-day by Phone
Northern Ireland	09065 222 355	09068 969 655
Clyde	09065 222 352	09068 969 652
North West	09065 222 351	09068 969 651
Wales	09065 222 350	09068 969 650
National (3-5 day)	09065 222 340	09068 969 640

Offshore	2-5 day by Fax	2-5 day by Phone
Northern North Sea	09065 222 362	09068 969 662
North West Scotland	09065 222 361	09068 969 661
Irish Sea	09065 222 359	09068 969 659
English Channel	09065 222 357	09068 969 657

09068 CALLS COST 60P PER MIN. 09065 CALLS COST £1.50 PER MIN.

Key to Marina Plans symbols

Bottled gas		P	Parking
Chandler			Pub/Restaurant
Disabled facilities			Pump out
Electrical supply			Rigging service
Electrical repairs			Sail repairs
Engine repairs			Shipwright
First Aid			Shop/Supermarket
Fresh Water			Showers
Fuel - Diesel			Slipway
Fuel - Petrol		WC	Toilets
Hardstanding/boatyard			Telephone
Internet Café			Trolleys
Laundry facilities		V	Visitors berths
Lift-out facilities			Wi-Fi

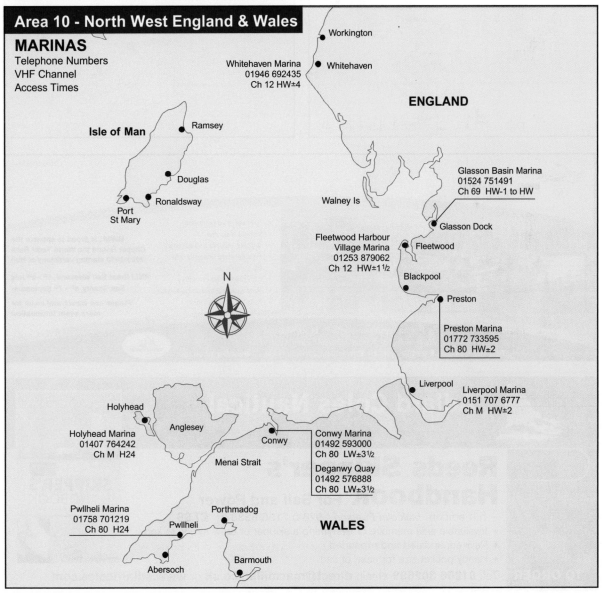

Area 10 - North West England & Wales

MARINAS
Telephone Numbers
VHF Channel
Access Times

Isle of Man
- Ramsey
- Douglas
- Ronaldsway
- Port St Mary

Workington

Whitehaven Marina
01946 692435
Ch 12 HW±4
- Whitehaven

ENGLAND

Walney Is

Glasson Basin Marina
01524 751491
Ch 69 HW-1 to HW
- Glasson Dock

Fleetwood Harbour
Village Marina
01253 879062
Ch 12 HW±1½
- Fleetwood

- Blackpool

- Preston

Preston Marina
01772 733595
Ch 80 HW±2

- Liverpool

Liverpool Marina
0151 707 6777
Ch M HW±2

Holyhead

Holyhead Marina
01407 764242
Ch M H24

Anglesey

- Conwy

Conwy Marina
01492 593000
Ch 80 LW±3½

Deganwy Quay
01492 576888
Ch 80 LW±3½

Menai Strait

Pwllheli Marina
01758 701219
Ch 80 H24

- Pwllheli

- Porthmadog

WALES

- Barmouth

- Abersoch

N

10

WHITEHAVEN MARINA

Whitehaven Harbour Commissioners, Pears House
1 Duke Street, Whitehaven, Cumbria, CA28 7HW
Tel: 01946 692435 Fax: 01946 61455
Email: office@whitehaven-harbour.co.uk
www.whitehaven-harbour.co.uk

VHF	Ch 12
ACCESS	HW±4

Whitehaven Marina can be found
at the south-western entrance
to the Solway Firth, providing
a strategic departure point for
those yachts heading for the
Isle of Man, Ireland or Southern
Scotland. The harbour is one
of the more accessible ports of
refuge in NW England, affording
a safe entry in most weathers. The approach channel across the outer
harbour is dredged to about 1.0m above chart
datum, allowing entry into the inner harbour via
a sea lock at around HW±4.

Conveniently situated for visiting the Lake
District, Whitehaven is an attractive Georgian town,
renowned in the C18 for its rum and slave imports.

FACILITIES AT A GLANCE

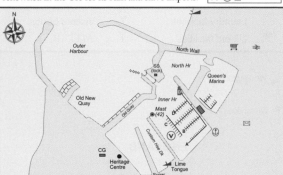

GLASSON BASIN MARINA

Glasson Basin Yacht Company Ltd
Glasson Dock, Lancaster, LA2 0AW
Tel: 01524 751491 Fax: 01524 752626
Email: info@glassonmarina.com
www.glassonmarina.com

VHF	Ch 69
ACCESS	HW-1 to HW

Glasson Dock Marina lies on the
River Lune, west of Sunderland
Point.   Access is via the outer
dock which opens 45 minutes
before H. W.Liverpool and thence
via BWB lock into the inner
basin. It is recommended to leave
Lune No. 1 Buoy approx 11/2
hrs. before H. W.. Contact the
dock on Channel 69.   The Marina can only be contacted by
telephone. All the necessary requirements can be
found either on site or within easy reach of
Glasson Dock, including boat, rigging and sail
repair services as well as a launderette, ablution
facilities, shops and restaurants.

FACILITIES AT A GLANCE

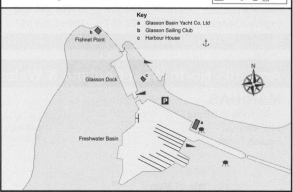

Key
a   Glasson Basin Yacht Co. Ltd
b   Glasson Sailing Club
c   Harbour House

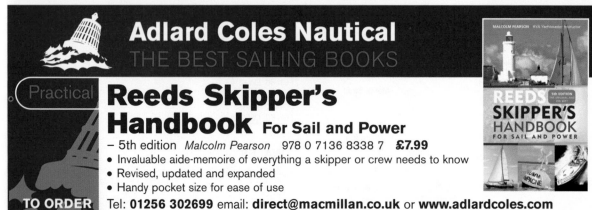

FLEETWOOD HARBOUR MARINA

Fleetwood Harbour Village Marina
The Dock Office, Wyre Dock, Fleetwood, FY7 6PP
Tel: 01253 879062 Fax: 01253 879043
Email: fleetwood@abports.co.uk

VHF Ch 12
ACCESS HW±1.5

Fleetwood Harbour Village Marina provides a good location from which to cruise Morecambe Bay and the Irish Sea. To the north west is the Isle of Man, to the north is the Solway Firth and the Clyde Estuary, while to the south west is Conwy, the Menai Straits and Holyhead.

Tucked away in a protected dock which dates back as far as 1835, Fleetwood Harbour Marina has 300 berths and offers extensive facilities. Overlooking the marina is a 15-acre retail and leisure park laid out in a popular American style.

FACILITIES AT A GLANCE

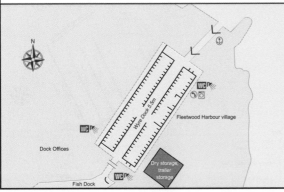

PRESTON MARINA

Preston Marine Services Ltd
The Boathouse, Navigation Way, Preston, PR2 2YP
Tel: 01772 733595 Fax: 01772 733595
Email: info@prestonmarina.co.uk www.prestonmarina.co.uk

VHF Ch 80
ACCESS HW±2

Preston Marina forms part of the comprehensive Riversway Docklands development, meeting all the demands of modern day boat owners. With the docks' history dating back over 100 years, today the marina comprises 40 acres of fully serviced pontoon berths sheltered behind the refurbished original lock gates. Lying 15 miles up the River Ribble, which itself is an interesting cruising ground with an abundance of wildlife,

Preston is well placed for sailing to parts of Scotland, Ireland or Wales. The Docklands development includes a wide choice of restaurants, shops and cinemas as well as being in easy reach of all the cultural and leisure facilities provided by a large town.

FACILITIES AT A GLANCE

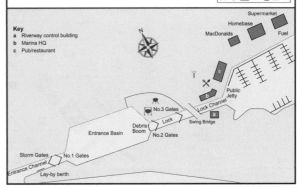

Key
a Riverway control building
b Marina HQ
c Pub/restaurant

LIVERPOOL MARINA

Liverpool Marina
Coburg Wharf, Sefton Street, Liverpool, L3 4BP
Tel: 0151 707 6777 Fax: 0151 707 6770
Email: harbourside@liverpoolmarina.co.uk

VHF Ch M
ACCESS HW±2

Liverpool Marina is ideally situated for yachtsmen wishing to cruise the Irish Sea. Access is through a computerised lock that opens two and a half hours either side of high water between 0600 and 2200 daily. Once in the marina, you can enjoy the benefits of the facilities on offer, including a first class club bar and restaurant.

Liverpool - recently announced Capital of Culture 2008 - is now a thriving cosmopolitan city, with attractions ranging from numerous bars and restaurants to museums, art galleries and the Beatles Story.

FACILITIES AT A GLANCE

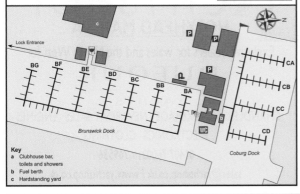

Key
a Clubhouse bar, toilets and showers
b Fuel berth
c Hardstanding yard

10

CONWY MARINA

Conwy Marina
Conwy, LL32 8EP
Tel: 01492 593000 Fax: 01492 572111
Email: jroberts@quaymarinas.com
www.quaymarinas.co.uk

VHF Ch 80
ACCESS LW±3.5

Situated in an area of outstanding natural beauty, with the Mountains of Snowdonia National Park providing a stunning backdrop, Conwy is the first purpose-built marina to be developed on the north coast of Wales. Enjoying a unique site next to the 13th century Conwy Castle, the third of Edward I's great castles, it provides a convenient base from which to explore the cruising grounds of the North Wales coast. The unspoilt coves of Anglesey and the beautiful Menai Straits prove a popular destination, while further afield are the Llyn Peninsula and the Islands of Bardsey and Tudwells.

The marina incorporates about 500 fully serviced berths which are accessible through a barrier gate between half tide and high water.

FACILITIES AT A GLANCE

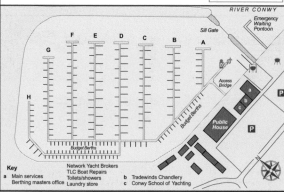

Key
a   Main services
    Berthing masters office
    Network Yacht Brokers
    TLC Boat Repairs
    Toilets/showers
    Laundry store
b   Tradewinds Chandlery
c   Conwy School of Yachting

HOLYHEAD MARINA

Holyhead Marina Ltd
Newry Beach, Holyhead, Gwynedd, LL65 1YA
Tel: 01407 764242 Fax: 01407 769152
Email: info@holyheadmarina.co.uk

VHF Ch M
ACCESS H24

One of the few natural deep water harbours on the Welsh coast, Anglesey is conveniently placed as a first port of call if heading to North Wales from the North, South or West. Its marina at Holyhead, accessible at all states of the tide, is sheltered by Holyhead Mountain as well as an enormous harbour breakwater and extensive floating breakwaters, therefore offering good protection from all directions.

Anglesey boasts numerous picturesque anchorages and beaches in addition to striking views over Snowdonia, while only a tide or two away are the Isle of Man and Eire.

FACILITIES AT A GLANCE

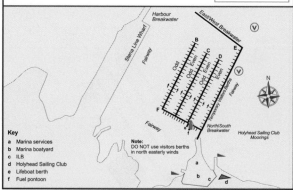

Key
a   Marina services
b   Marina boatyard
c   ILB
d   Holyhead Sailing Club
e   Lifeboat berth
f   Fuel pontoon

Note:
DO NOT use visitors berths
in north easterly winds

PWLLHELI MARINA

Pwllheli Marina
Glan Don, Pwllheli, North Wales, LL53 5YT
Tel: 01758 701219 Fax: 01758 701443
Email: hafanpwllheli@hafanpwllheli.co.uk

| VHF | Ch 80 |
| ACCESS | H24 |

Pwllheli is an old Welsh market town providing the gateway to the Llyn Peninsula, which stretches out as far as Bardsey Island to form an 'Area of Outstanding Natural Beauty'. Enjoying the spectacular backdrop of the Snowdonia Mountains,

Pwllheli's numerous attractions include an open-air market every Wednesday, 'Neuadd Dwyfor', offering a mix of live theatre and latest films, and beautiful beaches.

Pwllheli Marina is situated on the south side of the Llyn Peninsula. One of Wales' finest marinas and sailing centres, it has over 400 pontoon berths and excellent onshore facilities.

FACILITIES AT A GLANCE

Key
a   Marina offices
    Toilets
    Showers
    Baby change
    Launderette
b   Domestic refuse point
c   Dinghy park and slipway
d   Short stay boat park
e   Pwllheli sailing club
f   Chandlery

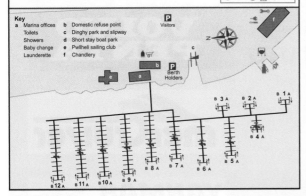

10

SOUTH WALES & BRISTOL CHANNEL - Bardsey Island to Land's End

ADLARD COLES NAUTICAL
WEATHER FORECASTS
BY FAX & TELEPHONE

Coastal/Inshore	2-day by Fax	5-day by Phone
North West	09065 222 351	09068 969 651
Wales	09065 222 350	09068 969 650
Bristol	09065 222 349	09068 969 649
South West	09065 222 348	09068 969 648
National (3-5 day)	09065 222 340	09068 969 640

Offshore	2-5 day by Fax	2-5 day by Phone
Irish Sea	09065 222 359	09068 969 659
English Channel	09065 222 357	09068 969 657
Biscay	09065 222 360	09068 969 660
North West Scotland	09065 222 361	09068 969 661

09068 CALLS COST 60P PER MIN. 09065 CALLS COST £1.50 PER MIN.

Key to Marina Plans symbols

	Bottled gas	**P**	Parking
	Chandler		Pub/Restaurant
	Disabled facilities		Pump out
	Electrical supply		Rigging service
	Electrical repairs		Sail repairs
	Engine repairs		Shipwright
	First Aid		Shop/Supermarket
	Fresh Water		Showers
	Fuel - Diesel		Slipway
	Fuel - Petrol	**WC**	Toilets
	Hardstanding/boatyard		Telephone
@	Internet Café		Trolleys
	Laundry facilities	**V**	Visitors berths
	Lift-out facilities		Wi-Fi

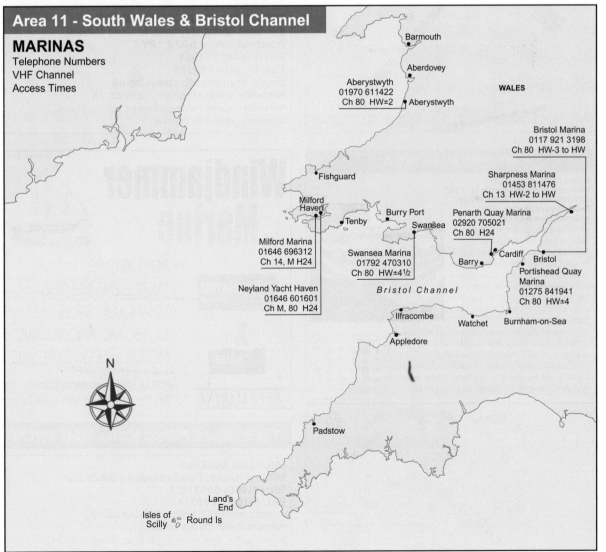

Area 11 - South Wales & Bristol Channel

MARINAS
Telephone Numbers
VHF Channel
Access Times

Barmouth

Aberdovey

Aberystwyth
01970 611422
Ch 80 HW±2 • Aberystwyth

WALES

Bristol Marina
0117 921 3198
Ch 80 HW-3 to HW

• Fishguard

Sharpness Marina
01453 811476
Ch 13 HW-2 to HW

Milford Haven

Burry Port

Penarth Quay Marina
02920 705021
Ch 80 H24

• Tenby

Swansea

Milford Marina
01646 696312
Ch 14, M H24

Cardiff

Swansea Marina
01792 470310
Ch 80 HW±4½

Barry • • Bristol

Neyland Yacht Haven
01646 601601
Ch M, 80 H24

Bristol Channel

Portishead Quay
Marina
01275 841941
Ch 80 HW±4

Ilfracombe

Watchet

Burnham-on-Sea

Appledore

N

Padstow

Land's
End

Isles of
Scilly Round Is

11

ABERYSTWYTH MARINA

Aberystwyth Marina, IMP Developments
Trefechan, Aberystwyth, Ceredigion, SY23 1AS
Tel: 01970 611422 Fax: 01970 624122
Email: enquiries@aberystwythmarina.com

VHF	Ch 80
ACCESS	HW±2

Aberystwyth is a picturesque university seaside town on the west coast of Wales. Its £9 million marina provides over 150 permanent pontoon berths and welcomes on average between 1,500 and 2,000 visiting yachts per year. Accessible two hours either side of high water, its facilities incorporate the usual marine services as well as an on-site pub and restaurant.

A short distance away are several pretty Welsh harbours, including Fishguard, Cardigan, Porthmadog and Abersoch, while the east coast of Ireland can be reached within a day's sail.

FACILITIES AT A GLANCE

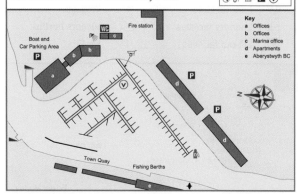

Key
a Offices
b Offices
c Marina office
d Apartments
e Aberystwyth BC

MILFORD MARINA

Milford Marina, Milford Docks
Milford Haven, Pembrokeshire SA73 3AF
Tel: 01646 696312 Fax: 01646 696314
Email: enquiries@mhpa.co.uk
www.milford-docks.co.uk

VHF	Ch 14, M
ACCESS	H24

Set within one of the deepest natural harbours in the world, Milford Marina was opened in 1991 by the Duke of York. Since then its facilities have gradually developed to include hard standing areas, secure boat yards, a diesel pump and chandlery as well as various bars and restaurants.

Accessed via an entrance lock (with waiting pontoons both inside and outside the lock), the marina is ideally situated for exploring the picturesque upper reaches of the River Cleddau or cruising out beyond St Ann's Head to the unspoilt islands of Skomer, Skokholm and Grassholm.

FACILITIES AT A GLANCE

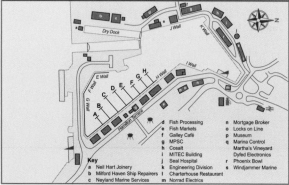

d Fish Processing	n Mortgage Broker
e Fish Markets	o Locks on Line
f Galley Café	p Museum
g MPSC	q Marina Control
h Cosalt	Martha's Vineyard
i MITEC Building	Dyfed Electronics
j Seal Hospital	r Phoenix Bowl
k Engineering Division	s Windjammer Marine
l Charterhouse Restaurant	
m Norrad Electrics	

Key
a Neil Hart Joinery
b Milford Haven Ship Repairers
c Neyland Marine Services

ABERYSTWYTH MARINA - IMP DEVELOPMENTS

Y Lanfa-Aberystwyth Marina, Trefechan,
Aberystwyth SY23 1AS
Tel: (01970) 611422
Fax: (01970) 624122
www.abermarina.com
Fully serviced marina. Diesel, gas, water, toilets and hot showers.

2009/L4/v

NEYLAND MARINE SERVICES
Tel: 01646 698968
Fax: 01646 695303
e-mail: neylandmarine@aol.com
www.neylandmarine.co.uk
We provide unequalled sales and service to the pleasure boating, fishing and shipping industry. Your complete repair and supply service for electrical and electronic equipment, engineering installations and components. Supply, service dealers for most manufacturers.

2009/L7/e

STEPHEN RATSEY SAILMAKERS
8 Brunel Quay, Neyland, Milford Haven,
Pembrokeshire SA73 1PY
Tel: (01646) 601561
Fax: (01646) 601968
Email: enquiries@ratseys.co.uk
Website: www.stephenratsey.co.uk
New sails, repairs, running, standing rigging, covers, upholstery, seldon & rotostay.

2009/L15/k

MILFORD MARINA
Milford Haven, Pembrokeshire SA73 3AF
Tel: (01646) 696312/3
Fax: (01646) 696314
e-mail: marina@milford-docks.co.uk
www.milford-docks.co.uk
Marina berths, boat storage, 16t hoist, diesel, VHF.CH.37, electricity, laundry, chandlery, boat & engine repairs, brokerage, engine sale, restaurants, retail park on site, 24 hour staff, 22 miles of sheltered estuary for all year round sailing.

2009/L16/e

NEYLAND YACHT HAVEN

Neyland Yacht Haven Ltd
Brunel Quay, Neyland, Pembrokeshire, SA73 1PY
Tel: 01646 601601 Fax: 01646 600713
Email: neyland@yachthavens.com

VHF Ch M, 80
ACCESS H24

Approximately 10 miles from the entrance to Milford Haven lies Neyland Yacht Haven. Tucked away in a well protected inlet just before the Cleddau Bridge, this marina has around 380 berths and

can accommodate yachts up to 25m LOA with draughts of up to 2.5m. The marina is divided into two basins, with the lower one enjoying full tidal access, while entry to the upper one is restricted by a tidal sill.

Offering a comprehensive range of services, Neyland Yacht Haven is within a five minute walk of the town centre where the various shops and takeaways cater for most everyday needs.

FACILITIES AT A GLANCE

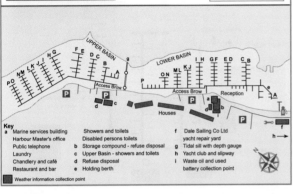

Key
a Marine services building
  Harbour Master's office
  Public telephone
  Laundry
  Chandlery and café
  Restaurant and bar
  Showers and toilets
  Disabled persons toilets
b Storage compound - refuse disposal
c Upper Basin - showers and toilets
d Refuse disposal
e Holding berth
f Dale Sailing Co Ltd
  yacht repair yard
g Tidal sill with depth gauge
h Yacht club and slipway
i Waste oil and used
  battery collection point

■ Weather information collection point

SWANSEA MARINA

Swansea Marina
Lockside, Maritime Quarter, Swansea, SA1 1WG
Tel: 01792 470310 Fax: 01792 463948
www.swansea.gov.uk/swanseamarina
Email: swanmar@swansea.gov.uk

VHF Ch 80
ACCESS HW±4.5

At the hub of the city's recently redeveloped and award winning Maritime Quarter, Swansea Marina can be accessed HW±4½ hrs via a lock. Surrounded by a plethora of shops, restaurants and marine businesses to cater for most yachtsmen's needs, the marina is in

close proximity to the picturesque Gower coast, where there is no shortage of quiet sandy beaches off which to anchor. It also provides the perfect starting point for cruising to Ilfracombe, Lundy Island, the North Cornish coast or West Wales.

Within easy walking distance of the marina is the city centre, boasting a covered shopping centre and market. For those who prefer walking or cycling, take the long promenade to the Mumbles fishing village from where there are plenty of coastal walks.

FACILITIES AT A GLANCE

Key
a Leisure Centre
b Maritime Museum
c Pumphouse Restaurant
d Yacht Club
e Repair shed
f Mariott Hotel

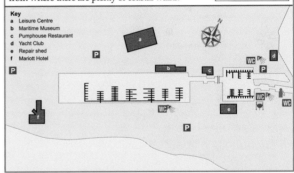

PENARTH QUAYS MARINA

Penarth Quays Marina
Penarth, Vale of Glamorgan, CF64 1TQ
Tel: 02920 705021 Fax: 02920 712170
www.quaymarinas.com
Email: sjones@quaymarinas.com

VHF Ch 80
ACCESS H24

Penarth Quays Marina has been established in the historic basins of Penarth Docks for over 20 years and is the premier boating facility in the region. The marina is Cardiff Bay's only 5 Gold Anchor marina and provides an ideal base for those using the Bay and the Bristol Channel. With 24hr access there is always water available for boating. Penarth and Cardiff boast an extensive range of leisure facilities, shops and restaurants making this marina an ideal base or destination.

FACILITIES AT A GLANCE

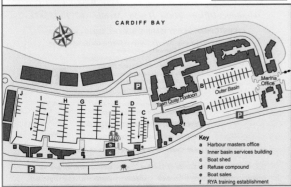

Key
a Harbour masters office
b Inner basin services building
c Boat shed
d Refuse compound
e Boat sales
f RYA training establishment

11

SHARPNESS MARINA

Sharpness Marina, Sharpness
Berkeley, Gloucestershire GR13 9UN
Tel: 01453 811476
Email: sharpnessmarina@ukonline.co.uk

VHF Ch 13
ACCESS HW-2

Sharpness is a small port on the
River Severn lying at the entrance
to the Gloucester and Sharpness
Canal. At the time of its
completion in 1827, the canal was
the largest and deepest ship canal
in the world. However, although
once an important commercial

waterway, it is now primarily used
by pleasure boats. Yachts approaching the marina from seaward can do
so via a lock two hours before high water, but note that the final arrival
should be timed as late as possible to avoid strong
tides in the entrance. From the lock, a passage under
two swing bridges and a turn to port brings you to
the marina, where pontoon berths are equipped

FACILITIES AT A GLANCE

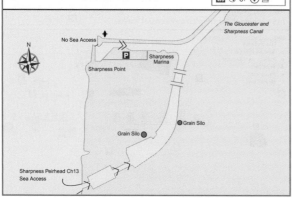

BRISTOL MARINA

Bristol Marina Ltd
Hanover Place, Bristol, BS1 6TZ
Tel: 0117 921 3198 Fax: 0117 929 7672
Email: info@bristolmarina.co.uk

VHF Ch 80
ACCESS HW-3 to HW

Situated in the heart of the city, Bristol is a fully serviced marina
providing over 100 pontoon berths for vessels up to 20m LOA.
Among the facilities are a new fuelling berth and pump out station
as well as an on site chandler and sailmaker. It is situated on the
south side of the Floating Harbour, about eight miles from the
mouth of the River Avon. Accessible from seaward via the
Cumberland Basin, passing through both Entrance Lock and Junction
Lock, it can be reached approximately three hours before HW.

Shops, restaurants, theatres and cinemas are all within easy
reach of the marina, while local attractions include the
SS *Great Britain*, designed by Isambard Kingdom
Brunel, and the famous Clifton Suspension Bridge,
which has an excellent visitors' centre depicting its
fascinating story.

FACILITIES AT A GLANCE

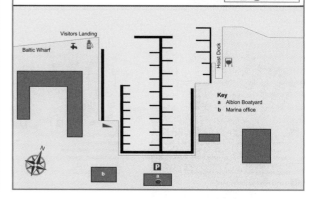

PORTISHEAD QUAYS MARINA

Portishead Quays Marina
The Docks, Portishead, Bristol BS20 7DF
Tel: 01275 841941 Fax: 01275 841942
Email: portisheadmarina@quaymarinas.com
www.quaymarinas.com

VHF Ch 80
ACCESS HW±4

Opened in May 2001, Portishead Quays
Marina, with its excellent facilities and 24
hour security, is becoming increasingly
popular with locals and visitors alike.
However, visiting yachtsmen should be
aware of the large tidal ranges and strong
tidal flows that they are likely to encounter
in this part of the Bristol Channel as well as
shipping plying to and from the Avonmouth
and Portbury Docks. The entrance to the
marina is via a lock, with
access for a 1.5m yacht
being at HW±4½ hrs on
neaps and HW±3¾ hrs
on springs – contact the marina on VHF Ch 80
ahead of time for the next available lock.

FACILITIES AT A GLANCE

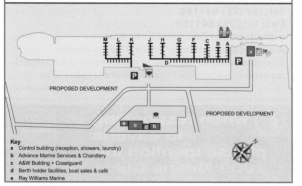

11

IRELAND'S LARGEST MARINA

1D2O0018 Photo: © Peter Barrow 14th July 2007. Tel: 0872-559638

Dun Laoghaire Marina

- 820 berth fully serviced marina
- Located in Dublin's major sailing centre
- Awarded ISO 14001 – Environment Management System
- Visitor berths available from €4 per metre per night
- 24 hour access
- Friendly, knowledgably and welcoming staff 24/7
- All visitor berths fully serviced, shore power supply metered.
- Petrol, diesel and holding tank pump out
- Laundry facilities onsite
- Oceanwave WiFi
- Full disabled access and facilities
- Direct access to UK with Stena HSS ferry and airport coach transfer
- Volvo Dun Laoghaire Regatta 9-12 July 2009

www.dlmarina.com
Contact: info@dlmarina.com

Marina Marketing & Management Ltd.

2009/MG168/z

SOUTH IRELAND - Malahide, south to Liscanor Bay

ADLARD COLES NAUTICAL
WEATHER FORECASTS
BY FAX & TELEPHONE

Coastal/Inshore	2-day by Fax	5-day by Phone
Northern Ireland	09065 222 355	09068 969 655
Wales	09065 222 350	09068 969 650
Bristol	09065 222 349	09068 969 649
South West	09065 222 348	09068 969 648
National (3-5 day)	09065 222 340	09068 969 640

Offshore	2-5 day by Fax	2-5 day by Phone
Irish Sea	09065 222 359	09068 969 659
English Channel	09065 222 357	09068 969 657
Biscay	09065 222 360	09068 969 660
North West Scotland	09065 222 361	09068 969 661

09068 CALLS COST 60P PER MIN. 09065 CALLS COST £1.50 PER MIN.

Key to Marina Plans symbols

Bottled gas		Parking	
Chandler		Pub/Restaurant	
Disabled facilities		Pump out	
Electrical supply		Rigging service	
Electrical repairs		Sail repairs	
Engine repairs		Shipwright	
First Aid		Shop/Supermarket	
Fresh Water		Showers	
Fuel - Diesel		Slipway	
Fuel - Petrol		Toilets	
Hardstanding/boatyard		Telephone	
Internet Café		Trolleys	
Laundry facilities		Visitors berths	
Lift-out facilities		Wi-Fi	

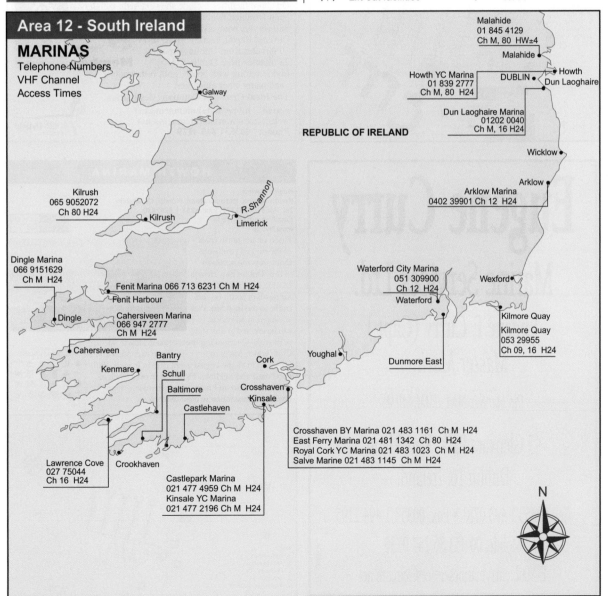

Area 12 - South Ireland

MARINAS
Telephone Numbers
VHF Channel
Access Times

REPUBLIC OF IRELAND

Malahide
01 845 4129
Ch M, 80 HW±4
Malahide

Howth YC Marina
01 839 2777
Ch M, 80 H24
DUBLIN
Howth
Dun Laoghaire

Dun Laoghaire Marina
01202 0040
Ch M, 16 H24

Wicklow

Arklow
Arklow Marina
0402 39901 Ch 12 H24

Galway

Kilrush
065 9052072
Ch 80 H24
Kilrush
R.Shannon
Limerick

Dingle Marina
066 9151629
Ch M H24

Fenit Marina 066 713 6231 Ch M H24
Fenit Harbour

Dingle

Cahersiveen Marina
066 947 2777
Ch M H24
Cahersiveen

Waterford City Marina
051 309900
Ch 12 H24
Waterford

Wexford

Kilmore Quay
Kilmore Quay
053 29955
Ch 09, 16 H24

Bantry
Schull
Baltimore
Castlehaven

Cork
Youghal
Dunmore East

Kenmare

Crosshaven
Kinsale

Crosshaven BY Marina 021 483 1161 Ch M H24
East Ferry Marina 021 481 1342 Ch 80 H24
Royal Cork YC Marina 021 483 1023 Ch M H24
Salve Marine 021 483 1145 Ch M H24

Lawrence Cove
027 75044
Ch 16 H24
Crookhaven

Castlepark Marina
021 477 4959 Ch M H24
Kinsale YC Marina
021 477 2196 Ch M H24

N

12

MALAHIDE MARINA

Malahide Marina
Malahide, Co. Dublin
Tel: +353 1 845 4129 Fax: +353 1 845 4255
Email: info@malahidemarina.net
www.malahidemarina.net

VHF	Ch M, 80
ACCESS	HW±4

Malahide Marina, situated just 10 minutes from Dublin Airport and 20 minutes north of Dublin's city centre, is a fully serviced marina accommodating up to 350 yachts. Capable of taking vessels of up to 75m in length, its first class facilities include a boatyard with hard standing for approximately 170 boats and a 30-ton mobile hoist. Its on site restaurant, Cruzzo, provides a large seating area in convivial surroundings. The village of Malahide has plenty to offer the visiting yachtsmen, with a wide variety of eating places, nearby golf courses and tennis courts as well as a historic castle and botanical gardens.

FACILITIES AT A GLANCE

Key
a Boat handling & storage area
b Refuelling bay
c Marina centre
d Boatyard
e Marina access bridge
f Restaurant
g Wash area

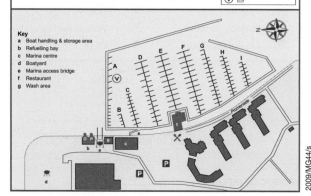

docklands

Dublin City Moorings
Custom House Quay, Docklands, Dublin I

the only mooring in the Centre of Dublin City

Beside the Custom House and IFSC.
Electricity/water. Showers/toilets. 24 hour security.
Swipe card access.
Telephone +353 I 8183300 Fax: +353 I 8183399

Email: info@dublindocklands.ie   Website: http://www.dublindocklands.ie

2009/MG5/e

MALAHIDE MARINA

Marina Centre, Malahide Marina Village, Malahide, Co. Dublin
350 Berths in fully serviced marina.
On-shore facilities include showers/bath, laundry
 and Disabled facilities.
Full service boatyard
Covered Repair Facility for re-fits.
10 minutes from Dublin Airport
25 minutes from Dublin City
Idyllic setting with beach, golf, restaurants
 and many other amenities.
The Ideal Cruise in Company destination.
e-mail: info@malahidemarina.net
website: www.malahidemarina.net
Phone: 003531 845 4129

Irish Marine Federation
Member

British Marine Federation

2009/MG44/s

Eugene Curry

Marine Services Ltd.

Eugene F. Curry (Capt.)

Master Mariner

Dip Mar Sur, MNI, IIMM, MIIMS

45 Glenvara Park, Knocklyon,
Dublin 16, Ireland.

Tel: 00353 1 493 9781 • Fax: 00353 1 494 2195

Mobile: 00 353 86 257 0730

E-Mail: currymarineservices@eircom.net

2009/MG167/s

HOWTH MARINA

Howth Marina
Howth Marina, Harbour Road, Howth, Co. Dublin
Tel: +353 1 8392777 Fax: +353 1 8392430
Email: marina@hyc.ie
www.hyc.ie

VHF	Ch M, 80
ACCESS	H24

Based on the north coast of the rugged peninsula that forms the northern side of Dublin Bay, Howth Marina is ideally situated for north or south-bound traffic in the Irish Sea. Well sheltered in all winds, it can be entered at any state of the tide. Overlooking the marina is Howth Yacht Club, which has in recent years been expanded and is now said to be the largest yacht club in Ireland. With good road and rail links, Howth is in easy reach of Dublin's airport and ferry terminal, making it an obvious choice for crew changeovers.

FACILITIES AT A GLANCE

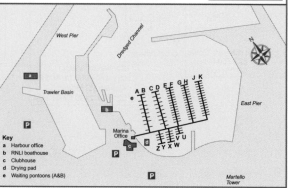

Key
a Harbour office
b RNLI boathouse
c Clubhouse
d Drying pad
e Waiting pontoons (A&B)

12

DUN LAOGHAIRE MARINA

Dun Laoghaire Marina
Harbour Road, Dun Laoghaire, Co Dublin, Eire
Tel: +353 1 202 0040 Fax: +353 1 202 0043
Email: info@dlmarina.com   www.dlmarina.com

VHF	Ch M, 16
ACCESS	H24

With over 800 berths Dun Laoghaire Marina is the largest in Ireland. The town centre is within 400m and with plenty of shops, supermarkets, restaurants, and chandlers. Berthing is available for yachts from 8 to 23m and linear berthing is available for yachts up to 35m. The minimum draught is 3.6m LWS. Dublin City centre is 12 kms away with frequent rail service. Dublin Airport is 22 km. Dun Laoghaire Marina is an ideal location for crew change or cruise rest. Berths are identified by access route, bay identification and number – ascending from bay entrance – odd numbers to port, even to starboard, eg SD10 indicates South Fairway, Bay D 5th berth on starboard hand. Visitor berths mainly located on

FACILITIES AT A GLANCE

Key
a Royal Irish Yacht Club
b Marina office
c WC
d Royal St George Yacht Club

ARKLOW MARINA

Arklow Marina
North Quay, Arklow, Co. Wicklow, Eire
Tel: +353 402 39901 Fax: +353 402 39902
Mobiles: 087 2375189 or 087 2515699
Email: technical@asl.ie
www.arklowmarina.com

VHF Ch12
ACCESS H24

Arklow is a popular fishing port and seaside town situated at the mouth of the River Avoca, just 16 miles south of Wicklow and 11 miles north east of Gorey. Historically noted for building wooden boats, the town is ideally placed for visiting the many beauty spots of County Wicklow including Glenmalure, Glendalough and Clara Lara, Avoca (Ballykissangel).

Lying on the north bank of the river, just upstream of the commercial quays, is Arklow Marina, which provides 42 berths in an inner harbour and 30 berths on pontoons outside the marina entrance. Note that vessels over 14m LOA should moor on the river pontoons. Just a five-minute walk from the town, the marina is within easy reach of as many as 19 pubs and several restaurants.

FACILITIES AT A GLANCE

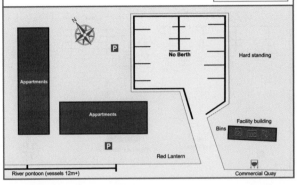

KILMORE QUAY

Kilmore Quay
Wexford, Ireland
Tel: +353 53 9129955 Fax: +353 53 9129915
Email: hmkilmorequay@eircom.net

VHF Ch 09, 16
ACCESS H24

Located in the SE corner of Ireland, Kilmore Quay is a small rural fishing village situated approximately 14 miles from the town of Wexford and 12 miles from Rosslare ferry port.

Its 55-berthed marina, offering shelter from the elements as well as various on shore facilities, has become a regular port of call for many cruising yachtsmen. Kilmore's fishing industry dates back over the last hundred years and among the species of fresh fish available are bass, shark, skate and whiting. With several nearby areas of either historical or natural significance, Kilmore is renowned for its 'green' approach to the environment.

FACILITIES AT A GLANCE

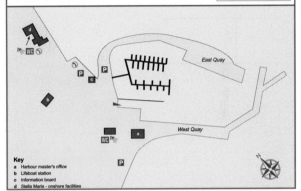

Key
a Harbour master's office
b Lifeboat station
c Information board
d Stella Maris - onshore facilities

WATERFORD CITY MARINA

Waterford City Marina
Waterford, Ireland
Tel: +353 51 309900 Fax: +353 51 870813

VHF Ch 12
ACCESS H24

Famous for its connections with Waterford Crystal, now manufactured on the outskirts of the city, Waterford is the capital of the south east region of Ireland. As a major city, it benefits from good rail links with Dublin, Limerick and Rosslare, a regional airport with daily flights to Britain and an extensive bus service to surrounding towns and villages. The marina can be located on the banks of the River Suir, in the heart of this historic Viking city dating back to the ninth century. Yachtsmen can therefore make the most of Waterford's wide range of shops, restaurants and bars without having to walk too far from their boats. With 150 fully serviced berths and first rate security, Waterford City Marina now provides shower, toilet and laundry facilities in its new reception building.

FACILITIES AT A GLANCE

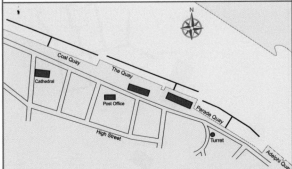

CROSSHAVEN BOATYARD MARINA

Crosshaven Boatyard Marina
Crosshaven, Co Cork, Ireland
Tel: +353 214 831161 Fax: +353 214 831603
Email: cby@eircom.net

VHF Ch M
ACCESS H24

One of three marinas at Crosshaven, Crosshaven Boatyard was founded in 1950 and originally made its name from the construction of some of the most world-renowned yachts, including *Gypsy Moth* and Denis Doyle's *Moonduster*. Nowadays, however, the yard has diversified to provide a wide range of services to both the marine leisure and professional industries. Situated on a safe and sheltered river only 12 miles from Cork City Centre, the marina boasts 100 fully-serviced berths along with the capacity to accommodate yachts up to 35m LOA with a 4m draught. In addition, it is ideally situated for cruising the stunning south west coast of Ireland.

FACILITIES AT A GLANCE

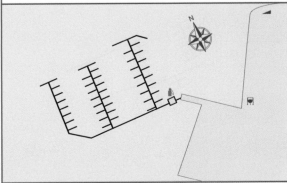

12

SALVE MARINE

Salve Marine
Crosshaven, Co Cork, Ireland
Tel: +353 214 831 145 Fax: +353 214 831 747
Email: salvemarine@eircom.net

VHF | Ch M
ACCESS | H24

Crosshaven is a picturesque seaside resort providing a gateway to Ireland's south and south west coasts. Offering a variety of activities to suit all types, its rocky coves and quiet sandy beaches stretch from Graball to Church Bay and from Fennell's Bay to nearby Myrtleville. Besides a selection of craft shops selling locally produced arts and crafts, there are plenty of pubs, restaurants and takeaways to suit even the most discerning of tastes. Lying within a few hundred metres of the village centre is Salve Marine, accommodating yachts up to 43m LOA with draughts of up to 4m. Its comprehensive services range from engineering and welding facilities to hull and rigging repairs.

FACILITIES AT A GLANCE

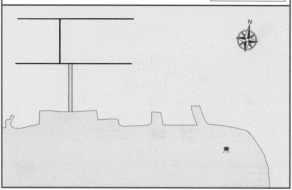

ROYAL CORK YACHT CLUB

Royal Cork Yacht Club Marina
Crosshaven, Co Cork, Ireland
Tel: +353 21 483 1023 Fax: +353 21 483 1586
Email: office@royalcork.com   www.royalcork.com

VHF | Ch M
ACCESS | H24

Founded in 1720, the Royal Cork Yacht Club is one of the oldest and most prominent yacht clubs in the world. Organising, among many other events, the prestigious biennial Ford Cork Week, it boasts a number of World, European and National sailors among its membership.

The Yacht Club's marina is situated at Crosshaven, which nestles on the hillside at the mouth of the Owenabue River just inside the entrance to Cork Harbour. The harbour is popular with yachtsmen as it is accessible and well sheltered in all weather conditions. It also benefits from the Gulf Stream producing a temperate climate practically all year round.

FACILITIES AT A GLANCE

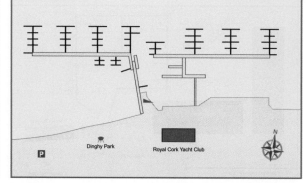

Dinghy Park   Royal Cork Yacht Club

EAST FERRY MARINA

East Ferry Marina
Cobh, Co Cork, Ireland
Tel: +353 21 481 1342 Fax: +353 21 481 1342

VHF | Ch 80
ACCESS | H24

East Ferry Marina lies on the east side of Great Island, one of three large islands in Cork Harbour which are now all joined by roads and bridges. Despite its remote, tranquil setting, it offers all the fundamental facilities including showers, water, fuel, electricity and that all important pub. The

nearest town is Cobh, which is a good five mile walk away, albeit a pleasant one.

Formerly known as Queenstown, Cobh (pronounced 'cove') reverted back to its original Irish name in 1922 and is renowned for being the place from where thousands of Irish men and women set off to America to build a new life for themselves, particularly during the famine years of 1844–48.

FACILITIES AT A GLANCE

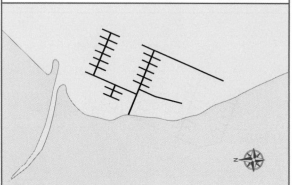

KINSALE YACHT CLUB MARINA

Kinsale Yacht Club Marina
Kinsale, Co Cork, Ireland
Tel: +353 21 4772196 Fax: +353 21 4774455
Email: kyc@iol.ie

VHF | Ch M
ACCESS | H24

Kinsale is a natural, virtually land-locked harbour on the estuary of the Bandon River, approximately 12 miles south west of Cork harbour entrance. Home to a thriving fishing fleet as well as frequented by commercial shipping, it boasts two fully serviced marinas, with the Kinsale Yacht Club & Marina being the closest to the town. Visitors to this marina automatically become temporary members of the club and are therefore entitled to make full use of the facilities, which include a fully licensed bar and restaurant serving evening meals on Wednesdays, Thursdays and Saturdays. Fuel, water and repairs services are also readily available.

FACILITIES AT A GLANCE

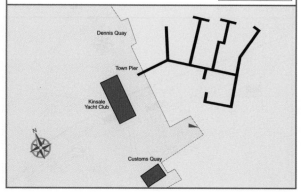

Dennis Quay

Town Pier

Kinsale
Yacht Club

Customs Quay

CASTLEPARK MARINA

Castlepark Marina Centre
Kinsale, Co Cork, Ireland
Tel: +353 21 4774959 Fax: +353 21 4774595
Email: maritime@indigo.ie

VHF Ch M
ACCESS H24

Situated on the south side of Kinsale Harbour, Castlepark is a small marina with deep water pontoon berths that are accessible at all states of the tide. Surrounded by rolling hills, it boasts its own beach as well as being in close proximity to the parklands of James Fort and a traditional Irish pub. The attractive town of Kinsale, with its narrow streets and slate-clad houses, lies just 1.5 miles away by road or five minutes away by ferry. Known as Ireland's 'fine food centre', it incorporates a number of gourmet food shops and high quality restaurants as well as a wine museum.

FACILITIES AT A GLANCE

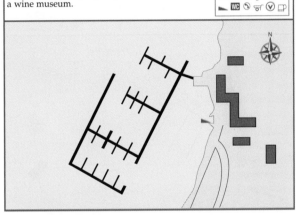

LAWRENCE COVE MARINA

Lawrence Cove Marina
Lawrence Cove, Bere Island, Co Cork, Ireland
Tel: +353 27 75044 Fax: +353 27 75044
Email: lcm@iol.ie
www.lawrencecovemarina.com

VHF Ch 16
ACCESS H24

Lawrence Cove enjoys a peaceful location on an island at the entrance to Bantry Bay. Privately owned and run, it offers sheltered and secluded waters as well as excellent facilities and fully serviced pontoon berths. A few hundred yards from the marina you will find a shop, pub and restaurant, while the mainland, with its various attractions, can be easily reached by ferry. Lawrence Cove lies at the heart of the wonderful cruising grounds of Ireland's south west coast and, just two hours from Cork airport, is an ideal place to leave your boat for long or short periods.

FACILITIES AT A GLANCE

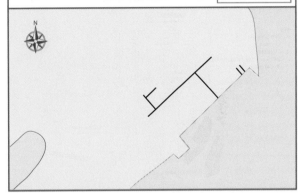

CAHERSIVEEN MARINA

Cahersiveen Marina
The Pier, Cahersiveen, Co. Kerry, Ireland
Tel: +353 66 9472777 Fax: +353 66 9472993
Email: info@cahersiveenmarina.ie
www.cahersiveenmarina.ie

VHF Ch M
ACCESS H24

Situated two miles up Valentia River from Valentia Harbour, Cahersiveen Marina is well protected in all wind directions and is convenient for sailing to Valentia Island and Dingle Bay as well as for visiting some of the spectacular uninhabited islands in the surrounding area. Boasting a host of sheltered sandy beaches, the region is renowned for salt and fresh water fishing as well as being good for scuba diving.

Within easy walking distance of the marina lies the historic town of Cahersiveen, incorporating an array of convivial pubs and restaurants.

FACILITIES AT A GLANCE

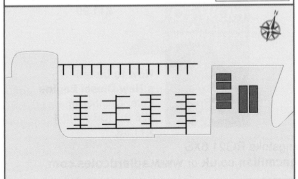

DINGLE MARINA

Dingle Marina
Strand Street, Dingle, Co Kerry, Ireland
Tel: +353 66 9151629 Fax: +353 69 5152546
Email:1dingle@eircom.net   www.dinglemarina.com

VHF Ch M
ACCESS H24

Dingle is Ireland's most westerly marina, lying at the heart of the sheltered Dingle Harbour, and is easily reached both day and night via a well buoyed approach channel. The surrounding area is an interesting and unfrequented cruising ground, with several islands, bays and beaches for the yachtsman to explore.

The marina lies in the heart of the old market town, renowned for its hospitality and traditional Irish pub music. Besides enjoying the excellent seafood restaurants and 52 pubs, other recreational pastimes include horse riding, golf, climbing and diving.

FACILITIES AT A GLANCE

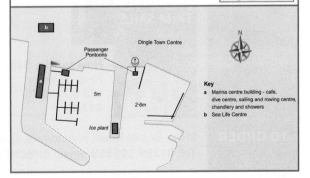

Key
a Marina centre building - cafe, dive centre, sailing and rowing centre, chandlery and showers
b Sea Life Centre

12

FENIT HARBOUR MARINA

Fenit Harbour
Fenit, Tralee, Co. Kerry, Republic of Ireland
Tel: +353 66 7136231 Fax: +353 66 7136473
Email: fenitmarina@eircom.net

VHF Ch M
ACCESS H24

Fenit Harbour Marina is tucked away in Tralee Bay, not far south of the Shannon Estuary. Besides offering a superb cruising ground, being within a day's sail of Dingle and Kilrush, the marina also

provides a convenient base from which to visit inland attractions such as the picturesque tourist towns of Tralee and Killarney. This 120-berth marina accommodates boats up to 15m LOA and benefits from deep water at all states of the tide.

The small village of Fenit incorporates a grocery shop as well a several pubs and restaurants, while among the local activities are horse riding, swimming from one of the nearby sandy beaches and golfing.

FACILITIES AT A GLANCE

Key
a Fenit Seaworld
b Fish store
c Warehouse
d Marina services, harbour office, lifeboat station

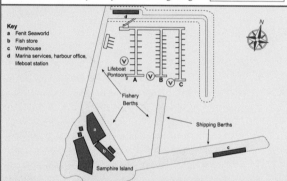

KILRUSH MARINA

Kilrush Creek Marina Ltd
Kilrush, Co. Clare, Ireland
Tel: +353 65 9052072 Fax: +353 65 9051692
Email: hehir@shannon.dev.ie

VHF Ch 80
ACCESS H24

Kilrush Marina and boatyard is strategically placed for exploring the unspoilt west coast of Ireland, including Galway Bay, Dingle, West Cork and Kerry. It also provides a gateway to over 150 miles of cruising on Lough Derg, the River Shannon and the Irish canal system. Accessed via lock gates, the

marina lies at one end of the main street in Kilrush, a vibrant market town with a long maritime history. A 15-minute ferry ride from the marina takes you to Scattery Island, once a sixth century monastic settlement but now uninhabited except by wildlife. The Shannon Estuary is reputed for being the country's first marine Special Area of Conservation (SAC) and is home to Ireland's only

FACILITIES AT A GLANCE

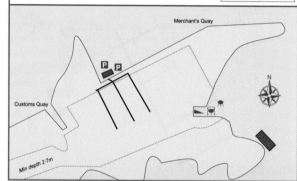

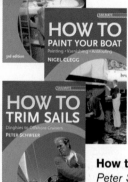

12

NORTH IRELAND - Lambay Island, north to Liscanor Bay

ADLARD COLES NAUTICAL
WEATHER FORECASTS
BY FAX & TELEPHONE

Coastal/Inshore	2-day by Fax	5-day by Phone
Caledonia	09065 222 353	09068 969 653
Northern Ireland	09065 222 355	09068 969 655
Clyde	09065 222 352	09068 969 652
North West	09065 222 341	09068 969 641
National (3-5 day)	09065 222 340	09068 969 640

Offshore	2-5 day by Fax	2-5 day by Phone
Irish Sea	09065 222 359	09068 969 659
English Channel	09065 222 357	09068 969 657
Biscay	09065 222 360	09068 969 660
North West Scotland	09065 222 361	09068 969 661

09068 CALLS COST 60P PER MIN. 09065 CALLS COST £1.50 PER MIN.

Key to Marina Plans symbols

	Bottled gas	P	Parking
	Chandler		Pub/Restaurant
	Disabled facilities		Pump out
	Electrical supply		Rigging service
	Electrical repairs		Sail repairs
	Engine repairs		Shipwright
	First Aid		Shop/Supermarket
	Fresh Water		Showers
	Fuel - Diesel		Slipway
	Fuel - Petrol	WC	Toilets
	Hardstanding/boatyard		Telephone
@	Internet Café		Trolleys
	Laundry facilities	V	Visitors berths
	Lift-out facilities		Wi-Fi

Area 13 - North Ireland

MARINAS
Telephone Numbers
VHF Channel
Access Times

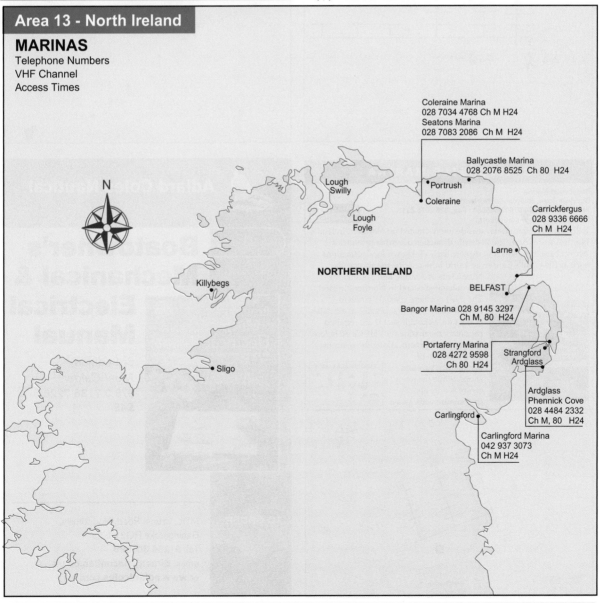

Coleraine Marina
028 7034 4768 Ch M H24
Seatons Marina
028 7083 2086 Ch M H24

Ballycastle Marina
028 2076 8525 Ch 80 H24

Lough Swilly

Portrush

Coleraine

Lough Foyle

Carrickfergus
028 9336 6666
Ch M H24

Larne

NORTHERN IRELAND

BELFAST

Killybegs

Bangor Marina 028 9145 3297
Ch M, 80 H24

Portaferry Marina
028 4272 9598
Ch 80 H24

Strangford
Ardglass

Ardglass
Phennick Cove
028 4484 2332
Ch M, 80 H24

Sligo

Carlingford

Carlingford Marina
042 937 3073
Ch M H24

COLERAINE MARINA

Coleraine Marina
64 Portstewart Road, Coleraine,
Co Londonderry, BT52 1RS
Tel: 028 7034 4768

| VHF | Ch M,16 |
| ACCESS | H24 |

Coleraine Marina complex enjoys a superb location in sheltered waters just one mile north of the town of Coleraine and four and a half miles south of the River Bann Estuary and the open sea. Besides accommodating vessels up to 18m LOA, this modern marina with 105 berths offers hard standing, fuel, a chandlery and shower facilities.

Among one of the oldest known settlements in Ireland, Coleraine is renowned for its linen, whiskey and salmon. Its thriving commercial centre includes numerous shops, a four-screen cinema and ice rink as well as a state-of-the-art leisure complex.

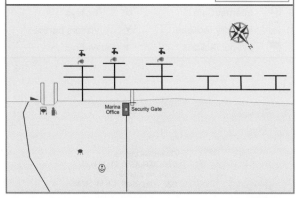

FACILITIES AT A GLANCE

SEATONS MARINA

Seatons Marina
Drumslade Rd, Coleraine, Londonderry, BT52 1SE
Tel: 028 7083 2086
Email: ssp@seatonsmarina.co.uk   www.seatonsmarina.co.uk

| VHF | Ch M |
| ACCESS | H24 |

Seatons Marina is a privately owned business on the north coast of Ireland, which was established by Eric Seaton in 1962. It lies on the east bank of the River Bann, approximately two miles downstream from Coleraine and three miles from the sea.

Although facilities are currently rather limited, plans are underway to improve the services available to yachtsmen. The pontoon berths are suitable for yachts up to 13.5m, with a minimum depth of 2.4m on the outer berths, although some of the inner berths do occasionally dry out. Seatons is also able to provide swinging moorings, all of which come with a galvanised chain riser passed over the stem roller.

FACILITIES AT A GLANCE

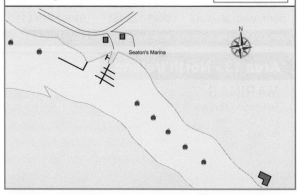

BALLYCASTLE MARINA

Ballycastle Marina
Bayview Road, Ballycastle, Northern Ireland
Tel: 028 2076 8525/07803 505084   Fax: 028 2076 6215
Email: info@moyle-council.org

| VHF | Ch 80 |
| ACCESS | H24 |

Ballycastle is a traditional seaside town situated on Northern Ireland's North Antrim coast. The 74-berthed, sheltered marina provides a perfect base from which to explore the well known local attractions such as the Giant's Causeway world heritage site, the spectacular

Nine Glens of Antrim, and Rathlin, the only inhabited island in Northern Ireland. The most northern coastal marina in Ireland, Ballycastle is accessible at all states of the tide, although yachts are required to contact the marina on VHF Ch 80 before entering the harbour. Along the seafront are a selection of restaurants, bars and shops, while the town centre is only about a five-minute walk away.

FACILITIES AT A GLANCE

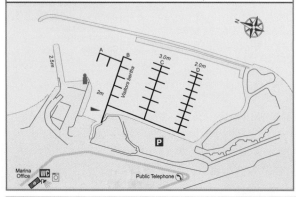

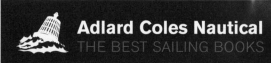
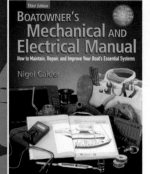

13

CARRICKFERGUS MARINA

Carrickferus Marina
3 Quayside, Carrickfergus, Co. Antrim, BT38 8BJ
Tel: 028 9336 6666 Fax: 028 9335 0505
Email: bwithers.marina@carrickfergus.org
www.carrickfergus.org

VHF Ch M
ACCESS H24

Located on the north shore of Belfast Lough, Carrickfergus Marina and harbour incorporates two sheltered areas suitable for leisure craft. The harbour is dominated by a magnificent 12th century Norman Castle which, recently renovated, includes a film theatre, banqueting room and outdoor models depicting the castle's chequered history.

The marina is located 250 metres west of the harbour and has become increasingly popular since its opening in 1985. A range of shops and restaurants along the waterfront caters for most yachtsmen's needs.

FACILITIES AT A GLANCE

Key
a Office space
b Development site
c Waterfront Administration Building
d Cinema/restaurant
e Retail superstore

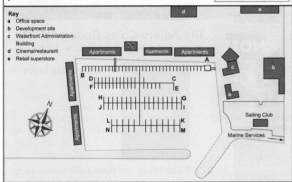

Carrickfergus Borough

Carrickfergus Marina

3 Quayside, Carrickfergus BT38 8BJ
T: +44 (0) 28 9336 6666   F: +44 (0) 28 9335 0505
E: marinarec@carrickfergus.org

SPECIAL OFFER

Upon presentation of this publication, you will receive a second night's accomodation free, subject to the first night being paid in advance.

BANGOR MARINA

Quay Marinas Limited
Bangor Marina, Bangor, Co. Down, BT20 5ED
Tel: 028 9145 3297 Fax: 028 9145 3450
Email: ajaggers@quaymarinas.com
www.quaymarinas.com

VHF Ch 80
ACCESS H24

Situated on the south shore of Belfast Lough, Bangor is located close to the Irish Sea cruising routes. The Marina is right at the town's centre, within walking distance of shops, restaurants, hotels and bars. The Tourist information centre is across the road from marina reception and there are numerous visitors' attractions in the Borough. The Royal Ulster Yacht Club and the Ballyholme Yacht Club are both nearby and welcome visitors.

QUAY MARINAS

FACILITIES AT A GLANCE

Key
a Boat hoist - BJ Marine
b Boat yard - BJ Marine
c Bregenz House
d Chandlery/brokerage BJ Marine
e Dinghy berths
f Access bridge
g Lifeboat slipway
h Domestic waste facilities
i Waste oil tank
j Disabled berthing
k Flare disposal

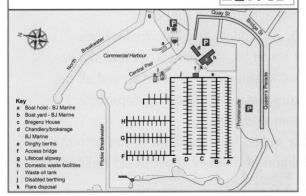

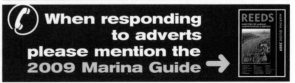

CARLINGFORD MARINA

Carlingford Marina
Co. Louth, Ireland
Tel: +353 (0)42 937 3073   Fax: +353 (0)42 937 3075
Email: cmarina@iol.ie
www.carlingfordmarina.ie

VHF	Ch M
ACCESS	H24

Carlingford Lough is an eight-mile sheltered haven between the Cooley Mountains to the south and the Mourne Mountains to the north. The marina is situated on the southern shore, about four miles from Haulbowline Lighthouse, and can be easily reached via a deep water shipping channel. Among the most attractive destinations in the Irish Sea, Carlingford is only 60 miles from the Isle of Man and within a day's sail from Strangford Lough and Ardglass. Full facilities in the marina include a first class bar and restaurant offering superb views across the water.

FACILITIES AT A GLANCE

Key
a   Bar and restaurant
b   Toilets, showers and laundry
c   Refuse
d   Office
e   Chandlery
f   Marina office
g   Waiting pontoon

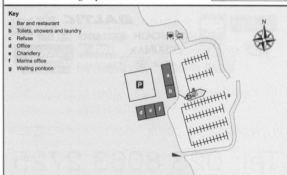

Carlingford Marina
North commons
Carlingford
Co. Louth
Ireland

Tel: +00353 (0)42 9373073
Fax: +00353 (0)42 9373075
Email: cmarina@iol.ie
Web: www.carlingfordmarina.ie
VHF Channel 37 or 16
Helipad Co-Ordinates
54°03'00.7"N/6°11'28.3"W

*Carlingford Marina...
where the world is
your Oyster*

Carlingford Marina is situated on the South Western side of Carlingford Lough.
Boasting a host of facilities to include;

• Over 200 berths most with power and water. Max LOA 30 metres.
• Diesel available on fuel quay
• Showers, toilets and laundry facilities
• 50T travel lift, winter storage and slipway
• Bar & Restaurant with food served all day
• Luxury 4 star Fàilte Ireland Approved Accommodation
• Easy access from land, air or sea with the addition of a newly constructed Helipad

2009/MG161/Z

PORTAFERRY MARINA

Portaferry Marina
11 The Strand, Portaferry, BT22 1PF
Tel: 028 4272 9598 Mobile: 07703 209 780 Fax: 028 4272 9784
Email: barholm.portaferry@virgin.net

VHF	Ch 80
ACCESS	H24

Portaferry Marina lies on the east shore of the Narrows, the gateway to Strangford Lough on the north east coast of Ireland. A marine nature reserve of outstanding natural beauty, the Lough offers plenty of recreational activities. The marina, which caters for draughts of up to 2.5m, is fairly small, accommodating around 30 yachts. The office is situated about 200m from the marina itself, where you will find ablution facilities along with a launderette.

Portaferry incorporates several pubs and restaurants as well as a few convenience stores, while one of its prime attractions is the Exploris Aquarium. Places of historic interest in the vicinity include Castleward, an 18th century mansion in Strangford, and Mount Stewart House & Garden in Newtownards.

FACILITIES AT A GLANCE

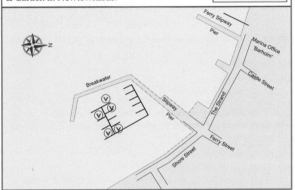

ARDGLASS MARINA

Ardglass Marina
19 Quay Street, Ardglass, BT30 7SA
Tel: 028 4484 2332 Fax: 028 4484 2332
Email: ardglassmarina@tiscali.co.uk
www.ardglassmarina.co.uk

VHF	Ch M, 80
ACCESS	H24

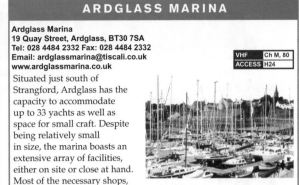

Situated just south of Strangford, Ardglass has the capacity to accommodate up to 33 yachts as well as space for small craft. Despite being relatively small in size, the marina boasts an extensive array of facilities, either on site or close at hand. Most of the necessary shops, including grocery stores, a post office, chemist and off-licence, are all within a five-minute walk from the marina. Among the local onshore activities are golf, mountain climbing in Newcastle, which is 18 miles south, as well as scenic walks at Ardglass and Delamont Park.

FACILITIES AT A GLANCE

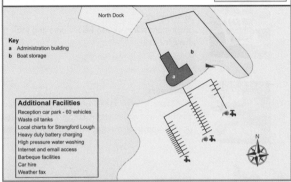

Key
a Administration building
b Boat storage

Additional Facilities
Reception car park - 60 vehicles
Waste oil tanks
Local charts for Strangford Lough
Heavy duty battery charging
High pressure water washing
Internet and email access
Barbeque facilities
Car hire
Weather fax

JACKSON YACHT SERVICES

Established for over 30 years, a traditional boatyard owned by Mike and Kay Jackson

Contact Mike about all aspects of yacht management, and Kay to discuss the sale of your vessel and for assistance in your search for the ideal yacht from the largest sailing vessel to the smallest dinghy. Also contact us for boat surveys.

 ZODIAC Zodiac Boat Sales and Service

What we do
Liferaft, Lifejacket, Sales, Hire and Service Jersey's only British Marine and Coastguard Agency (MCA) approved service station qualifying us to service commercial and yachting liferafts to the most stringent specifications. We pride ourselves on meticulous care and attention with your safety equipment and regularly attend manufacturers premises in order to keep abreast of the various liferaft packing methods so that your lifesaving apparatus will operate efficiently when required. We are sales agents and have been awarded servicing certificates for the following manufacturers: - Zodiac, Bombard, RFD, ML Lifeguard, BFA (XM), Plastimo, and Crewsaver. Owners of rafts are advised to have them serviced by a properly certificated service station as recommended by their manufacturer to ensure validity of guarantees.

Brokerage
Buying or selling, we can help. Come and look through our listings or visit our website for further details of the vessels we have for sale.

Chandlery
We stock a large range of traditional and modern chandlery including nautical publications, books and charts, paints, varnishes and antifouling. A complrehensive selection of ropes, blocks and shackles together with boat fishing tackle enables us to supply boat owners with most of their needs.

Clothing
Fashionable and conventional yachting clothing for adults and children by Le Glazic, Coude Maille, and St. James. Extensive leather deck shoe range by TBS and Sebago, as well as boots, offshore foul weather gear and equipment.

Boat Repairs and Maintenance
Motor & Sailing yacht repairs in GRP and timber, lifting out up to 65 Ton, cleaning and antifouling undertaken. All types of moorings made up and laid from deep water to marina berth.

Rigging Loft
Have your rigging checked, repaired or renewed by experienced staff. Masts, spars and furling gear supplied and fitted. Wire swageing machinery in workshop. Specialists in architectural rigging and wire work.

Sail Loft
All types of sails and covers supplied, valeted and repaired. Embroidery service for crew & team wear.

Yacht Management
Comprehensive management service ensuring smooth and cost effective running of your vessel. Marine consultancy and guardiennage service for non resident owners. We are a small, owner operated business and pride ourselves in the attention to detail commonly missing in large enterprises to-day. We look forward to meeting you and pledge our commitment to fulfil your boating requirements in connection with the smallest dinghy to the largest yacht.

Le Boulevard, St Aubin, Jersey, Channel Islands JE3 8AB
+44 (0) 1534 743819   +44 (0) 1534 745952
sales@jacksonyacht.com • www.jacksonyacht.com

CHANNEL ISLANDS - Alderney, Guernsey & Jersey

Key to Marina Plans symbols

Bottled gas		Parking	
Chandler		Pub/Restaurant	
Disabled facilities		Pump out	
Electrical supply		Rigging service	
Electrical repairs		Sail repairs	
Engine repairs		Shipwright	
First Aid		Shop/Supermarket	
Fresh Water		Showers	
Fuel - Diesel		Slipway	
Fuel - Petrol		Toilets	
Hardstanding/boatyard		Telephone	
Internet Café		Trolleys	
Laundry facilities		Visitors berths	
Lift-out facilities		Wi-Fi	

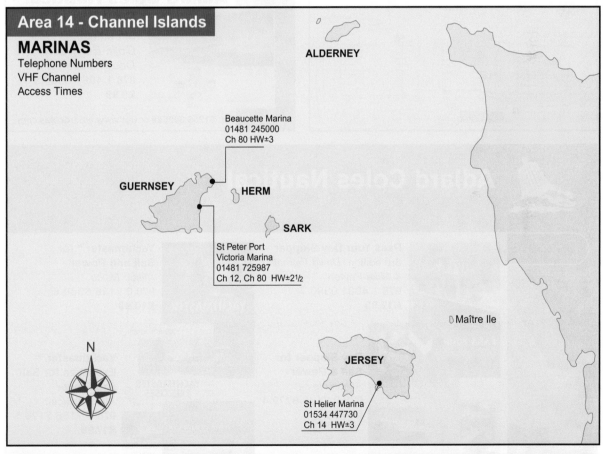

Area 14 - Channel Islands

MARINAS
Telephone Numbers
VHF Channel
Access Times

ALDERNEY

Beaucette Marina
01481 245000
Ch 80 HW±3

GUERNSEY

HERM

SARK

St Peter Port
Victoria Marina
01481 725987
Ch 12, Ch 80 HW±2½

Maître Ile

N

JERSEY

St Helier Marina
01534 447730
Ch 14 HW±3

BEAUCETTE MARINA

Beaucette Marina
Vale, Guernsey, GY3 5BQ
Tel: 01481 245000 Fax: 01481 247071
Mobile: 07781 102302
Email: info@beaucettemarina.com

VHF Ch 80
ACCESS HW±3

Situated on the north east tip of Guernsey, Beaucette enjoys a peaceful, rural setting in contrast to the more vibrant atmosphere of Victoria Marina. Now owned by a private individual and offering a high standard of service, the site was originally formed from an old quarry.

There is a general store close by, while the bustling town of St Peter Port is only 20 minutes away by bus.

FACILITIES AT A GLANCE

Key
a Harbour office   e Manager's cabin
b Restaurant   f Boatyard
c Showers/toilets
d Laundry & telephone

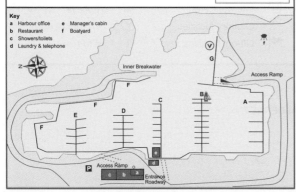

14

ST PETER PORT

Harbour Authority
PO Box 631, St Julian's Emplacement, St Peter Port
Tel: 01481 720229 Fax: 01481 714177
Email: guernsey.harbour@gov.gg

VHF	Ch 12, 80
ACCESS	HW±2.5

The harbour of St Peter Port comprises the Queen Elizabeth II Marina to the N and Victoria and Albert Marinas to the S, with visiting yachtsmen usually accommodated in Victoria Marina.

Renowned for being an international financial centre and tax haven, St Peter Port is the capital of Guernsey. Its regency architecture and picturesque cobbled streets filled with restaurants and boutiques help to make it one of the most attractive harbours in Europe. Among the places of interest are Hauteville House, home of the writer Victor Hugo, and Castle Cornet.

FACILITIES AT A GLANCE

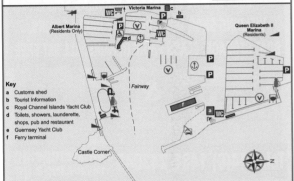

Key
a   Customs shed
b   Tourist Information
c   Royal Channel Islands Yacht Club
d   Toilets, showers, launderette, shops, pub and restaurant
e   Guernsey Yacht Club
f   Ferry terminal

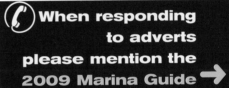

ST PETER PORT VICTORIA MARINA

Harbour Authority
PO Box 631, St Julian's Emplacement, St Peter Port
Tel: 01481 725987 Fax: 01481 714177
Email: guernsey.harbour@gov.gg

| VHF | Ch 80 |
| ACCESS | HW±2.5 |

Victoria Marina in St Peter Port accommodates approximately 300 visiting yachts. In the height of the season it gets extremely busy, but when full visitors can berth on 5 other pontoons in the Pool or pre-arrange a berth in the QE II or Albert marinas. There are no visitor moorings in the Pool. Depending on draught, the marina is accessible approximately two and a half hours either side of HW, with yachts crossing over a sill drying to 4.2m. The marina dory will direct you to a berth on arrival or else will instruct you to moor on one of the waiting pontoons just outside.

Once in the marina, you can benefit from its superb facilities as well as from its central location to St Peter Port's shops and restaurants.

Guernsey is well placed for exploring the rest of the Channel Islands, including the quiet anchorages off Herm and Sark, or making a short hop to one of the French ports such as St Malo,

FACILITIES AT A GLANCE

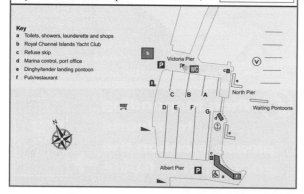

Key
a Toilets, showers, launderette and shops
b Royal Channel Islands Yacht Club
c Refuse skip
d Marina control, port office
e Dinghy/tender landing pontoon
f Pub/restaurant

ST HELIER HARBOUR

St Helier Harbour
Maritime House, La Route du Port Elizabeth
St Helier, Jersey, JE1 1HB
Tel: 01534 447730
www.jersey-harbours.com Email: s.marina@gov.je

VHF
ACCESS HW±3

Jersey is the largest of the Channel Islands, attracting the most number of tourists per year. Although St Helier can get very crowded in the height of the summer, if you hire a car and head out to the north coast in particular you will soon find isolated bays and pretty little fishing villages.

All visiting craft are directed to St Helier Marina, which may be entered three hours either side of HW via a sill. There is a long holding pontoon to port of the entrance accessible at any state of the tide. La Collette Yacht Basin is not for visitors but Elizabeth Marina may accept larger craft by prior arrangement.

FACILITIES AT A GLANCE

Key
a Marina office
b Water/toilets/public phone
c Tourism
d Harbour office and Customs
e Maritime house
f Waiting pontoon
g Passenger Terminal
h Trailer park
i Port control
j Marina shop
k Cafe

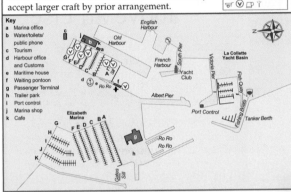

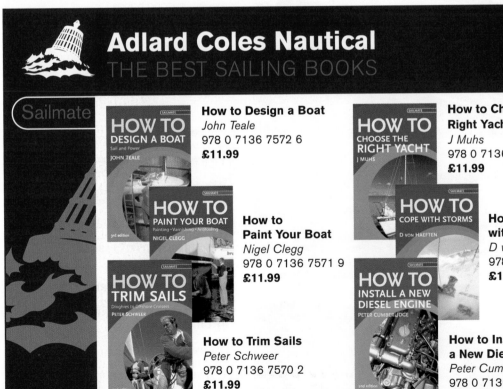

BEAUCETTE
M A R I N A

On an island paradise...

... one gem shines above all else

Accesible 3 hours either side of high water at St Peter Port, Beaucette Marina, situated on the North East of Guernsey, is the perfect base to discover the island.

All the services you would expect from a modern facility are on-hand to make your stay easy and ejoyable. Our staff are highly experienced and ready to help, so you can feel safe in the knowledge that your boat and your crew are in good hands.

Contact us by using the details below or call us on VHF 80 - call sign 'Beaucette Marina'. If you are unsure of the buoyed channel or the entrance to Beaucette, please call on VHF 80 and we will send a boat out to assist you.

For more information, please visit our website at: www.beaucettemarina.com

We look forward to welcoming you.

BEAUCETTE MARINA LTD,
VALE, GUERNSEY,
CHANNEL ISLANDS GY3 5BQ
T: +44 (0)1481 245000
F: +44 (0)1481 247071
E: INFO@BEAUCETTEMARINA.COM
M: +44 (0)7781 102302
W: WWW.BEAUCETTEMARINA.COM
VHF CHANNEL 80

VISITING & ANNUAL BERTHS | WATER & ELECTRICITY ON ALL BERTHS | FUEL & GAS | LAUNDERETTE RESTAURANT | SHOWERS & TOILETS | WEATHER FORECAST | FREE WIFI ACCESS | CAR HIRE

2009/MG134/z

Adhesives 134
Air Conditioning 134
Associations 134
Berths & Moorings 134
Boatbuilders & Repairs 134
Boatyard Services & Supplies 136
Boat Storage 138
Books & Charts/Publishers 138
Bow Thrusters 139
Breakdown 139
Chandlers 139
Chart Agents 142
Clothing 142
Code of Practice Examiners 143
Computers & Software 143
Deck Equipment 143
Diesel Marine/ Fuel Additives 143
Divers 143
Electrical & Electronic Engineers ..143
Electronic Devices & Equipment ..144

Engines & Accessories 144
Foul-Weather Gear 145
General Marine Equipment
& Spares 145
Harbour Masters 145
Harbours 147
Insurance & Finance 147
Liferaft & Inflatables 147
Marinas 147
Marine Consultants & Surveyors ..149
Marine Engineers 149
Masts/Spars & Rigging 151
Navigation Equipment - General ..152
Paint & Osmosis 152
Propellers & Sterngear/Repairs ...152
Radio Courses/Schools 152
Reefing Systems 152
Repair Materials & Accessories ...152
Rope & Wire 153
Safety Equipment 153

Sailmakers & Repairs 153
Solar Power 154
Sprayhoods & Dodgers 154
Surveyors & Naval Architects 154
Tape Technology 155
Transport/Yacht Deliveries 155
Tuition/Sailing Schools 155
Waterside Accommodation &
Restaurants 156
Weather Info 156
Wood Fittings 156
Yacht Brokers 156
Yacht Charters & Holidays 157
Yacht Clubs 157
Yacht Designers 160
Yacht Management 160
Yacht Valeting 160

SECTION 2
MARINE SUPPLIES AND SERVICES GUIDE

ADHESIVES

Adtech Ltd
Braintree   01376 346511

Bettabond Adhesives
Leeds   0113 278 5088

Casco Products Industrial Adhesives
St Neots   01480 476777

CC Marine Services Ltd
West Mersea   01206 381801

Industrial Self Adhesives Ltd
Nottingham   0115 9681895

Sika Ltd Garden City   01707 394444

Technix Rubber & Plastics Ltd
Southampton   01489 789944

Tiflex Liskeard   01579 320808

Trade Grade Products Ltd
Poole   01202 820177

UK Epoxy Resins
Burscough   01704 892364

Wessex Resins & Adhesives Ltd
Romsey   01794 521111

3M United Kingdom plc
Bracknell   01344 858315

ASSOCIATIONS/ AGENCIES

Cruising Association
London   020 7537 2828

Fishermans Mutual Association (Eyemouth) Ltd
Eyemouth   01890 750373

Maritime and Coastguard Agency
Southampton   0870 6006505

Royal Institute of Navigation
London   020 7591 3130

Royal National Lifeboat Institution
Poole   01202 663000

Royal Yachting Association (RYA)
Southampton   0845 345 0400

BERTHS & MOORINGS

ABC Powermarine
Beaumaris   01248 811413

Aqua Bell Ltd Norwich   01603 713013

Ardfern Yacht Centre
Lochgilphead   01852 500247/500636

Ardmair Boat Centre
Ullapool   01854 612054

Arisaig Marine Ltd
Inverness-shire   01687 450224

Bristol Boat Ltd Bristol   01225 872032

British Waterways Argyll
01546 603210

Burgh Castle Marine
Norfolk   01493 780331

Cambrian Marine Services Ltd
Cardiff   029 2034 3459

Chelsea Harbour Ltd
London   020 7225 9108

Clapson & Son (Shipbuilders) Ltd
Barton-on-Humber   01652 635620

Crinan Boatyard
Crinan   01546 830232

Dartside Quay Brixham   01803 845445

Douglas Marine Preston
01772 812462

Dublin City Moorings
Dublin   +353 1 8183300

Emsworth Yacht Harbour
Emsworth   01243 377727

Exeter Ship Canal   01392 274306

HAFAN PWLLHELI
Glan Don, Pwllheli, Gwynedd LL53 5YT
Tel: (01758) 701219
Fax: (01758) 701443 VHF Ch80
Hafan Pwllheli has over 400 pontoon berths and offers access at virtually all states of the tide. Ashore, its modern purpose-built facilities include luxury toilets, showers, launderette, a secure boat park for winter storage, 40-ton travel hoist, mobile crane and plenty of space for car parking. Open 24-hours a day, 7 days a week.   L14

Highway Marine
Sandwich   01304 613925

Iron Wharf Boatyard
Faversham   01795 537122

Jalsea Marine Services Ltd
Northwich   01606 77870

Jersey Harbours
St Helier   01534 885588

Jones (Boatbuilders), David
Chester   01244 390363

Lawrenny Yacht Station
Kilgetty   01646 651212

MacFarlane & Son
Glasgow   01360 870214

Maramarine
Helensburgh   01436 810971

MELFORT PIER & HARBOUR
Tel: 01852 200333
www.mellowmelfort.com
Swinging moorings on stunning Loch Melfort. Restaurant on site.   2009/L18/z

NEPTUNE MARINA LTD
Neptune Quay, Ipswich, Suffolk IP4 1AX
Tel: (01473) 215204
Fax: (01473) 215206
e-mail:
enquiries@neptune-marina.com
www.neptune-marina.com
Accessible through continuously operating lockgates (VHF Channel 68) Neptune Marina (VHF Channels 80 or 37) is located on the north side of Ipswich wet dock immediately adjacent to the town centre and part of the rapidly regenerating northern quays area.   2009/L8/e

Orkney Marinas Ltd
Kirkwall   07810 465835

PADSTOW HARBOUR COMMISSIONERS
Harbour Office, Padstow, Cornwall PL28 8AQ
Tel: (01841) 532239
Fax: (01841) 533346
e-mail:
padstowharbour@btconnect.com
www.padstow-harbour.co.uk
Inner harbour controlled by tidal gate - opens HW±2 hours. Minimum depth 3 metres at all times. Yachtsmen must be friendly as vessels raft together. Services include showers, toilets, diesel, water and ice. Wi-fi internet access. Security by CCTV.   2009/Ext1/ez

Surry Boatyard
Shoreham-by-Sea   01273 461491

Sutton Harbour Marina Plymouth
01752 204186

Wicor Marine Fareham   01329 237112

Winters Marine Ltd
Salcombe   01548 843580

Yarmouth Marine Service
Yarmouth   01983 760521

Youngboats Faversham   01795 536176

BOAT BUILDERS & REPAIRS

ABC Powermarine
Beaumaris   01248 811413

Aqua-Star Ltd
St Sampsons   01481 244550

Ardoran Marine
Oban   01631 566123

Baumbach Bros Boatbuilders
Hayle   01736 753228

BB Marine Restoration Services Ltd
Southampton   023 8045 4145

Beacon Boatyard
Rochester   01634 841320

Bedwell & Co
Walton on the Naze   01255 675873

Black Dog
Falmouth   01326 318058

Blackwell, Craig
Co Meath   +353 87 677 9605

Bluewater Horizons
Weymouth   01305 782080

Bowman Yachts Penryn   01326 376107

Brennan, John
Dun Laoghaire   +353 1 280 5308

Burghead Boat Centre
Findhorn   01309 690099

Camper & Nicholsons Yachting
Portsmouth   023 9258 0221

Carrick Marine Projects
Co Antrim   02893 355884

Chicks Marine Ltd
Guernsey   01481 724536

Cooks Maritime Craftsmen - Poliglow
Lymington   01590 675521

Creekside Boatyard (Old Mill Creek)
Dartmouth   01803 832649

CTC Marine & Leisure Middlesbrough	01642 372600
Davies Marine Services Ramsgate	01843 586172
Dickie & Sons Ltd, AM Bangor	01248 363400
Dickie & Sons Ltd, AM Pwllheli	01758 701828
East & Co, Robin - Frogmore BY Kingsbridge	01548 531257
East Llanion Marine Ltd Pembroke Dock	01646 686866
Emblem Enterprises East Cowes	01983 294243
Exe Leisure Exeter	01392 879055
Fairlie Quay Fairlie	01475 568267
Fairweather Marine Fareham	01329 283500
Fast Tack Plymouth	01752 255171
Fergulsea Engineering Ayr	01292 262978
Ferrypoint Boat Co Youghal	+353 24 94232
Floetree Ltd (Loch Lomond Marina) Balloch	01389 752069
Freshwater Boatyard Truro	01326 270443
Furniss Boat Building Falmouth	01326 311766
Gallichan Marine Ltd Jersey	01534 746387
Goodchild Marine Services Great Yarmouth	01493 782301
Gosport Boatyard Gosport	023 9252 6534
Gweek Quay Boatyard Helston	01326 221657
Halls Walton on the Naze	01255 675596
Hardway Marine Gosport	023 9258 0420
Harris Marine (1984) Ltd, Ray Barry	01446 740924
Haven Boatyard Lymington	01590 677073
Hayling Yacht Company Hayling Island	023 9246 3592
Hoare Ltd, Bob Poole	01202 736704
Holyhead Marine Services Ltd Holyhead	01407 760111
International Marine Designs Aberdyfi	01654 767572
Jackson Marine Whitehaven	01946 699332
Jackson Yacht Services Jersey	01534 743819
JEP Marine Canterbury	01227 710102
Jones (Boatbuilders), David Chester	01244 390363
JWS Marine Services Southsea	023 9275 5155
KG McColl Oban	01852 200248
Kimelford Yacht Haven Oban	01852 200248

Kingfisher Marine Weymouth	01305 766595
Kingfisher Ultraclean UK Ltd Tarporley	0800 085 7039
Kippford Slipway Ltd Dalbeattie	01556 620249
Langley Marine Services Ltd Eastbourne	01323 470244
Lavis & Son, CH Exmouth	01395 263095
Lawrenny Yacht Station Lawrenny	01646 651212
Lencraft Boats Ltd Dungarvan	+353 58 682220
Lifeline Marine Services Poole	01202 669676
Mackay Boatbuilders Arbroath	01241 872879
Marine Services Norwich	01692 582239
Mashford Brothers Torpoint	01752 822232
Mayor & Co Ltd, J Preston	01772 812250
McKellar's Slipway Ltd Helensburgh	01436 842334
Mears, HJ Axmouth	01297 23344
Medusa Marina Woolverstone	01473 780090
Moody Yachts International Ltd Swanwick	01489 885000
Morrison, A Killyleagh	028 44828215
Moss (Boatbuilders), David Thornton-Cleveleys	01253 893830
Multi Marine Composites Ltd Torpoint	01752 823513
Newing, Roy E Canterbury	01227 860345
Noble and Sons, Alexander Girvan	01465 712223
Northney Marine Services Hayling Island	023 9246 9246
Northshore Sport & Leisure King's Lynn	01485 210236
O'Sullivans Marine Ltd Tralee	+353 66 7124524
Oulton Manufacturing Ltd Lowestoft	01502 585631

Oyster Marine Ltd Ipswich	01473 688888
Pachol, Terry Brighton	01273 682724
Partington Marine Ltd, William Pwllheli	01758 612808
Pasco's Boatyard Truro	01326 270269
Penrhos Marine Aberdovey	01654 767478
Penzance Marine Services Penzance	01736 361081
Pepe Boatyard Hayling Island	023 9246 1968
PJ Bespoke Boat Fitters Ltd Crewe	01270 812244
Preston Marine Services Ltd Preston	01772 733595
Rampart Yachts Southampton	023 8023 4777
Red Bay Boats Ltd Cushendall	028 2177 1331
Reliance Marine Wirral	0151 625 5219
Retreat Boatyard Ltd Exeter	01392 874720/875934
Richards, Eddie East Cowes	01983 299740
Richardson Boatbuilders, Ian Stromness	01856 850321
Richardson Yacht Services Ltd Newport	01983 821095
River Tees Engineering & Welding Ltd Middlesbrough	01642 226226
Roberts Marine Ltd, S Liverpool	0151 707 8300
Rustler Yachts Penryn	01326 310120
Salterns Boatyard Poole	01202 707391
Sea & Shore Ship Chandler Dundee	01382 450666
Seamark-Nunn & Co Felixstowe	01394 275327
Seaquest Yachts Southampton	023 8045 4549
Searanger Yachts Peterborough	01832 274199

SEAWARD MARINE LTD
Prospect Road, Cowes,
Isle of Wight PO31 7AD
Tel: 01983 280333
Fax: 01983 295095
e-mail: sales@seawardboat.com
www.seawardboat.com
Builders of the Seaward brand of Nelson semi-displacement motor cruisers, renowned for their good seakeeping and traditional style. Custom building and repairs. Used Seaward craft also available. *2009/L6/v*

Slipway Cooperative Ltd
Bristol   0117 907 9938

Spencer Sailing Services, Jim
Brightlingsea   01206 302911

Spicer Boatbuilder, Nick
Weymouth Marina   01305 767118

Starlight Yachts Penryn 01326 310120

Storrar Marine Store
Newcastle upon Tyne   0191 266 1037

Tarquin Boat Co
Emsworth   01243 375211

Trio Mouldings Marine
Southampton   01489 787887

Troon Marine Services
Troon   01292 316180

TT Marine Ashwell   01462 742449

WA Simpson Marine Ltd
Dundee   01382 566670

Waterfront Marine
Bangor   01248 352513

WestCoast Marine
Troon   01292 318121

Western Marine
Dublin   +353 1 280 0321

Wigmore Wright Marine Services
Penarth   029 2070 9983

Williams, Peter
Fowey   01726 870987

Woodwind Composite Marine
Southampton   023 8033 7722

WQI Ltd
Bournemouth   01202 771292

Yarmouth Marine Service
        01983 760521

Youngboats Faversham 01795 536176

BOATYARD SERVICES & SUPPLIES

A & P Ship Care
Ramsgate   01843 593140

Abersoch Boatyard Services Ltd
Abersoch   01758 713900

Amble Boat Co Ltd
Amble   01665 710267

Amsbrisbeg Ltd
Port Bannatyne   01700 502719

Ardmair Boat Centre
Ullapool   01854 612054

Ardmaleish Boat Building Co
Rothesay   01700 502007
www.ardoran.co.uk
West coast Scotland. All marine facilities.

Ardrishaig Boatyard
Lochgilphead   01546 603280

Arklow Slipway
Arklow   +353 402 33233

Baltic Wharf Boatyard
Totnes   01803 867922

Baltimore Boatyard
Baltimore   +353 28 20444

Battricks Boatyard
St Aubin   01534 743412

Bedwell and Co
Walton-on-the-Naze   01255 675873

Berthon Boat Co
Lymington   01590 673312

Birch Boatbuilders, ER 01268 696094

Birdham Shipyard
Chichester   01243 512310

BJ Marine Ltd Bangor 028 91271434

Blagdon, A Plymouth   01752 561830

Boatworks + Ltd
St Peter Port   01481 726071

Booth W Kelly Ltd
Ramsey   01624 812322

Brennan, John
Dun Laoghaire   +353 1 280 5308

Brightlingsea Boatyard
Brightlingsea   01206 302003/8

Brighton Marina Boatyard
Brighton   01273 819919

Bristol Marina (Yard)
Bristol   0117 921 3198

Buchan & Son Ltd, J
Peterhead   01779 475395

Buckie Shipyard Ltd
Buckie   01542 831245

Bucklers Hard Boat Builders Ltd
Brockenhurst   01590 616214

Bure Marine Ltd
Great Yarmouth   01493 656996

C & J Marine Services
Newcastle Upon Tyne   0191 295 0072

Caley Marina Inverness 01463 236539

Cambrian Boat Centre
Swansea   01792 467263

Cambrian Marine Services Ltd
Cardiff   029 2034 3459

Cantell and Son Ltd
Newhaven   01273 514118

Carroll's Ballyhack Boatyard
New Ross   +353 51 389164

Castlepoint Boatyard
Crosshaven   +353 21 4832154

Chabot, Gary Newhaven 01273 611076

Chapman & Hewitt Boatbuilders
Wadebridge   01208 813487

Chippendale Craft Rye 01797 227707

Clapson & Son (Shipbuilders) Ltd
Barton on Humber   01652 635620

Coastal Marine Boatbuilders
(Berwick upon Tweed)
Eyemouth   01890 750328

Coastcraft Ltd
Cockenzie   01875 812150

Coates Marine Ltd
Whitby   01947 604486

Coombes, AA
Bembridge   01983 872296

Corpach Boatbuilding Company
Fort William   01397 772861

Craobh Marina
By Lochgilphead   01852 500222

Creekside Boatyard (Old Mill Creek)
Dartmouth   01803 832649

Crinan Boatyard
By Lochgilphead   01546 830232

Crosshaven Boatyard Co Ltd
Crosshaven   +353 21 831161

Dale Sailing Co Ltd
Neyland   01646 603110

Darthaven Marina
Kingswear   01803 752242

Dartside Quay Brixham 01803 845445

Dauntless Boatyard Ltd
Canvey Island   01268 793782

Davis's Boatyard Poole 01202 674349

Dinas Boat Yard Ltd
Y Felinheli   01248 671642

Dorset Yachts Poole 01202 674531

Douglas Boatyard
Preston   01772 812462

Dover Yacht Co Dover 01304 201073

Dun Laoghaire Marina
Dun Laoghaire   +353 1 2020040

Elephant Boatyard
Southampton   023 8040 3268

Elton Boatbuilding Ltd
Kirkcudbright   01557 330177

Farrow & Chambers Yacht Builders
Humberston   01472 632424

Felixstowe Ferry Boatyard
Felixstowe   01394 282173

Ferguson Engineering
Wexford   +353 6568 66822133

Ferry Marine South
Queensferry   0131 331 1233

Ferrybridge Marine Services Ltd
Weymouth   01305 781518

Findhorn Boatyard
Findhorn   01309 690099

Firmhelm Ltd Pwllheli 01758 612251

Fishbourne Quay Boatyard
Ryde   01983 882200

Fleming Engineering, J
Stornoway   01851 703488

Forrest Marine Ltd
Exeter   08452 308335

Fowey Boatyard Fowey 01726 832194

Fox's Marina Ipswich 01473 689111

Frank Halls & Son
Walton on the Naze   01255 675596

Freeport Marine Jersey 01534 888100

Furniss Boat Building
Falmouth   01326 311766

Goodchild Marine Services
Great Yarmouth   01493 782301

Gosport Boatyard
Gosport   023 9252 6534

Gweek Quay Boatyard
Helston   01326 221657

Haines Boatyard
Chichester   01243 512228

Harbour Marine
Plymouth   01752 204690/1

Harbour Marine Services Ltd
Southwold   01502 724721

Harris Marine Barry   01446 740924

Hartlepool Marine Engineering
Hartlepool   01429 867883

Hayles, Harold Yarmouth 01983 760373

Henderson, J Shiskine   01770 860259

Heron Marine
Whitstable   01227 361255

Hewitt, George Binham   01328 830078

Hillyard, David
Littlehampton   01903 713327

Holyhead Marina & Trinity Marine Ltd
Holyhead   01407 764242

Instow Marine Services
Bideford   01271 861081

Ipswich Haven Marina
Ipswich   01473 236644

Iron Wharf Boatyard
Faversham   01795 537122

Island Boat Services
Port of St Mary   01624 832073

Isle of Skye Yachts
Ardvasar   01471 844216

Jalsea Marine Services Ltd Weaver
Shipyard, Northwich   01606 77870

J B Timber Ltd
North Ferriby   01482 631765

Jersey Harbours Dept
St Helier   01534 885588

Kilnsale Boatyard
Kinsale   +353 21 4774774

Kilrush Marina & Boatyard – Ireland
                    +353 65 9052072

Kingfisher Ultraclean UK Ltd
Tarporley   0800 085 7039

Lake Yard Poole   01202 674531
Lallow, C Isle of Wight   01983 292112

Latham's Boatyard
Poole   01202 748029

Leonard Marine, Peter
Newhaven   01273 515987

Lincombe Marine
Salcombe   01548 843580

Lomax Boatbuilders
Cliffony   +353 71 66124

Lymington Yacht Haven
Lymington   01590 677071

MacDougalls Marine Services
Isle of Mull   01681 700294

Macduff Shipyard Ltd
Macduff   01261 832234

Madog Boatyard
Porthmadog   01766 514205/513435

Mainbrayce Marine
Alderney   01481 822772

Malakoff and Moore
Lerwick   01595 695544

Mallaig Boat Building and
Engineering Mallaig   01687 462304

Maramarine
Helensburgh   01436 810971

Marindus Engineering
Kilmore Quay   +353 53 29794

Marine Gleam
Lymington   0800 074 4672

Mariners Farm Boatyard
Gillingham   01634 233179

McCallum & Co Boat Builders, A
Tarbert   01880 820209

McCaughty (Boatbuilders), J
Wick   01955 602858

McGruar and Co Ltd
Helensburgh   01436 831313

Mitchell's Boatyard
Poole   01202 747857

Mooney Boats
Killybegs   +353 73 31152/31388

Moore & Son, J
St Austell   01726 842964

Morrison, A Killyleagh   028 44828215

Moss (Boatbuilders), David
Thornton-Cleveleys   01253 893830

New Horizons Rhu   01436 821555

Noble and Sons, Alexander
Girvan   01465 712223

North Pier (Oban) Oban01631 562892

North Wales Boat Centre
Conwy   01492 580740

Northshore Yacht Yard
Chichester   01243 512611

Oban Yachts and Marine Services
By Oban   01631 565333

Oulton Manufacturing Ltd
Lowestoft   01502 585631

Parker Yachts and Dinghys Ltd
Nr Boston   01205 722697

Pearn and Co, Norman
Looe   01503 262244

Penrhos Marine
Aberdovey   01654 767478

Penzance Dry Dock and Engineering
Co Ltd Penzance   01736 363838

Pepe Boatyard
Hayling Island   023 9246 1968

Philip & Son Dartmouth 01803 833351

Phillips, HJ Rye   01797 223234

Ponsharden Boatyard
Penryn   01326 372215

Powersail and Island Chandlers Ltd
East Cowes Marina   01983 299800

Pratt and Son, VJ
King's Lynn   01553 764058

Priors Boatyard
Burnham-on-Crouch   01621 782160

R K Marine Ltd
Swanwick   01489 583572

Rat Island Sailboat Company (Yard)
St Mary's   01720 423399

Retreat Boatyard Ltd
Exeter   01392 874720/875934

Rice and Cole Ltd
Burnham-on-Crouch   01621 782063

Richardson Boatbuilders, Ian
Stromness   01856 850321

Richardsons Boatbuilders
Binfield   01983 821095

Riverside Yard
Shoreham Beach   01273 592456

RJ Prior (Burnham) Ltd
Burnham-on-Crouch   01621 782160

Robertsons Boatyard
Woodbridge   01394 382305

Rossbrin Boatyard
Schull   +353 28 37352

Rossiter Yachts Ltd
Christchurch   01202 483250

Rossreagh Boatyard
Rathmullan   +353 74 51082

Rudders Boatyard & Moorings
Milford Haven   01646 600288

Ryan & Roberts Marine Services
Askeaton   +353 61 392198

Rye Harbour Marina Rye
                    01797 227667

Rynn Engineering, Pat
Galway   +353 91 562568

Salterns Boatyard
Poole   01202 707391

Sandbanks Yacht Company
Poole   01202 707500

Sandy Morrison Engineering
Uig   01470 542300

Scarborough Marine Engineering Ltd
Scarborough   01723 375199

Severn Valley Cruisers Ltd (Boatyard)
Stourport-on-Severn   01299 871165

Shepards Wharf Boatyard Ltd
Cowes   01983 297821

Shotley Marina Ltd Ipswich	01473 788982
Shotley Marine Services Ltd Ipswich	01473 788913
Silvers Marina Ltd Helensburgh	01436 831222
Skinners Boat Yard Baltimore	+353 28 20114
Smith & Gibbs Eastbourne	01323 833830
South Dock (Seaham Harbour Dock Co) Seaham	0191 581 3877
Sparkes Boatyard Hayling Island	023 92463572
Spencer Sailing Services, Jim Brightlingsea	01206 302911
Standard House Boatyard Wells-next-the-Sea	01328 710593
Storrar Marine Store Newcastle upon Tyne	0191 266 1037
Strand Shipyard Rye	01797 222070
Stratton Boatyard, Ken Bembridge	01983 873185
Surry Boatyard Shoreham-by-Sea	01273 461491
Titchmarsh Marina Walton-on-the-Naze	01255 672185
Tollesbury Marina Tollesbury	01621 869202
T J Rigging Conwy	07780 972411
Toms and Son Ltd, C Fowey	01726 870232
Tony's Marine Service Coleraine	028 7035 6422
Torquay Marina Torquay	01803 200210
Trinity Marine & Holyhead Marina Holyhead	01407 763855
Trouts Boatyard (River Exe) Topsham	01392 873044
Upson and Co, RF Aldeburgh	01728 453047
Versatility Workboats Rye	01797 224422
Weir Quay Boatyard Bere Alston	01822 840474
West Solent Boatbuilders Lymington	01590 642080
Wicor Marine Fareham	01329 237112
Woodrolfe Boatyard Maldon	01621 869202

Abersoch Boatyard Services Ltd Pwllheli	01758 713900
Ambrisbeg Ltd Port Bannatyne	01700 502719
Arisaig Marine Inverness-shire	01687 450224
Bedwell and Co Walton-on-the-Naze	01255 675873
Bembridge Boatyard Marine Works Bembridge	01983 872911

Berthon Boat Company Lymington	01590 673312
Bluewater Horizons Weymouth	01305 782080
Bure Marine Ltd Great Yarmouth	01493 656996
C & J Marine Services Newcastle upon Tyne	0191 295 0072
Caley Marine Inverness	01463 233437
Carrick Marine Projects Co Antrim	02893 355884
Challenger Marine Penryn	01326 377222
Coates Marine Ltd Whitby	01947 604486
Creekside Boatyard (Old Mill Creek) Dartmouth	01803 832649
Crinan Boatyard Ltd Crinan	01546 830232
Dale Sailing Co Ltd Neyland	01646 603110
Dartside Quay Brixham	01803 845445
Dauntless Boatyard Ltd Canvey Island	01268 793782
Debbage Yachting Ipswich	01473 601169
Douglas Marine Preston	01772 812462
East & Co, Robin Kingsbridge	01548 531257
Emsworth Yacht Harbour Emsworth	01243 377727
Exeter Ship Canal	01392 274306
Exmouth Marina	01395 2693146

Main Road
Fairlie
North Ayrshire
KA29 0AS

A prime facility just south of the town of Largs
• 80 ton hoist • 64,000sq.ft undercover storage
• 240v power available throughout shed • on-site contractors for all your maintenance needs •
clean concrete outside storage yard
• call VHF 80 call sign Fairlie Quay.

Visitors are welcome at this developing facility.

Tel: 01475 568267 Fax: 01475 568410
info@fairliequay.co.uk

website: www.fairliequay.co.uk

2009/MD6c/z

Firmhelm Ltd Pwllheli	01758 612244
Fowey Boatyard Fowey	01726 832194
Freshwater Boatyard Truro	01326 270443
Hafan Pwllheli Pwllheli	01758 701219
Gweek Quay Boatyard Helston	01326 221657
Iron Wharf Boatyard Faversham	01795 537122
Jalsea Marine Services Ltd Northwich	01606 77870
KG McColl Oban	01852 200248
Latham's Boatyard Poole	01202 748029
Lavis & Son, CH Exmouth	01395 263095

Lincombe Boat Yard Salcombe	01548 843580
Marine Resource Centre Ltd Oban	01631 720291
Marine & General Engineers Guernsey	01481 245808
Milford Marina Milford Haven	01646 696312/3
Northshore Yachts Chichester	01243 512611
Oulton Manufacturing Ltd Lowestoft	01502 585631
Pasco's Boatyard Truro	01326 270269
Pearn and Co, Norman Looe	01503 262244
Pepe Boatyard Hayling Island	023 9246 1968
Philip Leisure Group Dartmouth	01803 833351
Ponsharden Boatyard Penryn	01326 372215
Portsmouth Marine Engineering Fareham	01329 232854
Priors Boatyard Burnham-on-Crouch	01621 782160
Rossiter Yachts Christchurch	01202 483250
Shepards Wharf Boatyard Ltd Cowes	01983 297821
Silvers Marina Ltd Helensburgh	01436 831222
Waterfront Marine Bangor	01248 352513
Wicor Marine Fareham	01329 237112
Winters Marine Ltd Salcombe	01548 843580
Yacht Solutions Ltd Portsmouth	023 9220 0670
Yarmouth Marine Service Yarmouth	01983 760521
Youngboats Faversham	01795 536176

Adlard Coles Nautical London	0207 7580200
Brown Son & Ferguson Ltd Glasgow	0141 429 1234
Chattan Security Ltd Edinburgh	0131 555 3155
Cooke & Son Ltd, B Hull	01482 223454
Dubois Phillips & McCallum Ltd Liverpool	0151 236 2776
Imray, Laurie, Norie & Wilson Huntingdon	01480 462114
Kelvin Hughes Southampton	023 8063 4911
Lilley & Gillie Ltd, John	0191 257 2217
Marine Chart Services Wellingborough	01933 441629
Nautical Data Emsworth	01243 389352
Price & Co Ltd, WF Bristol	0117 929 2229

QPC
Fareham   01329 287880

SEA CHEST, THE
Admiralty Chart Agent
Queen Anne's Battery Marina,
Plymouth PL4 0LP
Tel: 01752 222012
Fax: 01752 252679
www.seachest.co.uk
Admiralty and Imray Chart Agent, Huge
stocks of Books and Charts, Rapid
dispatch. 2009/15/V**Smith AM (Marine) Ltd**
London   020 8529 6988

Stanford Charts
Bristol   0117 929 9966

Stanford Charts
London   020 7836 1321

Stanford Charts
Manchester   0870 890 3730

Wiley Nautical
Chichester   01243 779777

BOW THRUSTERS

ARS Anglian Diesels Ltd
Norfolk   01508 520555

Buckler's Hard Boat Builders Ltd
Beaulieu   01590 616214

JS Mouldings International
Bursledon   023 8063 4400

BREAKDOWN

BJ Marine Ltd
Bangor, Ireland   028 9127 1434

Seafit Marine Services
Falmouth   01326 313713

CHANDLERS

ABC Powermarine
Beaumaris   01248 811413

Acamar Marine Services/Sirius Yacht
Training Christchurch   01202 488030

Admiral Marine Supplies
Bootle   01469 575909

Aladdin's Cave Chandlery Ltd
(Deacons) Bursledon   023 8040 2182

Aladdin's Cave Chandlery Ltd
Chichester   01243 773788

Aladdin's Cave Chandlery Ltd (Hamble
Point) Southampton   023 80455 058

Aladdin's Cave Chandlery Ltd
(Mercury) Southampton   023 8045 4849

Aladdin's Cave Chandlery Ltd (Port
Hamble) Southampton   023 8045 4858

Aladdin's Cave Chandlery Ltd
(Swanwick) Swanwick   01489 555999

Alderney Boating Centre
Alderney   01481 823725

Allgadgets.co.uk
Basingstoke   01256 478000

Alpine Room & Yacht Equipment
Chemsford   01245 223563

Aquatogs Cowes   01893 247890

Arbroath Fishermen's Association
Arbroath   01241 873132

Ardfern Yacht Centre Ltd
Argyll   01852 500247

Ardoran Marine Oban   01631 566123

Arthurs Chandlery
Gosport   023 9252 6522

Arun Aquasports
Littlehampton   01903 713553

Arun Canvas and Rigging Ltd
Littlehampton   01903 732561

Arun Nautique
Littlehampton   01903 730558

Aruncraft Chandlers
Littlehampton   01903 713327

ASAP Supplies – Equipment &
Spares Worldwide
Beccles   0845 1300870

Auto Marine Sales
Southsea   023 9281 2263

Bayside Marine
Brixham   01803 856771

Bedwell and Co
Walton on the Naze   01255 675873

BJ Marine Ltd Bangor 028 9127 1434

Bluecastle Chandlers
Portland   01305 822298

Bluewater Horizons
Weymouth   01305 782080

Blue Water Marine Ltd
Pwllheli   01758 614600

Boatshop Chandlery
Brixham   01803 882055

Boatacs
Westcliffe on Sea   01702 475057

Boathouse, The Penryn 01326 374177

Boston Marina   01205 364420

Bosun's Locker, The
Falmouth   01326 312212

Bosun's Locker, The
Milford Haven   01646 697834

Bosun's Locker, The
Ramsgate   01843 597158

Bosuns Locker, The
South Queensferry 0131 331 3875/4496

Brancaster Sailing and Sailboard
Centre Kings Lynn   01485 210236

Bridger Marine, John
Exeter   01392 216420

Brigantine Teignmouth   01626 872400

Brighton Chandlery
Brighton   01273 612612

Bristol Boat Ltd Bristol 01225 872032

Brixham Chandlers
Brixham   01803 882055

Brixham Yacht Supplies Ltd
Brixham   01803 882290

Brundall Angling Centre
Norwich   01603 715289

Brunel Chandlery Ltd
Neyland   01646 601667

Bucklers Hard Boat Builders
Beaulieu   01590 616214

Burghead Boat Centre
Findhorn   01309 690099

Bussell & Co, WL
Weymouth   01305 785633

Buzzard Marine
Yarmouth   01983 760707

C & M Marine
Bridlington   01262 672212

Cabin Yacht Stores
Rochester   01634 718020

Caley Marina Inverness   01463 236539

Cambrian Boat Centre
Swansea   01792 467263

Cantell & Son Ltd
Newhaven   01273 514118

Carne (Sales) Ltd, David
Falmouth   01326 318314

Carne (Sales) Ltd, David
Penryn   01326 374177

Carrickcraft
Malahide   +353 1 845 5438

Caters Carrick Ltd
Carrickfergus   028 93351919

CH Marine (Cork)
Cork   +353 21 4315700

CH Marine Skibbereen +353 28 23190

Charity & Taylor Ltd
Lowestoft   01502 581529

Chertsey Marine Ltd
Penton Hook Marina   01932 565195

Chicks Marine Ltd
Guernsey   01481 724536

Christchurch Boat Shop
Christchurch   01202 482751

Churcher Marine
Worthing   01903 230523

Clapson & Son (Shipbuilders) Ltd
South Ferriby Marina   01652 635620

Clarke, Albert
Newtownards   01247 872325

Coastal Marine Boatbuilders Ltd
(Dunbar) Eyemouth   01890 750328

Coates Marine Ltd
Whitby   01947 604486

Collins Marine St Helier 01534 732415

Compass Marine
Lancing   01903 761773

Cosalt International Ltd Aberdeen 01224 588327	**Eccles Marine Co** Middlesbrough 01642 372600	**Green Marine, Jimmy** Fore St Beer 01297 20744
Cosalt International Ltd Southampton 023 8063 2824	**Ely Boat Chandlers** Hayling Island 023 9246 1968	**Greenham Marine** Emsworth 01243 378314
Cotter, Kieran Baltimore +353 28 20106	**Emsworth Chandlery** Emsworth 01243 375500	**Gunn Navigation Services, Thomas** Aberdeen 01224 595045
Cox Yacht Charter Ltd, Nick Lymington 01590 673489	**Exe Leisure** Exeter 01392 879055	**Hale Marine, Ron** Portsmouth 023 92732985
C Q Chandlers Ltd Poole 01202 682095	**Express Marine Services** Chichester 01243 773788	**Harbour Marine Services Ltd (HMS)** Southwold 01502 724721
Crinan Boats Ltd Lochgilphead 01546 830232	**Fairways Chandlery** Burnham-on-Crouch 01621 782659	**Hardware & Marine Supplies** Wexford +353 53 29791
CTC Marine & Leisure Middlesbrough 01642 230123	**Fairweather Marine** Fareham 01329 283500	**Hardway Marine** Gosport 023 9258 0420
Dale Sailing Co Ltd Milford Haven 01646 603110	**Fal Chandlers** Falmouth Marina 01326 212411	**Harris Marine (1984) Ltd, Ray** Barry 01446 740924
Danson Marine Sidcup 0208 304 5678	**Ferrypoint Boat Co** Youghal +353 24 94232	**Hartlepool Marine Supplies** Hartlepool 01429 862932
Dartside Quay Brixham 01803 845445	**Findhorn Marina & Boatyard** Findhorn 01309 690099	**Harwich Chandlers Ltd** Harwich 01255 504061
Dauntless Boatyard Ltd Canvey Island 01268 793782	**Firmhelm Ltd** Pwllheli 01758 612244	**Harwoods** Yarmouth 01983 760258
Davis's Yacht Chandler Littlehampton 01903 722778	**Fisherman's Mutual Asssociation (Eyemouth) Ltd** Eyemouth 01890 750373	**Hawkins Marine Shipstores, John** Rochester 01634 840812
Denholm Fishselling Scrabster 01847 896968	**Fleetwood Trawlers' Supply Co Ltd, The** Fleetwood 01253 873476	**Hayles, Harold** Yarmouth 01983 760373
Denney & Son, EL Redcar 01642 483507	**Floetree Ltd (Loch Lomond Marina)** Balloch 01389 752069	**Herm Seaway Marine Ltd** St Peter Port 01481 726829
Deva Marine Conwy 01492 572777	**Foc'sle, The** Exeter 01392 874105	**Highway Marine** Sandwich 01304 613925
Dickie & Sons Ltd, AM Bangor 01248 363400	**Freeport Marine** Jersey 01534 888100	**Hill Head Chandlers** Hill Head 01329 664621
Dickie & Sons Ltd, AM Pwllheli 01758 701828	**French Marine Motors Ltd** Brightlingsea 01206 302133	**Hoare Ltd, Bob** Poole 01202 736704
Dinghy Supplies Ltd/Sutton Marine Ltd Sutton +353 1 832 2312	**Furneaux Riddall & Co Ltd** Portsmouth 023 9266 8621	**Hornsey (Chandlery) Ltd, Chris** Southsea 023 9273 4728
Diverse Yacht Services Hamble 023 80453399	**Gallichan Marine Ltd** Jersey 01534 746387	**Hunter & Combes** Cowes 01983 299599
Dixon Chandlery, Peter Exmouth 01395 273248	**Galway Marine Chandlers Ltd** Galway +353 91 566568	**Iron Stores Marine** St Helier 01534 877755
Doling & Son, GW Barrow In Furness 01229 823708	**GB Attfield & Company** Dursley 01453 547185	**Isles of Scilly Steamship Co** St Mary's 01720 422710
Dovey Marine Aberdovey 01654 767581	**Gibbons Ship Chandlers Ltd** Sunderland 0191 567 2101	**Jackson Yacht Services** Jersey 01534 743819
Down Marine Co Ltd Belfast 028 9048 0247	**Gibbs Chandlery** Shepperton 01932 242977	**Jamison and Green Ltd** Belfast 028 9032 2444
Douglas Marine Preston 01772 812462	**Glaslyn Marine Supplies Ltd** Porthmadog 01766 513545	**Jeckells and Son Ltd** Lowestoft 01502 565007
Dubois Phillips & McCallum Ltd Liverpool 0151 236 2776	**Goodwick Marine** Fishguard 01348 873955	**JF Marine Chandlery** Rhu 01436 820584
Duncan Ltd, JS Wick 01955 602689	**Gorleston Marine Ltd** Great Yarmouth 01493 661883	**JNW Services** Aberdoon 01224 594050
Duncan Yacht Chandlers Ely 01353 663095	**GP Barnes Ltd** Shoreham 01273 591705/596680	**JNW Services** Peterhead 01779 477346
East Anglian Sea School Ipswich 01473 659992		**Johnston Brothers** Mallaig 01687 462215
		Johnstons Marine Stores Lamlash 01770 600333
		Kearon Ltd, George Arklow +353 402 32319
		Kelpie Boats Pembroke Dock 01646 683661
		Kelvin Hughes Ltd Southampton 023 80634911
		Kildale Marine Hull 01482 227464
		Kingfisher Marine Weymouth 01305 766595
		Kings Lock Chandlery Middlewich 01606 737564
		Kip Chandlery Inverkip Greenock 01475 521485

www.kipmarina.co.uk
e-mail: dduffield@kipmarina.co.uk

Huge variety of stock covering virtually every aspect of boat maintenance. Yanmar dealers for Scotland with extensive range of maintenance parts and spares available. Open 7 days a week.
Tel: 01475 521485

The Yacht Harbour, Inverkip, Renfrewshire PA16 0AS

2009/MG82/zz

Kirkcudbright Scallop Gear Ltd
Kirkcudbright   01557 330399
Kyle Chandlers Troon   01292 311880
Landon Marine, Reg
Truro   01872 272668
Largs Chandlers Largs 01475 686026
Lencraft Boats Ltd
Dungarvan   +353 58 68220
Lincoln Marina Lincoln 01522 526896
Looe Chandlery
West Looe   01503 264355
Lynch Ltd, PA Morpeth 01670 512291
Mackay Boatbuilders (Arbroath) Ltd
Aberdeen   01241 872879
Mackay Marine Services
Aberdeen   01224 575772
Mailspeed Marine
Burnham-on-Crouch   01621 781120
Mailspeed Marine
Southsea Marina   023 9275 5450
Mailspeed Marine
Warrington   01925 838858
Manx Marine Ltd
Douglas   01624 674842
Marine & Leisure Europe Ltd
Plymouth   01752 268826
Marine Instruments
Falmouth   01326 312414
Marine Scene Cardiff   029 2070 5780
Marine Services Jersey 01534 626930
Marine Store Wyatts
West Mersea   01206 384745
Marine Store Maldon   01621 854380
Marine Store
Walton on the Naze   01255 679028
Marine Superstore Port Solent
Chandlery Portsmouth 023 9221 9843
MarineCo Looe   01503 265444
Maryport Harbour and Marina
Maryport   01900 814431
Matchett Ltd, HC
Widnes   0151 423 4420
Matthews Ltd, D
Cork   +353 214 277633
Mayflower Chandlery
Plymouth   01752 500121
McCready Sailboats Ltd
Holywood   028 9042 1821
Moore & Son, J
Mevagissey   01726 842964
Morgan & Sons Marine, LH
Brightlingsea   01206 302003

Mount Batten Boathouse
Plymouth   01752 482666
MR Marine Ltd Brighton 01273 668900
Murphy, Nicholas
Dunmore East   +353 51 383259
Mylor Chandlery & Rigging
Falmouth   01326 375482
Nancy Black Oban   01631 562550
Nautical World Bangor 028 91460330
New World Yacht Care
Helensburgh   01436 820586
Newhaven Chandlery
Newhaven   01273 612612
Nifpo Ardglass   028 4484 2144
Norfolk Marine
Great Yarmouth   01692 670272
Norfolk Marine Chandlery Shop
Norwich   01603 783150
Northshore Sport & Leisure
Brancaster Staithe   01485 210236
Ocean Leisure Ltd
London   020 7930 5050
One Stop Chandlery
Maldon   01621 853558
Partington Marine Ltd, William
Pwllheli   01758 612808
Pascall Atkey & Sons Ltd
Isle of Wight   01983 292381
Peculiar's Chandlery
Gosport   023 9258 9953
Pennine Marine Ltd
Skipton   01756 792335
Penrhos Marine
Aberdovey   01654 767478

Penzance Marine Services
Penzance   01736 361081
Perry Marine, Rob
Axminster   01297 631314
Pepe Boatyard
Hayling Island   023 9246 1968
Peters PLC Chichester 01243 511033
Pinnell & Bax
Northampton   01604 592808
Piplers of Poole Poole 01202 673056
Pirate's Cave, The
Rochester   01634 295233
Powersail Island Chandlers Ltd
East Cowes Marina   01983 299800
Preston Marine Services Ltd
Preston   01772 733595
Price & Co Ltd, WF
Bristol   0117 929 2229
PSM Ltd Alderney   01481 824968
Purple Sails & Marine
Walsall   01922 614787
Quay West Chandlers
Poole   01202 742488
Quayside Marine
Salcombe   01548 844300
Racecourse Yacht Basin (Windsor)
Ltd Windsor   01753 851501
Rat Rigs Water Sports
Cardiff   029 2062 1309
Reliance Marine Wirral 0151 625 5219
RHP Marine Cowes   01983 290421
Rhu Chandlery Rhu   01436 820584
RNS Marine Northam   01237 474167
Sail Loft Bideford   01271 860001
Sailaway St Anthony   01326 231357
Salcombe Boatstore
Salcombe   01548 843708
Salterns Chandlery
Poole   01202 701556
Sand & Surf Chandlery
Salcombe   01548 844555
Sandrock Marine Rye   01797 222679
Schull Watersports Centre
Schull   +353 28 28554
Sea & Shore Ship Chandler
Dundee   01382 450666
Sea Cruisers of Rye Rye 01797 222070
Sea Span Edinburgh   0131 552 2224
Sea Teach Ltd Emsworth 01243 375774
Seafare Tobermory   01688 302277

Yacht Chandlers
The Tongue Building, The Tongue, Douglas Harbour, Douglas IM1 5AO
The Islands leading and most established Yacht Chandlery. Stockists of quality foul weather clothing and thermal wear. Large stock holding of s/steel fixtures and fittings and a comprehensive range of general chandlery including rigging facilities
Telephone: 01624 674842
Web: www.manxmarine.com
E-mail: manxmarine@mcb.net
2009/MG33/v

MARINE SUPPLIES AND SERVICES GUIDE

CHANDLERS

Seahog Boats Preston   01772 633016

Seamark-Nunn & Co
Felixstowe   01394 451000

Seaquest Marine Ltd
St Peter Port   01481 721773

Seaware Ltd Penryn   01326 377948

Seaway Marine Macduff 01261 832877

Severn Valley Boat Centre
Stourport-on-Severn   01299 871165

Shamrock Chandlery
Southampton   023 8063 2725

Sharp & Enright Dover   01304 206295

Shearwater Engineering Services Ltd
Dunoon   01369 706666

Shipmates Chandlery
Dartmouth   01803 839292

Shipshape Marine
King's Lynn   01553 764058

Ship Shape
Ramsgate   01843 597000

Shipsides Marine Ltd
Preston   01772 797079

Shorewater Sports
Chichester   01243 672315

Simpson Marine Ltd
Newhaven   01273 612612

Simpson Marine Ltd, WA
Dundee   01382 566670

Sketrick Marine Centre
Killinchy   028 9754 1400

Smith & Gibbs
Eastbourne   01323 723824

Smith AM (Marine) Ltd
London   020 8529 6988

Solent Marine Chandlery Ltd
Gosport   023 9258 4622

South Coast Marine
Christchurch   01202 482695

South Pier Shipyard
St Helier   01534 711000

Southampton Yacht Services Ltd
Southampton   023 803 35266

Southern Masts & Rigging
Brighton   01273 818189

S Roberts Marine Ltd
Liverpool   0151 707 8300

Standard House Chandlery
Wells-next-the-Sea   01328 710593

Stornoway Fishermen's Co-op
Stornoway   01851 702563

Sunset Marine & Watersports
Sligo   +353 71 9162792

Sussex Marine
St Leonards on Sea   01424 425882

Sussex Marine Centre
Shoreham   01273 454737

Sutton Marine (Dublin)
Sutton   +353 1 832 2312

SW Nets Newlyn   01736 360254

Tarbert Ltd, JSB Tarbert 01880 820180

TCS Chandlery Grays   01375 374702

TCS Chandlery
Southend   01702 444423

Thulecraft Ltd Lerwick   01595 693192

The Monkeys Fist
Hayling Island   023 9246 1610

Torbay Boating Centre
Paignton   01803 558760

Torquay Chandlers
Torquay   01803 211854

Trafalgar Yacht Services
Fareham   01329 822445

Trident UK N Shields   0191 490 1736

Union Chandlery
Cork   +353 21 4554334

Uphill Boat Services
Weston-Super-Mare   01934 418617

Upper Deck Marine and Outriggers
Fowey   01726 832287

V Ships (Isle of Man)
Douglas   01624 688886

V F Marine Rhu   01436 820584

Viking Marine Ltd
Dun Laoghaire   +353 1 280 6654

Waterfront Marine
Bangor   01248 352513

Wayne Maddox Marine
Margate   01843 297157

Western Marine
Dalkey   +353 1280 0321

Whitstable Marine
Whitstable   01227 274168

Williams Ltd, TJ Cardiff 029 20 487676

Work & Leisure
Arbroath   01241 431134

XM Yachting
Southampton   0870 751 4666

Yacht & Boat Chandlery
Faversham   01795 531777

Yacht Parts Plymouth   01752 252489

Yacht Shop, The
Fleetwood   01253 879238

Yachtmail Ltd Lymington 01590 672784

CHART AGENTS

Brown Son & Ferguson Ltd
Glasgow   0141 429 1234

Chattan Security Ltd
Edinburgh   0131 554 7527

Cooke & Son Ltd, B
Hull   01482 223454

Dubois Phillips & McCallum Ltd
Liverpool   0151 236 2776

Imray Laurie Norie and Wilson Ltd
Huntingdon   01480 462114

Kelvin Hughes
Southampton   023 8063 4911

Lilley & Gillie Ltd, John
North Shields   0191 257 2217

Marine Chart Services
Wellingborough   01933 441629

Morgan Mapping
Exeter   01392 255788

Price & Co, WF Bristol 0117 929 2229

Sea Chest Nautical Bookshop
Plymouth   01752 222012

Seath Instruments (1992) Ltd
Lowestoft   01502 573811

Small Craft Deliveries
Woodbridge   01394 382655

Smith (Marine) Ltd, AM
London   020 8529 6988

South Bank Marine Charts Ltd
Grimsby   01472 361137

Stanford Charts
Bristol   0117 929 9966

Stanford Charts
London   020 7836 1321

Stanford Charts
Manchester   0161 831 0250

Todd Chart Agency Ltd
County Down   028 9146 6640

UK Hydrographics Office
Taunton   01823 337900

Warsash Nautical Bookshop
Warsash   01489 572384

CLOTHING

Absolute
Gorleston on Sea   01493 442259

Aquatogs Cowes   01493 247890

Crew Clothing London 020 8875 2300

Crewsaver Gosport   023 9252 8621

Douglas Gill Nottingham 0115 9460844

Fat Face   fatface.com

Gul International Ltd
Bodmin   01208 262400

Guy Cotten UK Ltd
Liskeard   01579 347115

Harwoods Yarmouth   01983 760258

Helly Hansen
Nottingham   0115 9608797

Henri Lloyd Manchester 0161 799 1212

Joules
Market Harborough   01858 461156

Mad Cowes Clothing Co
Cowes   0845 456 5158

Matthews Ltd, D
Cork   +353 214 277633

Mountain & Marine
Stockport — 0800 093 5793

Musto Ltd Laindon — 01268 491555

Ocean World Ltd Cowes 01983 291744

Purple Sails & Marine Walsall
01922 614787

Quba Sails Cowes — 01983 299004

Quba Sails Lymington — 01590 689362

Quba Sails Salcombe — 01548 844599

Ravenspring Ltd Totnes — 01803 867092

Shorewater Sports
Chichester — 01243 672315

Splashdown Leeds — 0113 270 7000

Yacht Parts
Plymouth — 01752 252489

CODE OF PRACTICE EXAMINERS

Booth Marine Surveys, Graham
Birchington-on-Sea — 01843 843793

Cannell & Associates, David M
Wivenhoe — 01206 823337

COMPUTERS & SOFTWARE

C-map Ltd Fareham — 01329 517777

Dolphin Maritime Software
White Cross — 01524 841946

Forum Software Ltd
Nr Haverfordwest — 01646 636363

Kelvin Hughes Ltd
Southampton — 023 8063 4911

Maptech-Marine
Aldermaston — 0870 740 9040

PC Maritime Plymouth — 01752 254205

Sea Information Systems Ltd
Aberdeen — 01224 621326

Square Mile Marlow — 0870 1202536

DECK EQUIPMENT

Aries Van Gear Spares
Penryn — 01326 377467

Frederiksen Boat Fittings (UK) Ltd
Gosport — 023 9252 5377

Harken UK Lymington — 01590 689122

Kearon Ltd George — +353 402 32319

Marine Maintenance
Tollesbury — 01621 860441

Nauquip Warsash — 01489 885336

Pro-Boat Ltd
Burnham-on-Crouch — 01621 785455

Ryland, Kenneth
Stanton — 01386 584270

Smith, EC & Son Ltd
Luton — 01582 729721

Timage & Co Ltd
Braintree — 01376 343087

DIESEL MARINE/ FUEL ADDITIVES

Corralls Poole — 01202 674551

Cotters Marine & General Supplies
Baltimore — +353 28 20106

Diesel Dialysis
St Austelll — 0800 389 7874

Expresslube Henfield — 01444 881883

Gorey Marine Fuel Supplies
Gorey — 07797 742384

Hammond, George
Dover — 01304 206809

Iron Wharf Boatyard
Faversham — 01795 536296

Lallow, Clare Cowes — 01983 760707

Marine Support & Towage
Cowes — 01983 200716/07860 297633

Quayside Fuel
Weymouth — 07747 182181

Rossiter Yachts
Christchurch — 01202 483250

Sleeman & Hawken
Shaldon — 01626 872750

DIVERS

Abco Divers Belfast — 028 90610492

Andark Diving So'ton — 01489 581755

Argonaut Marine
Aberdeen — 01224 706526

Baltimore Diving and Watersports Centre West Cork — +353 28 20300

C & C Marine Services
Largs — 01475 687180

Cardiff Commercial Boat Operators Ltd Cardiff — 029 2037 7872

C I Diving Services Ltd
Invergordon — 01349 852500

Clyde Diving Centre
Inverkip — 01475 521281

Divesafe Sunderland — 0191 567 8423

Divetech UK King's Lynn — 01485 572323

Diving & Marine Engineering
Barry — 01446 721553

Donnelly, R South Shields 07973 119455

DV Diving — 028 9146 4671

Falmouth Divers Ltd
Penryn — 01326 374736

Fathom Diving (Chislehurst)
Chislehurst — 020 8289 8237

Fathoms Ltd Wick — 01955 605956

Felixarc Marine Ltd
Felixstowe — 01394 676497

Grampian Diving Services
New Deer — 01771 644206

Higgins, Noel — +353 872027650

Hudson, Dave
Trearddur Bay — 01407 860628

Hunt, Kevin Tralee — +353 6671 25979

Kaymac Diving Services
Swansea — 01792 301818

Keller, Hilary
Buncrana — +353 77 62146

Kilkee Diving Centre
Kilkee — +353 6590 56707

Leask Marine Kirkwall — 01856 874725

Looe Divers Hannafore — 01503 262727

MacDonald, D Nairn — 01667 455661

Medway Diving Contractors Ltd
Gillingham — 01634 851902

Mojo Maritime Penzance 01736 762771

Murray, Alex Stornoway — 01851 704978

New Dawn Dive Centre
Lymington — 01590 675656

New Tec Diving Services
Blackpool — 01253 691665

Northern Divers (Engineering) Ltd
Hull — 01482 227276

Offshore Marine Services Ltd
Bembridge — 01983 873125

Parkinson (Sinbad Marine Services), J Killybegs — +353 73 31417

Port of London Authority
Gravesend — 01474 560311

Purcell, D – Crouch Sailing School
Burnham — 01621 784140/0585 33

Salvesen UK Ltd
Liverpool — 0151 933 6038

Sea-Lift Diving Dover — 01304 829956

Southern Cylinder Services
Fareham — 01329 221125

Sub Aqua Services
North Ormesby — 01642 230209

Teign Diving Centre
Teignmouth — 01626 773965

Thorpe, Norman Portree 01478 612274

Tuskar Rock Marine
Rosslare — +353 53 33376

Underwater Services
Dyffryn Arbwy — 01341 247702

Wilson Alan c/o Portrush Yacht Club
Portrush — 028 2076 2225

Woolford, William
Bridlington — 01262 671710

ELECTRICAL AND ELECTRONIC ENGINEERS

Allworth Riverside Services, Adrian
Chelsea Harbour Marina — 07831 574774

Belson Design Ltd, Nick
Southampton — 077 6835 1330

Biggs, John Weymouth Marina,
Weymouth — 01305 778445

BJ Marine Ltd Bangor — 028 9127 1434

Calibra Marine
Dartmouth — 01803 833094

Campbell & McHardy Lossiemouth
Marina, Lossiemouth — 01343 812137

CES Sandown Sparkes Marina,
Hayling Island — 023 9246 6005

Colin Coady Marine
Malahide — +353 87 265 6496

Contact Electrical
Arbroath — 01241 874528

DDZ Marine Ardossan — 01294 607077

EC Leisure Craft
North Fambridge — 01621 744424

Energy Solutions
Rochester — 01634 290772

Enterprise Marine Electronic & Technical Services Ltd
Aberdeen — 01224 593281

Eurotex Brighton 01273 818990

Floetree Ltd (Loch Lomond Marina)
Balloch 01389 752069

HNP Engineers (Lerwick) Ltd
Lerwick 01595 692493

Index Marine
Bournemouth 01202 470149

Jackson Yacht Services
Jersey 01534 743819

Jedynak, A Salcombe 01548 843321

Kippford Slipway Ltd
Dalbeattie 01556 620249

Land & Sea Electronics
Aberdeen 01224 593281

Lifeline Marine Services
Dolphin Haven, Poole 01202 669676

Lynch Ltd, PA Morpeth 01670 512291

Mackay Boatbuilders (Arbroath) Ltd
Aberdeen 01241 872879

Marine, AW Gosport 023 9250 1207

Marine Electrical Repair Service
London 020 7228 1336

MES Falmouth Marina,
Falmouth 01326 378497

Mount Batten Boathouse
Plymouth 01752 482666

New World Yacht Care
Rhu 01436 820586

Neyland Marine Services Ltd
Milford Haven 01646 698968

Powell, Martin Shamrock Quay,
Southampton 023 8033 2123

R & J Marine Electricians Suffolk Yacht
Harbour Ltd, Ipswich 01473 659737

Radio & Electronic Services Beaucette
Marina, Guernsey 01481 728837

Redcar Fish Company
Stockton-on-Tees 01642 633638

RHP Marine Cowes 01983 290421

Rothwell, Chris
Torquay Marina 01803 850960

Rutherford, Jeff Largs 01475 568026

Sea Electric Hamble 023 8045 6255

SM International
Plymouth 01752 662129

Sussex Fishing Services
Rye 01797 223895

Ultra Marine Systems
Mayflower International Marina, Plymouth
07989 941020

WESTERN MARINE POWER LTD
Eastern Hangar, Shaw Way,
Mount Batten, Plymouth, PL9 9XH
TEL: (01752) 408804 FAX: (01752) 408807
e-mail: info@wmp.co.uk

Suppliers and installers of:-
Watermakers, Air Conditioning,
Generators, Electrical Systems,
Trim tabs, Electronic Engine Controls,
Bow and Stern Thrusters, Teak Decks,
Davits, Passarelles and Cranes,
Galley and Sanitation Equipment.
ISO 9001 Quality Assurance.
Website: www.wmp.co.uk/
2009/MD15/v

Upham, Roger
Chichester 01243 528299

Volspec Ipswich 01473 780144

Waypoint Marine
Plymouth 01752 661913

Weyland Marine Services
Milford Haven 01646 698968

Yoldings Marine
Eastbourne 01323 470882

ELECTRONIC DEVICES AND EQUIPMENT

Anchorwatch UK
Edinburgh 0131 447 5057

Aquascan International Ltd
Newport 01633 841117

Atlantis Marine Power Ltd
Plymouth 01752 225679

Autosound Marine
Bradford 01274 688990

AW Marine Gosport 023 9250 1207

Brookes & Gatehouse
Romsey 01794 518448

Boat Electrics & Electronics Ltd
Troon 01292 315355

Cactus Navigation & Communication
London 020 7833 3435

CDL Aberdeen 01224 706655

Charity & Taylor Ltd
Lowestoft 01502 581529

Diverse Yacht Services
Hamble 023 8045 3399

Dyfed Electronics Ltd
Milford Haven 01646 694572

Echopilot Marine Electronics Ltd
Ringwood 01425 476211

Euronav Ltd Portsmouth 023 9237 3855

Furuno (UK) Ltd
Denmead 023 9223 0303

Garmin (Europe) Ltd
Romsey 0870 850 1242

Golden Arrow Marine Ltd
Southampton 023 8071 0371

Greenham Regis Marine Electronics
Emsworth 01243 378314

Greenham Regis Marine Electronics
Lymington 01590 671144

Greenham Regis Marine Electronics
Poole 01202 676363

Greenham Regis Marine Electronics
Southampton 023 8063 6555

ICS Electronics Arundel 01903 731101

JG Technologies Ltd
Weymouth 0845 458 9616

KM Electronics
Lowestoft 01502 569079

Kongsberg Simrad Ltd
Aberdeen 01224 226500

Kongsberg Simrad Ltd
Wick 01955 603606

Landau UK Ltd Hamble 02380 454040

Land & Sea Electronics
Aberdeen 01224 593281

Marathon Leisure
Hayling Island 023 9263 7711

Marine Instruments
Falmouth 01326 375483

Maritek Ltd Glasgow 0141 571 9164

Microcustom Ltd Ipswich 01473 780724

Nasa Marine Instruments
Stevenage 01438 354033

Navcom Chichester 01243 776625

Navionics UK Plymouth 01752 204735

Ocean Leisure Ltd
London 020 7930 5050

Plymouth Marine Electronics
Plymouth 01752 227711

Radio & Electronic Services Ltd
St Peter Port 01481 728837

Raymarine Ltd
Portsmouth 023 9269 3611

Redfish Car Company
Stockton-on-Tees 01642 633638

Robertson, MK Oban 01631 563836

Satcom Distribution Ltd
Salisbury 01722 410800

Sea Information Systems Ltd
Aberdeen 01224 621326

Seaquest Marine Ltd
Guernsey 01481 721773

Seatronics Aberdeen 01224 853100

Selenia Communications
Aberdeen 01224 585334

Selenia Communications
Brixham 01803 851993

Selenia Communications
Fraserburgh 01346 518187

Selenia Communications
Lowestoft 01502 572365

Selenia Communications
Newlyn 01736 361320

Selenia Communications
Newcastle upon Tyne 0191 265 0374

Selenia Communications
Penryn 01326 378031

Selenia Communications
Southampton 023 8051 1868

Silva Ltd Livingston 01506 419555

SM International
Plymouth 01752 662129

Sperry Marine Ltd
Peterhead 01779 473475

Stenmar Ltd Aberdeen 01224 827288

STN Atlas Marine UK Ltd
Peterhead 01779 478233

Tacktick Ltd Emsworth 01243 379331

Transas Nautic
Portsmouth 023 9267 4016

Veripos Precise Navigation
Fraserburgh 01346 511411

Wema (UK) Bristol 01454 316103

Western Battery Service
Mallaig 01687 462044

Wilson & Co Ltd, DB
Glasgow 0141 647 0161

Woodsons of Aberdeen Ltd
Aberdeen 01224 722884

Yeoman Romsey 01794 521079

ENGINES AND ACCESSORIES

Airylea Motors
Aberdeen 01224 872891

Amble Boat Co Ltd
Amble 01665 710267

Anchor Marine Products
Benfleet 01268 566666

Aquafac Ltd Luton 01582 568700

Attfield & Company, GB
Dursley 01453 547185

Barrus Ltd, EP Bicester 01869 363636

Brigantine
Teignmouth 01626 872400

British Polar Engines Ltd
Glasgow 0141 445 2455

Bukh Diesel UK Ltd
Poole 01202 668840

Caledonian Marine
Rhu 01436 821184

CJ Marine Mechanical
Troon 01292 313400

Cleghorn Waring Ltd
Letchworth 01462 480380

Cook's Diesel Service Ltd
Faversham 01795 538553

Felton Marine Engineering
Brighton 01273 601779

Felton Marine Engineering
Eastbourne 01323 470211

Fender-Fix Maidstone 01622 751518

Fettes & Rankine Engineering
Aberdeen 01224 573343

Fleetwood & Sons Ltd, Henry
Lossiemouth 01343 813015

Gorleston Marine Ltd
Great Yarmouth 01493 661883

Halyard Salisbury 01722 710922

Interseals (Guernsey) Ltd
Guernsey 01481 246364

Kelpie Boats
Pembroke Dock 01646 683661

Keypart Watford 01923 330570

Lancing Marine Brighton 01273 410025

Lencraft Boats Ltd
Dungarvan +353 58 68220

Lewmar Ltd Havant 023 9247 1841

Liverpool Power Boats
Bootle 0151 944 1163

Lynch Ltd, PA Morpeth 01670 512291

MacDonald & Co Ltd, JN
Glasgow 0141 334 6171

Marine Maintenance
Tollesbury 01621 860441

Mariners Weigh
Shaldon 01626 873698

Mooring Mate Ltd
Bournemouth 01202 421199

Nauquip Warsash 01489 885336

Newens Marine, Chas
Putney 020 8788 4587

Ocean Safety
Southampton 023 8072 0800

Outboard Centre
Fareham 01329 234277

Riley Marine Dover 01304 214544

RK Marine Ltd Hamble 01489 583585

RK Marine Ltd Swanwick 01489 583572

Rule – ITT Industries
Hoddesdon 01992 450145

Sillette Sonic Ltd
Sutton 020 8337 7543

Smith & Son Ltd, EC
Luton 01582 729721

Sowester Simpson-Lawrence Ltd
Poole 01202 667700

Timage & Co Ltd
Braintree 01376 343087

Trident UK Gateshead 0191 259 6797

Vetus Den Ouden Ltd
Totton 023 8086 1033

Western Marine
Dublin +353 1 280 0321

Whitstable Marine
Whitstable 01227 262525

Yates Marine, Martin
Galgate 01524 751750

Ynys Marine Cardigan 01239 613179

FOUL-WEATHER GEAR

Aquatogs Cowes 01983 295071

Century Finchampstead 0118 9731616

Crewsaver Gosport 023 9252 8621

Douglas Gill Nottingham 0115 9460844

Gul International Ltd
Bodmin 01208 262400

Helly Hansen
Nottingham 0115 9608797

Henri Lloyd Manchester 0161 799 1212

Musto Ltd Laindon 01268 491555

Pro Rainer Windsor 07752 903882

Splashdown Leeds 0113 270 7000

GENERAL MARINE EQUIPMENT & SPARES

Ampair Ringwood 01425 480780

Aries Vane Gear Spares
Penryn 01326 377467

Arthurs Chandlery, R
Gosport 023 9252 6522

Barden UK Ltd Fareham 01489 570770

Calibra Marine International Ltd
Southampton 08702 400358

CH Marine (Cork)
Cork +353 21 4315700

Chris Hornsey (Chandlery) Ltd
Southsea 023 9273 4728

Compass Marine (Dartmouth)
Dartmouth 01803 835915

Cox Yacht Charter Ltd, Nick
Lymington 01590 673489

CTC Marine & Leisure
Middlesbrough 01642 372600

Docksafe Ltd Bangor 028 9147 0453

Frederiksen Boat Fittings (UK) Ltd
Gosport 023 9252 5377

Furneaux Riddall & Co Ltd
Portsmouth 023 9266 8621

Hardware & Marine Supplies
Co Wexford +353 (53) 29791

Index Marine
Bournemouth 01202 470149

Kearon Ltd, George
Arklow +353 402 32319

Marathon Leisure
Hayling Island 023 9263 7711

Pro-Boat Ltd
Burnham-on-Crouch 01621 785455

Pump International Ltd
Cornwall 01209 831937

Quay West Chandlers
Poole 01202 742488

Rogers, Angie Bristol 0117 973 8276

Ryland, Kenneth
Stanton 01386 584270

Tiflex Liskeard 01579 320808

Vetus Boating Equipment
Southampton 023 8086 1033

Western Marine Power Ltd
Plymouth 01752 408804

Whitstable Marine
Whitstable 01227 262525

Yacht Parts Plymouth 01752 252489

HARBOUR MASTERS

Aberaeron 01545 571645
Aberdeen 01224 597000
Aberdovey 01654 767626
Aberystwyth 01970 611433
Alderney & Burhou 01481 822620
Amble 01665 710306
Anstruther 01333 310836
Appledore 01237 474569
Arbroath 01241 872166
Ardglass 028 4484 1291
Ardrossan Control Tower 01294 463972
Arinagour Piermaster 01879 230347
Arklow +353 402 32466
Baltimore +353 28 22145
Banff 01261 815544
Bantry Bay +353 27 53277
Barmouth 01341 280671
Barry 01446 732665
Beaucette 01481 245000
Beaulieu River 01590 616200
Belfast Lough 028 90 553012
Belfast River Manager 028 90 328507
Bembridge 01983 872828
Berwick-upon-Tweed 01289 307404
Bideford 01237 346131
Blyth 01670 352678
Boston 01205 362328
Bridlington 01262 670148/9
Bridport 01308 423222
Brighton 01273 819919
Bristol 0117 926 4797
Brixham 01803 853321
Buckie 01542 831700
Bude 01288 353111
Burghead 01343 835337
Burnham-on-Crouch 01621 783602
Burnham-on-Sea 01278 782180
Burtonport +353 075 42155
Caernarfon 01286 672118
Caernarfon 07786 730865
Camber Berthing Offices – Portsmouth 023 92297395
Campbeltown 01586 552552
Canal Off. (Inverness) 01463 233140
Cardiff 029 20400500
Carnlough Harbour 07703 606763
Castletown Bay 01624 823549

Charlestown	01726 67526	Kettletoft Bay	01857 600227	Queens Gareloch/Rhu	01436 674321
Chichester Harbour	01243 512301	Killybegs	+353 73 31032	Ramsey	01624 812245
Christchurch	01202 495061	Kilmore Quay	+353 53 912 9955	Ramsgate	01843 572100
Conwy	01492 596253	Kinlochbervie	01971 521235	River Bann & Coleraine	
Cork	+353 21 4273125	Kinsale	+353 21 4772503		028 7034 2012
Corpach Canal Sea Lock	01397 772249	Kirkcudbright	01557 331135	River Blackwater	01621 856487
Courtmacsherry	+353 23 46311/46600	Kirkwall	01856 872292	River Colne (Brightlingsea)	01206 302200
Coverack	01326 380679	Langstone Harbour	023 9246 3419	River Dart	01803 832337
Cowes	01983 293952	Larne	02828 872100	River Deben	01394 270106
Crail	01333 450820	Lerwick	01595 692991	River Exe Dockmaster	01392 274306
Craobh Haven	01852 502222	Littlehampton	01903 721215	River Humber	01482 327171
Crinan Canal Office	01546 603210	Liverpool	0151 949 6134/5	River Medway	01795 596593
Cromarty Firth	01381 600479	Loch Gairloch	01445 712140	River Orwell	01473 231010
Cromarty Harbour	01381 600493	Loch Inver	01571 844265	River Roach	01621 783602
Crookhaven	+353 28 35319	Looe	01503 262839	River Stour	01255 243000
Cullen	01261 842477		07918728955	River Tyne/North Shields	0191 257 2080
Dingle	+353 66 9151629	Lossiemouth	01343 813066	River Yealm	01752 872533
Douglas	01624 686628	Lough Foyle	028 7186 0555	Rivers Alde & Ore	01473 450481
Dover	01304 240400 Ext 4520	Lowestoft	01502 572286	Rosslare Europort	+353 53 915 7921
Dublin	+353 1 874871	Lyme Regis	01297 442137	Rothesay	01700 503842
Dun Laoghaire	+353 1 280 1130/8074	Lymington	01590 672014		07799 724225
Dunbar	01368 863206	Lyness	01856 791387	Ryde	01983 613879
Dundee	01382 224121	Macduff	01261 832236	Salcombe	01548 843791
Dunmore East	+353 51 383166	Maryport	01900 814431	Sark	01481 832323
East Loch Tarbert	01859 502444	Menai Strait	01248 712312	Scalloway	01595 880574
Eastbourne	01323 470099	Methil	01333 462725	Scarborough	01723 373530
Eigg Harbour	01687 482428	Mevagissey	01726 843305	Scrabster	01847 892779
Elie	01333 330051	Milford Haven	01646 696100	Seaham	0191 581 3246
Estuary Control - Dumbarton	01389 726211	Minehead	01643 702566	Sharpness	01453 811862/64
Exe	01392 274306	Montrose	01674 672302	Shoreham	01273 598100
Eyemouth	01890 750223	Mousehole	01736 731511	Silloth	016973 31358
Falmouth	01326 312285	Mullion Cove	01326 240222	Sligo	+353 71 61197
Findochty	01542 831466	Nairn	01667 454330	Southampton	023 8033 9733
	7900 920445	Newhaven	01273 612868	Southend-on-Sea	01702 611889
Fisherrow	0131 665 5900	Newlyn	01736 362523	Southwold	01502 724712
Fishguard (Lower Hbr)	01348 874726	Newquay	01637 872809	St Helier	01534 447788
Fishguard	01348 404425	Newport Harbour Office	01983 525994	St Ives	01736 795018
Fleetwood	01253 879060	Oban	01631 562892	St Margaret's Hope	01856 831454
Flotta	01856 701411	Padstow	01841 532239	St Mary's	01720 422768
Folkestone	01303 715354	Par	01726 818337	St Michael's Mount	07870 400282
Fowey	01726 832471/2.	Peel	01624 842338	St Monans	01333 350055
Fraserburgh	01346 515858	Penrhyn Bangor	01248 352525	St Peter Port	01481 720229
Galway Bay	+353 91 561874	Penzance	01736 366113	Stonehaven	01569 762741
Garlieston	01988 600274	Peterhead	01779 483630	Stornoway	01851 702688
Glasson Dock	01524 751724	Pierowall	01857 677216	Strangford Lough	028 44 881637
Gorey	01534 447788	Pittenweem	01333 312591	Stromness	01856 850744
Gourdon	01569 762741	Plockton	01599 534589	Stronsay	01857 616317
Great Yarmouth	01493 335501	Polperro	01503 272809	Sullom Voe	01806 242551
Grimsby Dockmaster	01472 359181	Poole	01202 440233	Sunderland	0191 567 2626
Groomsport Bay	028 91 278040	Port St Mary	01624 833205	Swale	01795 561234
Hamble River	01489 576387	Porth Dinllaen	01758 720276	Swansea	01792 653787
Hayle	01736 754043	Porthleven	01326 574207	Tees & Hartlepool Port Authority	01429 277205
Helford River	01326 250749	Porthmadog	01766 512927	Teignmouth	01626 773165
Helmsdale	01431 821692	Portknockie	01542 840833	Tenby	01834 842717
Holy Island	01289 389217	Portland	01305 824044	Thames Estuary	01474 562200
Holyhead	01407 763071	Portpatrick	01776 810355	Tobermory Port Manager	01688 302017
Hopeman	01343 835337	Portree	01478 612926	Torquay	01803 292429
Howth	+353 1 832 2252	Portrush	028 70822307	Troon	01292 281687
Ilfracombe	01271 862108	Portsmouth Harbour Commercial Docks	023 92297395	Truro	01872 272130
Inverness	01463 715715	Portsmouth Harbour Control	023 92723694	Ullapool	01854 612091
Irvine	01294 487286	Portsmouth Harbour	023 92723124		
Johnshaven	01561 362262	Preston	01772 726711		
		Pwllheli	01758 704081		
		Queenborough	01795 662051		

Walton-on-the-Naze	01255 851899
Watchet	01984 631264
Waterford	+353 51 874907
Wells-next-the-Sea	01328 711646
Wexford	+353 53 912 2039
Weymouth	01305 206423
Whitby	01947 602354
Whitehaven	01946 692435
Whitehills	01261 861291
Whitstable	01227 274086
Wick	01955 602030
Wicklow	+353 404 67455
Workington	01900 602301
Yarmouth	01983 760321
Youghal	+353 24 92626

HARBOURS

Bristol Harbour	0117 922 2000
Clyde Marina – Ardrossan	01294 607077
Jersey Harbours	
St Helier	01534 885588
Maryport Harbour and Marina	
Maryport	01900 818447/4431

QUAY MARINAS
A & W Building, The Docks,
Portishead, N. Somerset
BS20 7DF
Tel: (01275) 841188
Fax: (01275) 841189
e-mail: sriggs@quaymarinas.com
A wholly owned subsidary of Quay
Marinas, operate comprehensive yachting
facilities at 5 locations in the UK and are
marketing agents for Malahide Marina in
Dublin Bay.   2009/EXT3/e

**PADSTOW HARBOUR
COMMISSIONERS**
Harbour Office, Padstow,
Cornwall PL28 8AQ
Tel: (01841) 532239
Fax: (01841) 533346
e-mail:
padstowharbour@btconnect.com
www.padstow-harbour.co.uk
Inner harbour controlled by tidal gate -
opens HW±2 hours. Minimum depth 3
metres at all times. Yachtsmen must be
friendly as vessels raft together. Services
include showers, toilets, diesel, water and
ice. Security by CCTV.   2009/Ext1/e

Peterhead Bay Authority	
Peterhead	01779 474020
Sark Moorings – Channel Islands	
	01481 832260

INSURANCE/FINANCE

Admiral Marine Ltd	
Salisbury	01722 416106
Bigfish London	020 8651 4096
Bishop Skinner Boat Insurance	
London	0800 7838057
Bristol Channel Marine	
Cardiff	029 2063 1163
Carter Boat Insurance, RA	
	0800 174061

Castlemain Ltd	
St Peter Port	01481 721319
Clark Insurance, Graham	
Tyneside	0191 455 8089
Craftinsure.com	
Orpington	01689 889507
Craven Hodgson Associates	
Leeds	0113 243 8443
Giles Insurance Brokers	
Irvine	01294 315481
GJW Direct Liverpool	0151 473 8000
Haven Knox-Johnston	
West Malling	01732 223600
Lombard Southampton	023 8024 2171
Mardon Insurance	
Shrewsbury	0800 515629
Marine & General Insurance Services Ltd Maidstone	01622 201106
Mercia Marine Malvern	01684 564457
Nautical Insurance Services Ltd	
Leigh-on-Sea	01702 470811
Navigators & General	
Brighton	01273 863400
Pantaenius UK Ltd	
Plymouth	01752 223656
Porthcawl Insurance Consultants	
Porthcawl	01656 784866
Saga Boat Insurance Folkestone	01303 771135
St Margarets Insurances	
London	020 8778 6161
Weysure Ltd Weymouth	07000 939787

LIFERAFTS & INFLATABLES

A B MARINE LTD
Castle Walk, St Peter Port,
Guernsey, Channel Islands
GY1 1AU.
Tel: (01481) 722378
Fax: (01481) 711080
We specialise in safety and survival
equipment and are a M.C.A. approved
service station for liferafts including
R.F.D., Beaufort/Dunlop, Zodiac, Avon,
Plastimo and Lifeguard. We also carry a
full range of new liferafts, dinghies and
lifejackets and distress flares.   2009/L1/e

Adec Marine Ltd	
Croydon	020 8686 9717
Avon Inflatables Llanelli	01554 882000
Cosalt International Ltd	
Aberdeen	01224 588327

Glaslyn Marine Supplies Ltd	
Porthmadog	01766 513545
Hale Marine, Ron	
Portsmouth	023 9273 2985
Herm Seaway Marine Ltd	
St Peter Port	01481 722838
IBS Boats South Woodham Ferrers	01245 323211/425551
KTS Seasafety Kilkeel	028 918 28405
Nationwide Marine Hire	
Warrington	01925 245788
Norwest Marine Ltd	
Liverpool	0151 207 2860
Ocean Safety	
Southampton	023 8072 0800
Polymarine Ltd Conwy	01492 583322
Premium Liferaft Services	
Burnham-on-Crouch	0800 243673
Ribeye Dartmouth	01803 832060
Secumar Swansea	01792 280545
South Eastern Marine Services Ltd	
Basildon	01268 534427
Suffolk Sailing Ipswich	01473 833010
Whitstable Marine	
Whitstable	01227 262525

MARINAS

Aberystwyth Marina	01970 611422
Amble Marina	01665 712168
Arbroath Harbour	01241 872166
Ardfern Yacht Centre Ltd	01852 500247
Ardglass Marina	028 44842332
Arklow Marina	+353 402 39901
Ballycastle Marina	028 2076 8525
Bangor Marina	028 91 453297
Beaucette Marina	01481 245000
Bembridge Harbour	01983 872828
Berthon Lymington Marina	01590 647405
Birdham Pool Marina	01243 512310
Blackwater Marina	01621 740264
Boston Marina	01205 364420
Bradwell Marina	01621 776235
Bray Marina	01628 623654
Brentford Dock Marina	020 8232 8941
Bridgemarsh Marine	01621 740414
Brighton Marina	01273 819919
Bristol Marina	0117 9213198

Brixham Marina	01803 882929
Bucklers Hard Marina	01590 616200
Burnham Yacht Harbour Marina Ltd	
	01621 782150
Cahersiveen Marina	
	+353 66 947 2777
Caley Marina	01463 236539
Carlingford Marina	+353 42 9373073
Carrickfergus Marina	028 9336 6666
Castlepark Marina	+353 21 477 4959
Chatham Maritime Marina	
	01634 899200
Chelsea Harbour Marina	
	020 7225 9157
Chichester Marina	01243 512731
Clyde Marina Ltd	01294 607077
Cobbs Quay Marina	01202 674299
Coleraine Marina	028 703 44768
Conwy Marina	01492 593000
Cowes Yacht Haven	01983 299975
Craobh Marina	01852 500222
Crosshaven Boatyard Marina	
	+353 21 483 1161
Dart Marina Yacht Harbour	
	01803 833351
Darthaven Marina	01803 752545
Dartside Quay	01803 845445
Deganwy Quay	01492 583984
Dingle Marina	+353 66 915 1629
Dover Marina	01304 241663
Dublin City Marina	
Dun Laoghaire Marina	
	+353 1 202 0040
Dunstaffnage Marina Ltd	
	01631 566555
East Cowes Marina	01983 293983
East Ferry Marina	+353 21 483 1342
Emsworth Yacht Harbour	
	01243 377727
Essex Marina	01702 258531
Falmouth Marina	01326 316620
Falmouth Visitors Yacht Haven	
	01326 310991
Fambridge Yacht Haven	
	01621 740370
Fenit Harbour Marina	
	+353 66 7136231
Fleetwood Harbour Village	
	01253 879062
Fox's Marina Ipswich Ltd	
	01473 689111
Gallions Point Marina	0207 476 7054
Gillingham Marina	01634 280022
Glasson Dock Marina	01524 751491
Gosport Marina	023 9252 4811
Gunwharf Quays	02392 836732
Hafan Pwllheli	01758 701219
Hamble Point Marina	023 8045 2464
Harbour of Rye	01797 225225
Hartlepool Marina	01429 865744
Haslar Marina	023 9260 1201
Heybridge Basin	01621 853506
Hillyards	01903 713327
Holy Loch Marina	01369 701800

Holyhead Marina	01407 764242
Hoo Marina	01634 250311
Howth Marina	+353 1839 2777
Hull Marina	01482 609960
Hythe Marina	023 8020 7073
Inverness Marina	07526 446348
Ipswich Haven Marina	01473 236644
Island Harbour Marina	01983 822999
Kemps Quay Marina	023 8063 2323
Kilmore Quay Marina	
	+353 5391 29955
Kilrush Creek Marina	
	+353 65 9052072
Kinsale Yacht Club Marina	
	+353 21 477 2196
Kip Marina	01475 521485
Kirkwall Marina	07810 465835
La Collette Yacht Basin	01534 885588
Lady Bee Marina	01273 593801
Lake Yard Marina	01202 674531
Largs Yacht Haven	01475 675333
Lawrence Cove Marina	
	+353 27 75044
Limehouse Marina	020 7308 9930
Littlehampton Marina	01903 713553
Liverpool Marina	0151 707 6777
Lossiemouth Marina	01343 813066
Lowestoft Haven Marina	
	01502 580300
Lymington Yacht Haven	01590 677071
Malahide Marina	+353 1 845 4129
Maryport Harbour and Marina	
	01900 814431
Mayflower International Marina	
	01752 556633
Melfort Pier & Harbour	01852 200333
Mercury Yacht Harbour	
	023 8045 5994
Meridian Quay Marina	01472 268424
Milford Marina	01646 696312
Multihull Centre	01752 823900
Mylor Yacht Harbour	01326 372121
Nairn Marina	01667 456008
Neptune Marina Ltd	01473 215204
Newhaven Marina	01273 513881
Neyland Yacht Haven	01646 601601
Northney Marina	023 9246 6321
Noss Marina	01803 839087

Ocean Village Marina	023 8022 9385
Parkstone Yacht Club Haven	
	01202 743610
Penarth Quays Marina	02920 705021
Penton Hook	01932 568681
Peterhead Bay Marina	01779 477868
Plymouth Yacht Haven	01752 404231
Poole Quay Boat Haven	
	01202 649488
Poplar Dock Marina	0207 308 9930
Port Edgar Marina & Sailing School	
	0131 331 3330
Port Ellen Marina	01496 300301
Port Falmouth Marina	01326 212100
Port Hamble Marina	023 8045 2741
Port Pendennis Marina	01326 211211
Port Solent Marina	02392 210765
Portaferry Marina	028 4272 9598
Portavadie Marina	01700 811075
Portishead Quays Marina	
	01275 841941
Portland Marina	08454 30 2012
Preston Marina	01772 733595
Queen Anne's Battery Marina	
	01752 671142
Rhu Marina Ltd	01436 820238
Ridge Wharf Yacht Centre	
	01929 552650
Royal Cork Yacht Club Marina	
	+353 21 483 1023
Royal Harbour Marina, Ramsgate	
	01843 572100
Royal Harwich Yacht Club Marina	
	01473 780319
Royal Norfolk and Suffolk Yacht Club	
	01502 566726
Royal Northumberland Yacht Club	
	01670 353636
Royal Quays Marina	0191 272 8282
Ryde Leisure Harbour	01983 613879
Salterns Marina Boatyard & Hotel	
	01202 709971
Salve Engineering Marina	
	+353 21 483 1145

Sandpoint Marina (Dumbarton)	01389 762396
Saxon Wharf Marina	023 8033 9490
Seaport Marina	01463 725500
Seaton's Marina	028 703 832086
Shamrock Quay Marina	023 8022 9461
Sharpness Marine	01453 811476
Shepherds Wharf Boatyard Ltd	01983 297821
Shotley Marina	01473 788982
South Dock Marina	020 7252 2244
South Ferriby Marina	01652 635620
Southdown Marina	01752 823084
Southsea Marina	023 9282 2719
Sovereign Harbour Marina	01323 470099
Sparkes Marina	023 92463572
St Helier Marina	01534 447730
St Katharine Marina Ltd	0207 264 5312
St Peter Port Marinas	01481 720229
St Peter's Marina	0191 265 4472

Stromness Marina	07810 465825
Suffolk Yacht Harbour Ltd	01473 659240
Sunderland Marina	0191 514 4721
Sutton Harbour	01752 204702
Swansea Marina	01792 470310
Swanwick Marina	01489 884081
Titchmarsh Marina	01255 672185
Tollesbury Marina	01621 869202
Torpoint Yacht Harbour	01752 813658
Torquay Marina	01803 200210
Troon Yacht Haven	01292 315553
Victoria Marina	01481 725987
Walton Yacht Basin	01255 675873
Waterford City Marina	+353 51 309900
Weymouth Harbour	01305 838423
Weymouth Marina	01305 767576
Whitby Marina	01947 600165
Whitehaven Harbour Marina	01946 692435
Whitehills Marina	01261 861291
Windsor Marina	01753 853911

Wisbech Yacht Harbour	01945 588059
Woolverstone Marina	01473 780206
Yarmouth Harbour	01983 760321

MARINE CONSULTANTS AND SURVEYORS

Amble Boat Company Ltd Amble	01665 710267
Ark Surveys East Anglia/South Coast	01621 857065/01794 521957
Atkin and Associates Lymington	01590 688633
Barbican Yacht Agency Ltd Plymouth	01752 228855
Booth Marine Surveys, Graham Birchington-on-Sea	01843 843793
Bureau Maritime Ltd Maldon	01621 859181
Byrde & Associates Kimmeridge	01929 480064
Cannell & Associates, David M Wivenhoe	01206 823337
Clarke Designs LLP, Owen Dartmouth	01803 770495
Davies, Peter Wivenhoe	01206 823289
Down Marine Co Ltd Belfast	028 90480247
Green, James Plymouth	01752 660516
Greening Yacht Design Ltd, David Chichester	023 9263 1806
Hansing & Associates North Wales/Midlands	01248 671291
JP Services – Marine Safety & Training Chichester	01243 537552
Marintec Lymington	01590 683414
Norwood Marine Margate	01843 835711
Quay Consultants Ltd West Wittering	01243 673056
Scott Marine Surveyors & Consultants Conwy	01248 680759
Staton-Bevan, Tony Lymington	01590 645755
Swanwick Yacht Surveyors Southampton	01489 564822
Thomas, Stephen Southampton	023 8048 6273
Victoria Yacht Surveys Cornwall	0800 093 2113
Ward & McKenzie Woodbridge	01394 383222
Ward & McKenzie (North East) Pocklington	01759 304322
Yacht Designers & Surveyors Association Bordon	0845 0900 162

MARINE ENGINEERS

Allerton Engineering Lowestoft	01502 537870
APAS Engineering Ltd Southampton	023 8063 2558
Ardmair Boat Centre Ullapool	01854 612054

Arisaig Marine
Inverness-shire   01687 450224
Arun Craft Littlehampton 01903 723667
Attrill & Sons, H
Bembridge   01983 872319
Auto & Marine Services
Botley   01489 785009
Auto Marine Southsea 023 9282 5601
BJ Marine Ltd Bangor 028 9127 1434
Bristol Boat Ltd Bristol 01225 872032
Buzzard Marine Engineering
Yarmouth   01983 760707
C & B Marine Ltd
Chichester Marina   01243 511273
Caddy, Simon Falmouth Marina,
Falmouth   01326 372682
Caledonian Marine
Rhu Marina   01436 821184
Cardigan Outboards
Cardigan   01239 613966
Channel Islands Marine Ltd
Guernsey   01481 716880
Channel Islands Marine Ltd
Jersey   01534 767595
Clarence Marine Engineering
Gosport   023 9251 1555
Cook's Diesel Service Ltd
Faversham   01795 538553
Cragie Engineering
Kirkwall   01856 874680
Wartsila
Havant   023 9240 0121
Crinan Boatyard Ltd
Crinan   01546 830232
Cutler Marine Engineering, John
Emsworth   01243 375014
Dale Sailing Co Ltd
Milford Haven   01646 603110
Davis Marine Services
Ramsgate   01843 586172
Denney & Son, EL
Redcar   01642 483507
DH Marine (Shetland) Ltd
Shetland   01595 690618
Emark Marine Ltd
Emsworth   01243 375383
Evans Marine Engineering, Tony
Pwllheli   01758 703070
Fairways Marine Engineers
Maldon   01376 572866
Felton Marine Engineering
Brighton   01273 601779
Felton Marine Engineering
Eastbourne   01323 470211
Ferrypoint Boat Co
Youghal   +353 24 94232
Fettes & Rankine Engineering
Aberdeen   01224 573343
Fleetwood & Sons Ltd, Henry
Lossiemouth   01343 813015
Fleming Engineering, J
Stornoway   01851 703488

Floetree Ltd (Loch Lomond Marina)
Balloch   01389 752069
Fowey Harbour Marine Engineers
Fowey   01726 832806
Fox Marine Services Ltd
Jersey   01534 721312
Freeport Marine Jersey 01534 888100
French Marine Motors Ltd
Colchester   01206 302133
GH Douglas Marine Services
Fleetwood Harbour Village Marina,
Fleetwood   01253 877200
Golden Arrow Marine
Southampton   023 8071 0371
Goodchild Marine Services
Great Yarmouth   01493 782301
Goodwick Marine
Fishguard   01348 873955
Gosport Boat Yard
Gosport   023 9252 4811
Griffins Garage Dingle Marina,
Co Kerry   +353 66 91 51178
Hale Marine, Ron
Portsmouth   023 9273 2985
Hamnavoe Engineering
Stromness   01856 850576
Hampshire Marine Ltd
Stubbington   01329 665561
Harbour Engineering
Itchenor   01243 513454
Hardway Marine Store
Gosport   023 9258 0420
Hartlepool Marine Engineering
Hartlepool   01429 867883
Hayles, Harold
Yarmouth   01983 760373
Herm Seaway Marine Ltd
St Peter Port   01481 726829
HNP Engineers (Lerwick Ltd)
Lerwick   01595 692493
Home Marine Emsworth Yacht Harbour,
Emsworth   01243 374125
Hook Marine Ltd
Troon   01292 679500
Humphrey, Chris
Teignmouth   01626 772324
Instow Marine Services
Bideford   01271 861081
Jones (Boatbuilders), David
Chester   01244 390363
Keating Marine Engineering Ltd, Bill
Jersey   01534 733977
Kingston Marine Services
Cowes   01983 299385
Kippford Slipway Ltd
Dalbeattie   01556 620249
Lansdale Pannell Marine
Chichester   01243 512374
Lencraft Boats Ltd
Dungarvan   +353 58 68220
Lifeline Marine Services
Dolphin Haven, Poole   01202 669676

Llyn Marine Services
Pwllheli   01758 612606
Lynx Engineering
St Helens, Isle of Wight 01983 873711
M&G Marine Services
Mayflower International Marina, Plymouth
    01752 563345
MacDonald & Co Ltd, JN
Glasgow   0141 334 6171
Mackay Marine Services
Aberdeen   01224 575772
Mainbrayce Marine
Alderney   01481 722772
Malakoff and Moore
Lerwick   01595 695544
**Mallaig Boat Building and
Engineering** Mallaig 01687 462304
Marindus Engineering
Kilmore Quay   +353 53 29794
Marine Engineering Looe
Brixham   01803 844777
Marine Engineering Looe
Looe   01503 263009
Marine General Engineers Beaucette
Marina, Guernsey 01481 245808
Marine Maintenance
Portsmouth   023 9260 2344
Marine Maintenance
Tollesbury   01621 860441
Marine Propulsion
Hayling Island   023 9246 1694
Marine & General Engineers
St. Sampsons Harbour, Guernsey
    01481 245808
Marine-Trak Engineering Mylor Yacht
Harbour, Falmouth 01326 376588
Marlec Marine
Ramsgate   01843 592176
Martin (Marine) Ltd, Alec
Birkenhead   0151 652 1663
Medusa Marine Ipswich 01473 780090
Mobile Marine Engineering Liverpool
Marina, Liverpool 01565 733553
Motortech Marine Engineering
Portsmouth   023 9251 3200
Mount's Bay Engineering
Newlyn   01736 363095
MP Marine Maryport 01900 810299
New World Yacht Care
Helensburgh   01436 820586
North Western Automarine Engineers
Largs   01475 687139
Noss Marine Services
Dart Marina, Dartmouth 01803 833343
Owen Marine, Robert
Porthmadog   01766 513435
Pace, Andy Newhaven 01273 516010
**Penzance Dry Dock and Engineering
Co Ltd** Penzance 01736 363838

Pirie & Co, John S
Fraserburgh   01346 513314

Portavon Marine
Keynsham   0117 986 1626

Power Afloat, Elkins Boatyard
Christchurch   01202 489555

Powerplus Marine Cowes Yacht Haven,
Cowes   01983 200036

Pro-Marine Queen Anne's Battery
Marina, Plymouth   01752 267984

PT Marine Engineering
Hayling Island   023 9246 9332

QUAY MARINAS
A & W Building, The Docks,
Portishead, N. Somerset
BS20 7DF
Tel: (01275) 841188
Fax: (01275) 841189
e-mail: sriggs@quaymarinas.com
A wholly owned subsidiary of Quay
Marinas, operate comprehensive yachting
facilities at 5 locations in the UK and are
marketing agents for Malahide Marina in
Dublin Bay.   2009/EXT3/e

R & M Marine
Portsmouth   023 9273 7555

R & S Engineering Dingle Marina,
Ireland   +353 66 915 1189

Reddish Marine
Salcombe   01548 844094

Reynolds, Cliff
Hartlepool   01429 272049

RHP Marine
Cowes   01983 290421

River Tees Engineering & Welding Ltd
Middlesbrough   01642 226226

RK Marine Ltd Hamble   01489 583585

RK Marine Ltd
Swanwick   01489 583572

Rossiter Yachts Ltd
Christchurch   01202 483250

Ryan & Roberts Marine Services
Askeaton   +353 61 392198

Salve Marine Ltd
Crosshaven   +353 21 4831145

Seaguard Marine Engineering Ltd
Goodwick   01348 872976

Seamark-Nunn & Co
Felixstowe   01394 275327

Seaward Engineering
Glasgow   0141 632 4910

Seaway Marine
Gosport   023 9260 2722

Shearwater Engineering Services Ltd
Dunoon   01369 706666

Silvers Marina Ltd
Helensburgh   01436 831222

Starey Marine
Salcombe   01548 843655

Strickland Marine Engineering, Brian
Chichester   01243 513454

Tarbert Marine Arbroath 01241 872879

Tollesbury Marine Engineering
Tollesbury Marina,
Tollesbury   01621 869919

Troon Marine Services Ltd
Troon   01292 316180

Vasey Marine Engineering, Gordon
Fareham   07798 638625

Volspec Ltd Ipswich Marina,
Ipswich   01473 219651

Wallis, Peter Torquay Marina,
Torquay   01803 844777

WB Marine Chichester   01243 512857

West, Mick Brighton   01273 626656

West Point Marine Services
Fareham   01329 232881

Western Marine Power Ltd
Plymouth   01752 408804

Weymouth Marina Mechanical
Services Weymouth   01305 779379

Whittington, G Lady Bee Marine,
Shoreham   01273 593801

Whitewater Marine
Malahide   +353 1 816 8473

Wigmore Wright Marine Services
Penarth Marina   029 2070 9983

Wright, M Manaccan   01326 231502

Wyko Industrial Services
Inverness   01463 224747

Yates Marine, Martin
Galgate   01524 751750

Ynys Marine
Cardigan   01239 613179

Yoldings Marine
Eastbourne   01323 470882

Youngboats
Faversham   01795 536176

1° West Marine Ltd
Portsmouth   023 9283 8335

MASTS, SPARS & RIGGING

1° Degree West Ltd
Portsmouth   02392 200670

A2 Rigging
Falmouth   01326 312209

Allspars Plymouth   01752 266766

Amble Boat Co Ltd
Morpeth   01665 710267

ATLANTIC SPARS LTD
Brixham   01803 843322
                           2008/M&WL13/e

Arun Canvas & Rigging
Littlehampton   1903 732561

Buchanan, Keith
St Mary's   01720 422037

Bussell & Co, WL
Weymouth   01305 785633

Carbospars Ltd Hamble 023 8045 6736

Cable & Rope Works
Pevensey   01323 763019

Coates Marine Ltd
Whitby   01947 604486

Composite Rigging
Southampton   023 8023 4488

Dauntless Boatyard Ltd
Canvey Island   01268 793782

Davies Marine Services
Ramsgate   01843 586172

Eurospars Ltd Plymouth 01752 550550

Exe Leisure Exeter   01392 879055

Fox's Marine Ipswich Ltd
Ipswich   01473 689111

Freeland Yacht Spars Ltd
Dorchester on Thames   01865 341277

Gordon, AD Portland   01305 821569

Harris Rigging Totnes   01803 840160

Heyn Engineering
Belfast   028 9035 0022

Holman Rigging
Chichester   01243 514000

Irish Spars and Rigging
Malahide   +353 86 209 5996

Lowestoft Yacht Services
Lowestoft   01502 585535

Marine Resource Centre
Oban   01631 720291

Martin Leaning Masts & Rigging
Hayling   023 9237 1157

Mast & Rigging Services
Largs   01475 670110

Mast & Rigging Services
Largs   01475 670110

MP Marine Maryport   01900 810299

Ocean Rigging Lymington	01590 676292
Owen Sails Oban	01631 720485
Premier Spars Poole	01202 677717
Pro Rig S Ireland	+353 87 298 3333
Rig Magic Ipswich	01473 655089
Rig Shop Southampton	023 8033 8341
Roberts Marine Ltd, S Liverpool	0151 707 8300
Sailspar Ltd Brightlingsea	01206 302679
Salcombe Boatstore Salcombe	01548 843708
Seldén Mast Ltd Southampton	01489 484000
Silvers Marina Ltd Helensburgh	01436 831222
Silverwood Yacht Services Ltd Portsmouth	023 9232 7067
Southern Spar Services Northam	023 8033 1714
Southern Masts & Rigging Brighton	01273 668902
Storrar Marine Store Newcastle upon Tyne	0191 266 1037
Tedfords Rigging & Rafts Belfast	028 9032 6763
TJ Rigging Conwy	07780 972411
TS Rigging Malden	01621 874861
Windjammer Marine Milford Marina	01646 699070
Yacht Rigging Services Plymouth	01752 226609
Yacht Shop, The Fleetwood	01253 879238
Yacht Solutions Ltd Portsmouth	023 9220 0670
XW Rigging Gosport	023 9251 3553
Z Spars UK Hadleigh	01473 822130
1° West Marine Ltd Portsmouth	023 9283 8335

NAVIGATION EQUIPMENT – GENERAL

Belson Design Ltd, Nick Southampton	077 6835 1330
B & G UK Romsey	01794 510010
Brown Son & Ferguson Ltd Glasgow	0141 429 1234
Cooke & Son Ltd, B Hull	01482 223454
Diverse Yacht Services Hamble	023 8045 3399
Dolphin Maritime Software Ltd Lancaster	01524 841946
Dubois Phillips & McCallum Ltd Liverpool	0151 236 2776
Eland Exeter	01392 255788
Garmin Romsey	01794 519944
Geonav UK Ltd Poole	0870 240 4575
Imray Laurie Norie and Wilson Ltd St Ives, Cambs	01480 462114
Kelvin Hughes Southampton	023 8063 4911
Lilley & Gillie Ltd, John North Shields	0191 257 2217

Marine Chart Services Wellingborough	01933 441629
PC Maritime Plymouth	01752 254205
Navimo UK Hedge End	01489 778850
Precision Navigation Romsey	01794 521079
Price & Co, WF Bristol	0117 929 2229
Raymarine Ltd Portsmouth	023 9269 3611
Robbins Marine Electronics Liverpool	0151 709 5431
Royal Institute of Navigation London	020 7591 3130
Sea Chest Nautical Bookshop Plymouth	01752 222012
Seath Instruments (1992) Ltd Lowestoft	01502 573811
Smith (Marine) Ltd, AM London	020 8529 6988
South Bank Marine Charts Ltd Grimsby	01472 361137
Southcoasting Navigators Devon	01626 335626
Stanford Charts Bristol	0117 929 9966
London	020 7836 1321
Manchester	0870 890 3730
Todd Chart Agency Ltd County Down	028 9146 6640
UK Hydrographic Office Taunton	01823 337900
Warsash Nautical Bookshop Warsash	01489 572384
Yachting Instruments Ltd Sturminster Newton	01258 817662

PAINT & OSMOSIS

Advanced Blast Cleaning Paint Tavistock	01822 617192/07970 407911
Blakes Paints Southampton	01489 864440
Herm Seaway Marine Ltd St Peter Port	01481 726829
Gillingham Marina	01634 280022
International Coatings Ltd Southampton	023 8022 6722
Marineware Ltd Southampton	023 8033 0208
NLB Marine Ardrossan	01563 521509
Pro-Boat Ltd Burnham on Crouch	01621 785455
Rustbuster Ltd Peterborough	0870 9090093
Smith & Son Ltd, EC Luton	01582 729721
SP Systems Isle of Wight	01983 828000
Teal & Mackrill Ltd Hull	01482 320194
Troon Marine Services Ltd Troon	01292 316180

PROPELLERS & STERNGEAR/REPAIRS

CJR Propulsion Ltd Southampton	023 8063 9366

Darglow Engineering Ltd Wareham	01929 556512
Gori Propellers Poole	01202 621631
Propeller Revolutions Poole	01202 671226
Sillette – Sonic Ltd Sutton	020 8337 7543
Vetus Den Ouden Ltd Southampton	023 8086 1033

RADIO COURSES / SCHOOLS

Bisham Abbey Sailing & Navigation School Bisham	01628 474960
East Coast Offshore Yachting – Les Rant Perry	01480 861381
Hamble School of Yachting Hamble	023 8045 6687
Pembrokeshire Cruising Neyland	01646 602500
Plymouth Sailing School Plymouth	01752 493377
Southern Sailing Swanwick	01489 575511
Start Point Sailing Kingsbridge	01548 810917

REEFING SYSTEMS

Atlantic Spars Ltd Brixham	01803 843322
Calibra Marine International Ltd Southampton	08702 400358
Eurospars Ltd Plymouth	01752 550550
Holman Rigging Chichester	01243 514000
Navimo UK Ltd Hedge End	01489 778850
Sea Teach Ltd Emsworth	01243 375774
Southern Spar Services Northam	023 8033 1714
Wragg, Chris Lymington	01590 677052
Z Spars UK Hadleigh	01473 822130

REPAIR MATERIALS AND ACCESSORIES

Akeron Ltd Southend on Sea	01702 297101
Howells & Son, KJ Poole	01202 665724
JB Timber Ltd North Ferriby	01482 631765
Robbins Timber Bristol	0117 9633136
Sika Ltd Welwyn Garden City	01707 394444
SP Systems Newport, Isle of Wight	01983 828000
Technix Rubber & Plastics Ltd Southampton	01489 789944
Tiflex Liskeard	01579 320808
Timage & Co Ltd Braintree	01376 343087
Trade Grade Products Ltd Poole	01202 820177
Wessex Resins & Adhesives Ltd Romsey	01794 521111

ROPE AND WIRE

Cable & Rope Works
Pevensey   01323 763019

Euro Rope Ltd
Scunthorpe   01724 280480

Marlow Ropes Hailsham 01323 444444

Mr Splice Leicester   0800 1697178

Spinlock Ltd Cowes   01983 295555

TJ Rigging Conwy   07780 972411

SAFETY EQUIPMENT

AB Marine Ltd
St Peter Port   01481 722378

Adec Marine Ltd
Croydon   020 8686 9717

Anchorwatch UK
Edinburgh 0131 447 5057

Avon Inflatables
Llanelli   01554 882000

Cosalt International Ltd
Aberdeen   01224 588327

Crewsaver Gosport   023 9252 8621

Glaslyn Marine Supplies Ltd
Porthmadog   01766 513545

Guardian Fire Ltd
Norwich   01603 787679

Hale Marine, Ron
Portsmouth   023 9273 2985

Herm Seaway Marine Ltd
St Peter Port   01481 722838

IBS Boats South Woodham Ferrers
                    01245 323211/425551

KTS Seasafety Kilkeel 028 41762655

McMurdo Pains Wessex
Portsmouth   023 9262 3900

Met Office Bracknell 0845 300 0300

Nationwide Marine Hire
Warrington   01925 245788

Norwest Marine Ltd
Liverpool   0151 207 2860

Ocean Safety So'ton   023 8072 0800

Navimo UK Ltd
Hedge End   01489 778850

Polymarine Ltd Conwy 01492 583322

Premium Liferaft Services
Burnham-on-Crouch   0800 243673

Ribeye Dartmouth   01803 832060

Secumar Swansea   01792 280545

South Eastern Marine Services Ltd
Basildon   01268 534427

Suffolk Sailing
Ipswich   01473 833010

Whitstable Marine
Whitstable   01227 262525

Winters Marine Ltd
Salcombe   01548 843580

SAILMAKERS & REPAIRS

Allison-Gray Dundee   01382 505888

Alsop Sailmakers, John
Salcombe   01548 843702

Arun Canvas & Rigging
Littlehampton   01903 732561

Arun Sails Chichester 01243 573185

Bank Sails, Bruce
Southampton   01489 582444

Barford Sails Weymouth 01305 768282

Batt Sails Bosham   01243 575505

Bissett and Ross
Aberdeen   01224 580659

Breaksea Sails Barry 01446 730785

Bristol Sails Bristol 0117 922 5080

Buchanan, Keith
St Mary's   01720 422037

C&J Marine Textiles
Chichester   01243 782629

Calibra Sails Dartmouth 01803 833094

Canard Sails Swansea 01792 367838

Coastal Covers
Portsmouth   023 9252 0200

Covercare Fareham   01329 311878

Crawford, Margaret
Kirkwall   01856 875692

Crusader Sails Poole 01202 670580

Cullen Sailmakers
Galway   +353 91 771991

Dawson (Sails), J
Port Dinorwic   01248 670103

Dolphin Sails Harwich 01255 243366

Doyle Sails Southampton 023 8033 2622

RESTAURANTS/PUBS

Downer International Sails & Chandlery
Dun Laoghaire +353 1 280 0231

Duthie Marine Safety, Arthur
Glasgow 0141 429 4553

Dynamic Sails
Emsworth 01243 374495

East Coast Sails
Walton-on-the-Naze 01255 678353

Flew Sailmakers
Portchester 01329 822676

Fylde Coast Sailmaking Co
Fleetwood 01253 873476

Garland Sails Bristol 0117 935 3233

Goldfinch Sails
Whitstable 01227 272295

Gowen Ocean Sailmakers
West Mersea 01206 384412

Green Sailmakers, Paul
Plymouth 01752 660317

Henderson Sails & Covers
Southsea 023 9229 4700

Hood Sailmakers
Lymington 01590 675011

Hooper, A Plymouth 01752 830411

Hyde Sails Southampton 01489 563420

Jackson Yacht Services
Jersey 01534 743819

Jeckells and Son Ltd (Wroxham)
Wroxham 01603 782223

Jessail Ardrossan 01294 467311

JKA Sailmakers
Pwllheli 01758 613266

Kemp Sails Ltd
Wareham 01929 554308/554378

Lawrence Sailmakers, J
Brightlingsea 01206 302863

Leitch, WM Tarbert 01880 820287

Leith UK
Berwick on Tweed 01289 307264

Lodey Sails Newlyn 01736 719359

Lossie Sails
Lossiemouth 07989 956698

Lucas Sails Portchester 023 9237 3699

Malakoff and Moore
Lerwick 01595 695544

Malcolm Sails Fairlie 01475 568500

McCready and Co Ltd, J
Belfast 028 90232842

McKillop Sails, John
Kingsbridge 01548 852343

McKillop Sails (Sail Locker)
Ipswich 01255 678353

McNamara Sails, Michael
Great Yarmouth 01692 584186

McWilliam Sailmaker (Crosshaven)
Crosshaven +353 21 4831505

Mitchell Sails Fowey 01726 833731

Montrose Rope and Sails
Montrose 01674 672657

Mountfield Sails
Hayling Island 023 9246 3720

Mouse Sails Holyhead 01407 763636

Nicholson Hughes Sails
Rosneath 01436 831356

North Sea Sails
Tollesbury 01621 869367

North West Sails
Keighley 01535 652949

Northrop Sails
Ramsgate 01843 851665

Ösen Sails Ltd
Plymouth 01752 563666

Owen Sails (Gourock)
Gourock 01475 636196

Owen Sails By Oban 01631 720485

Parker & Kay Sailmakers –
East Ipswich 01473 659878

Parker & Kay Sailmakers –
South Hamble 023 8045 8213

Penrose Sailmakers
Falmouth 01326 312705

Pinnell & Bax
Northampton 01604 592808

Pollard Marine
Port St Mary 01624 835831

Quantum Sails
Ipswich Haven Marina 01473 659878

Quantum-Parker & Kay Sailmakers
Hamble 023 8045 8213

Quay Sails (Poole) Ltd
Poole 01202 681128

Ratsey & Lapthorn
Isle of Wight 01983 294051

Ratsey Sailmakers, Stephen
Milford Haven 01646 601561

Relling One Design
Portland 01305 826555

Richardson Sails
Southampton 023 8045 5106

Rig Shop, The
Southampton 023 8033 8341

Rockall Sails
Chichester 01243 573185

Sail Locker
Woolverstone Marina 01473 780206

Sail Style Hayling Is 023 9246 3720

Sails & Canvas Exeter 01392 877527

Saltern Sail Co
West Cowes 01983 280014

Saltern Sail Company
Yarmouth 01983 760120

Sanders Sails
Lymington 01590 673981

Saturn Sails Largs 01475 689933

Scott & Co, Graham
St Peter Port 01481 259380

Shore Sailmakers
Swanwick 01489 589450

SKB Sails Falmouth 01326 372107

Sketrick Sailmakers Ltd
Killinchy 028 9754 1400

Storrar Marine Store
Newcastle upon Tyne 0191 266 1037

Suffolk Sails
Woodbridge 01394 386323

Sunset Sails Sligo +353 71 62792

Teltale Sails Prestwick 01355 500001

Torquay Marina Sails and Canvas
Exeter 01392 877527

Trident UK Gateshead 0191 490 1736

UK McWilliam Cowes 01983 281100

Underwood Sails Queen Anne's
Battery, Plymouth 01752 229661

W Sails Leigh-on-Sea 01702 714550

Watson Sails
Dublin 13 +353 1 846 2206

WB Leitch and Son
Tarbert 01880 820287

Westaway Sails
Plymouth Yacht Haven 01752 892560

Wilkinson, Ursula
Brighton 01273 677758

Wilkinson Sails
Burnham-on-Crouch 01621 786770

Wilkinson Sails
Teynham 01795 521503

Yacht Shop, The
Fleetwood 01253 879238

SOLAR POWER

Ampair Ringwood 01425 480780

Barden UK Ltd Fareham 01489 570770

Marlec Engineering Co Ltd
Corby 01536 201588

SPRAYHOODS & DODGERS

A & B Textiles
Gillingham 01634 579686

Allison–Gray Dundee 01382 505888

Arton, Charles
Milford-on-Sea 01590 644682

Arun Canvas and Rigging Ltd
Littlehampton 01903 732561

Buchanan, Keith
St Mary's 01720 422037

C & J Marine Textiles
Chichester 01243 785485

Covercare Fareham 01329 311878

Covercraft Southampton 023 8033 8286

Jeckells and Son Ltd
Wroxham 01603 782223

Jessail Ardrossan 01294 467311

Lomond Boat Covers
Alexandria 01389 602734

Lucas Sails
Portchester 023 9237 3699

Poole Canvas Co Ltd
Poole 01202 677477

Saundersfoot Auto Marine
Saundersfoot 01834 812115

Teltale Sails Prestwick 01355 500001

Trident UK Gateshead 0191 490 1736

SURVEYORS AND NAVAL ARCHITECTS

Amble Boat Company Ltd
Amble 01665 710267

Ark Surveys East Anglia/South Coast
01621 857065/01794 521957

Atkin & Associates
Lymington 01590 688633

Barbican Yacht Agency Ltd
Plymouth 01752 228855

Battick, Lee
St Helier 01534 611143

Booth Marine Surveys, Graham
Birchington-on-Sea 01843 843793

Byrde & Associates
Kimmeridge — 01929 480064

Bureau Maritime Ltd
Maldon — 01621 859181

Cannell & Associates, David M
Wivenhoe — 01206 823337

Cardiff Commercial Boat Operators Ltd Cardiff — 029 2037 7872

CE Proof Hamble — 023 8045 3245

Clarke Designs LLP, Owen
Dartmouth — 01803 770495

Cox, David Penryn — 01326 340808

Davies, Peter N
Wivenhoe — 01206 823289

Down Marine Co Ltd
Belfast — 028 90480247

Evans, Martin
Kirby le Soken — 01255 677883

Goodall, JL
Whitby — 01947 604791

Green, James
Plymouth — 01752 660516

Greening Yacht Design Ltd, David
Chichester — 023 9263 1806

Hansing & Associates
North Wales/Midlands — 01248 671291

JP Services – Marine Safety & Training Chichester — 01243 537552

MacGregor, WA
Felixstowe — 01394 676034

Mahoney & Co, KPO
Co Cork — +353 21 477 6150

Norwood Marine
Margate — 01843 835711

Quay Consultants Ltd
West Wittering — 01243 673056

Scott Marine Surveyors & Consultants Conwy — 01492 573001

S Roberts Marine Ltd
Liverpool — 0151 707 8300

Staton-Bevan, Tony
Lymington 01590 645755/07850 315744

Swanwick Yacht Surveyors
Southampton — 01489 564822

Thomas, Stephen
Southampton — 023 8048 6273

Ward & McKenzie
Woodbridge — 01394 383222

Ward & McKenzie (North East)
Pocklington — 01759 304322

YDSA Yacht Designers & Surveyors Association Bordon — 0845 0900162

TAPE TECHNOLOGY

Adhesive Technologies
Braintree — 01376 346511

CC Marine Services (Rubbaweld) Ltd
London — 020 7402 4009

Trade Grade Products Ltd
Poole — 01202 820177

UK Epoxy Resins
Burscough — 01704 892364

3M United Kingdom plc
Bracknell — 01344 858315

TRANSPORT/YACHT DELIVERIES

Anglo European Boat Transport
Devon — 01803 868691

Boat Shifters
— 07733 344018/01326 210548

Convoi Exceptionnel Ltd
Hamble — 023 8045 3045

Debbage Yachting
Ipswich — 01473 601169

East Coast Offshore Yachting
— 01480 861381

Forrest Marine Ltd
Exeter — 08452 308335

Hainsworth's UK and Continental
Bingley — 01274 565925

Houghton Boat Transport
Tewkesbury — 07831 486710

Moonfleet Sailing
Poole — 01202 682269

Performance Yachting
Plymouth — 01752 565023

Peters & May Ltd
Southampton — 023 8048 0480

Reeder School of Seamanship, Mike
Lymington — 01590 674560

Seafix Boat Transfer
North Wales — 01766 514507

Sealand Boat Deliveries Ltd
Liverpool — 01254 705225

Shearwater Sailing
Southampton — 01962 775213

Southcoasting Navigators
Devon — 01626 335626

West Country Boat Transport
— 01566 785651

Wolff, David — 07659 550131

Sealand Boat Deliveries Ltd

Nationwide and worldwide yacht transport 36 years. Storage, salvage. lifting 24/7 ops room **01254 705225** fax 776582
ros@poptel.org
www.btx.co.uk

2009/MD6/s

TUITION/SAILING SCHOOLS

Association of Scottish Yacht Charterers Argyll — 07787 363562
01880 820012

Bisham Abbey Sailing & Navigation School Bisham — 01628 474960

Blue Baker Yachts
Ipswich — 01473 780008

Britannia Sailing (East Coast)
Ipswich — 01473 787019

British Offshore Sailing School
Hamble — 023 8045 7733

Coastal Sea School
Weymouth — 0870 321 3271

Conwy School of Yachting
Conwy — 01492 572999

Corsair Sailing
Banstead — 01737 211466

Dart Sailing School
Dartmouth — 01803 833973

Dartmouth Sailing
Dartmouth — 01803 833399

Drake Sailing School
Plymouth — 01635 253009

East Anglian Sea School
Ipswich — 01473 659992

East Coast Offshore Yachting – Les Rant Perry — 01480 861381

Five Star Sailing
Southampton — 01489 885599

Gibraltar Sailing Centre
Gibraltar — 00350 78554

Go Sail Ltd East
Cowes — 01983 280220

Hamble School of Yachting
Hamble — 023 8045 6687

Haslar Sea School
Gosport — 023 9252 0099

Hobo Yachting
Southampton — 023 8033 4574

Hoylake Sailing School
Wirral — 0151 632 4664

Ibiza Sailing School — 07092 235 853

International Yachtmaster Academy
Southampton — 0800 515439

Island Sea School
Port Dinorwic — 01248 352330

JP Services – Marine Safety & Training Chichester — 01243 537552

Lymington Cruising School
Lymington — 01590 677478

Marine Leisure Association (MLA)
Southampton — 023 8029 3822

Menorca Cruising School
— 01995 679240

Moncur Sailing School, Bob
Newcastle upon Tyne — 0191 265 4472

Moonfleet Sailing Poole 01202 682269

National Marine Correspondence School Birkenhead — 0151 647 6777

Northshore King's Lynn 01485 210236

On Deck Sailing
Southampton — 023 8033 3887

Pembrokeshire Cruising
Neyland — 01646 602500

Performance Yachting
Plymouth — 01752 565023

Plain Sailing Dartmouth 01803 853843

Plymouth Sailing School
Plymouth — 01752 493377

Port Edgar Marina & Sailing School
Port Edgar — 0131 331 3330

Portsmouth Outdoor Centre
Portsmouth — 023 9266 3873

Portugal Sail & Power 01473 833001

Rainbow Sailing School
Swansea 01792 467813

Reeder School of Seamanship, Mike
Lymington 01590 674560

Safe Water Training Sea School Ltd
Wirral 0151 630 0466

Sail East Harwich 01473 689344

Sally Water Training
East Cowes 01983 299033

Sea 'N' Ski Portsmouth 023 9246 6041

Seafever 01342 316293

Solaris Mediterranean Sea School
  01925 642909

Solent School of Yachting
Southampton 023 8045 7733

Southcoasting Navigators
Devon 01626 335626

Southern Sailing
Southampton 01489 575511

Start Point Sailing
Dartmouth 01548 810917

Sunsail
Port Solent/Largs 0870 770 6314

Team Sailing Gosport 023 9252 4370

The Dream Or Two Experience of
Yachting Portsmouth 0800 970 7845

Tiller School of Navigation
Banstead 01737 211466

Workman Marine School
Portishead 01275 845844

Wride School of Sailing, Bob
North Ferriby 01482 635623

Abbey, The Penzance 01736 330680

Arun View Inn, The
Littlehampton 01903 722335

Baywatch on the Beach
Bembridge 01983 873259

Beaucette Marina Restaurant
Guernsey 01481 247066

Bella Napoli
Brighton Marina 01273 818577

Bembridge Coast Hotel
Bembridge 01983 873931

Budock Vean Hotel
Porth Navas Creek 01326 252100

Café Mozart Cowes 01983 293681

Caffé Uno Port Solent 023 9237 5227

Chandlers Bar & Bistro Queen Anne's
Battery Marina, Plymouth 01752 257772

Chiquito Port Solent 023 9220 1181

Cruzzo Malahide Marina, Co Dublin
  +353 1 845 0599

Cullins Yard Bistro
Dover 01304 211666

Custom House, The
Poole 01202 676767

Dart Marina River Lounge
Dartmouth 01803 832580

Deer Leap, The Exmouth 01395 265030

Doghouse Swanwick Marina,
Hamble 01489 571602

Dolphin Restaurant
Gorey 01534 853370

Doune Knoydart 01687 462667

El Puertos
Penarth Marina 029 2070 5551

Falmouth Marina Marine Bar and
Restaurant Falmouth 01326 313481

Ferry Boat Inn West Wick Marina,
Nr Chelmsford 01621 740208

Ferry Inn, The (restaurant)
Pembroke Dock 01646 682947

First and Last, The Braye,
Alderney 01481 823162

Fisherman's Wharf
Sandwich 01304 613636

Folly Inn Cowes 01983 297171

Gaffs Restaurant Fenit Harbour Marina,
County Kerry +353 66 71 36666

Godleys Hotel Fenit,
County Kerry +353 66 71 36108

Harbour Lights Restaurant
Walton on the Naze 01255 851887

Haven Bar and Bistro, The
Lymington Yacht Haven 01590 679971

Haven Hotel Poole 01202 707333

HMS Ganges Restaurant
Mylor Yacht Harbour 01326 374320

Jolly Sailor, The
Bursledon 023 8040 5557

Kames Hotel Argyll 01700 811489

Ketch Rigger, The Hamble Point Marina
Hamble 023 8045 5601

Kota Restaurant
Porthleven 01326 562407

La Cala Lady Bee Marina,
Shoreham 01273 597422

Le Nautique
St Peter Port 01481 721714

Lighter Inn, The
Topsham 01392 875439

Mariners Bistro Sparkes Marina,
Hayling Island 023 9246 9459

Mary Mouse II Haslar Marina,
Gosport 023 9252 5200

Martha's Vineyard
Milford Haven 01646 697083

Master Builder's House Hotel
Buckler's Hard 01590 616253

Millstream Hotel
Bosham 01243 573234

Montagu Arms Hotel
Beaulieu 01590 612324

Olivo Port Solent 023 9220 1473

Oyster Quay Mercury Yacht Harbour,
Hamble 023 8045 7220

Paris Hotel Coverack 01326 280258

Pebble Beach, The
Gosport 023 9251 0789

Petit Champ Sark 01481 832046

Philip Leisure Group
Dartmouth 01803 833351

Priory Bay Hotel Seaview,
Isle of Wight 01983 613146

Quayside Hotel
Brixham 01803 855751

Queen's Hotel Kirkwall 01856 872200

Sails Dartmouth 01803 839281

Shananagans
Yarmouth 01983 760054

Shell Bay Seafood Restaurant
Poole Harbour 01929 450363

Simply Italian Sovereign Harbour,
Eastbourne 01323 470911

Slackwater Jacques
Port Solent 023 9278 0777

Spinnaker, The
Chichester Marina 01243 511032

Spit Sand Fort
The Solent 01329 242077

Steamboat Inn Lossiemouth Marina,
Lossiemouth 01343 812066

Taps Shamrock Quay,
Southampton 023 8022 8621

Tayvallich Inn, The
Argyll 01546 870282

Villa Adriana Newhaven Marina
Newhaven 01903 722335

Warehouse Brasserie, The
Poole 01202 677238

36 on the Quay
Emsworth 01243 375592

Met Office Exeter 0870 900 0100

Howells & Son, KJ
Poole 01202 665724

Onward Trading Co Ltd
Southampton 01489 885250

Robbins Timber
Bristol 0117 963 3136

Sheraton Marine Cabinet
Witney 01993 868275

ABC Powermarine
Beaumaris 01248 811413

ABYA Association of Brokers & Yacht Agents Bordon 0845 0900162

Adur Boat Sales
Southwick 01273 596680

Ancasta International Boat Sales
Southampton 023 8045 0000

Anglia Yacht Brokerage
Bury St Edmunds 01359 271747

Ardmair Boat Centre
Ullapool 01854 612054

Assured Boating Egham 01784 473300

Barbican Yacht Agency, The
Plymouth 01752 228855

Bates Wharf Marine Sales Ltd
01932 571141

BJ Marine
Bangor 028 9127 1434

Bluewater Horizons
Weymouth 01305 782080

Boatworks + Ltd
St Peter Port 01481 726071

Caley Marina Inverness 01463 236539

Calibra Marine International Ltd
Southampton 08702 400358

Clarke & Carter Interyacht Ltd
Ipswich/Burnham on Crouch
01473 659681/01621 785600

Coastal Leisure Ltd
Southampton 023 8033 2222

Dale Sailing Brokerage
Neyland 01646 603105

Deacons
Southampton 023 8040 2253

Exe Leisure
Essex Marina 01702 258190

Ferrypoint Boat Co
Youghal +353 24 94232

Gweek Quay Boatyard
Helston 01326 221657

International Barge & Yacht Brokers
Southampton 023 8045 5205

Iron Wharf Boatyard
Faversham 01795 537122

Jackson Yacht Services
Jersey 01534 743819

Kings Yacht Agency
Beaulieu/Southampton
01590 616316/023 8033 1533

Kippford Slipway Ltd
Dalbeattie 01556 620249

Knox-Johnston, Paul
Southsea 023 9286 4524

Lencraft Boats Ltd
Dungarvan +353 58 68220

Liberty Yachts Ltd
Plymouth 01752 227911

Lucas Yachting, Mike
Torquay 01803 212840

Network Yacht Brokers
Dartmouth 01803 834864

Network Yacht Brokers
Plymouth 01752 605377

New Horizon Yacht Agency
Guernsey 01481 726335

Oyster Brokerage Ltd
Ipswich 01473 602263

Pearn and Co, Norman
(Looe Boatyard) Looe 01503 262244

Performance Boat Company
Maidenhead 07768 464717

Peters Chandlery
Chichester 01243 511033

Portavon Marina
Keynsham 0117 986 1626

Prosser Marine Sales Ltd
Glasgow 0141 552 2005

Retreat Boatyard
Topsham 01392 874720

Scanyachts
Southampton 023 8045 5608

SD Marine Ltd
Southampton 023 8045 7278

Sea & Shore Ship Chandler
Dundee 01382 202666

South Pier Shipyard
St Helier 01534 519700

South West Yacht Brokers Group
Plymouth 01752 551991

Sunbird Marine Services
Fareham 01329 842613

Trafalgar Yacht Services
Fareham 01329 823577

Transworld Yachts
Hamble 023 8045 7704

WA Simpson Marine Ltd
Dundee 01382 566670

Walton Marine Sales
Brighton 01273 670707

Walton Marine Sales
Portishead 01275 840132

Walton Marine Sales
Wroxham 01603 781178

Watson Marine, Charles
Hamble 023 8045 6505

Western Marine
Dublin +353 1280 0321

Westways of Plymouth Ltd
Plymouth 01752 670770

Woodrolfe Brokerage
Maldon 01621 868494

Youngboats Faversham 01795 536176

YACHT CHARTERS & HOLIDAYS

Ardmair Boat Centre
Ullapool 01854 612054

Association of Scottish Yacht Charterers Argyll 01880 820012

Blue Baker Yachts
Ipswich 01473 780111/780008

Coastal Leisure Ltd
Southampton 023 8033 2222

Crusader Yachting
Turkey 01732 867321

Dartmouth Sailing
Dartmouth 01803 833399

Dartmouth Yacht Charters
Dartmouth 01803 883718

Doune Marine Mallaig 01687 462667

Four Seasons Yacht Charter
Gosport 023 9251 1789

Golden Black Sailing
Cornwall 01209 715757

Hamble Point Yacht Charters
Hamble 023 8045 7110

Haslar Marina & Victory Yacht Charters Gosport 023 9252 0099

Indulgence Charters
Wendover 01296 696006

Liberty Yachts West Country, Greece, Mallorca & Italy 01752 227911

Nautilus Yachting Mediterranean & Caribbean 01732 867445

Ondeck
Ryde 01983 612642

Patriot Charters & Sail School
Milford Haven 01437 741202

Plain Sailing Yacht Charters
Dartmouth 01803 853843

Portway Yacht Charters
Plymouth/Falmouth
01752 606999/01326 212320

Puffin Yachts
Port Solent 01483 420728

Rainbow Sailing School
Swansea 01792 467813

Sailing Holidays Ltd
Mediterranean 020 8459 8787

Sailing Holidays in Ireland
Kinsale +353 21 477 2927

Setsail Holidays Greece, Turkey, Croatia, Majorca 01787 310445

Shannon Sailing Ltd
Tipperary +353 67 24499

Sleat Marine Services
Isle of Skye 01471 844216

Smart Yachts
Mediterranean 01425 614804

Sunsail Worldwide 0870 770 0102

Templecraft Yacht Charters
Lewes 01273 812333

Top Yacht Charter Ltd
Worldwide 01243 520950

Victory Yacht Charters
Gosport 023 9252 0099

West Wales Yacht Charter
Pwllheli 07748 634869

Westways of Plymouth Ltd
Plymouth 01752 481200

39 North (Mediterranean)
Kingskerwell 07071 393939

YACHT CLUBS

Aberaeron YC
Aberdovey 01545 570077

Aberdeen and Stonehaven SC
Nr Inverurie 01569 764006

Aberdour BC 01383 860632

Abersoch Power BC
Abersoch 01758 712027

Aberystwyth BC	
Aberystwyth	01970 624575
Aldeburgh YC	01728 452562
Alderney SC	01481 822959
Alexandra YC	
Southend-on-Sea	01702 340363
Arklow SC	+353 402 33100
Arun YC Littlehampton	01903 716016
Axe YC Axemouth	01297 20043
Ayr Yacht and CC	01292 476034
Ballyholme YC Bangor	028 91271467
Baltimore SC	+353 28 20426
Banff SC	01464 820308
Bantry Bay SC	+353 27 50081
Barry YC	01446 735511
Beaulieu River SC	
Brockenhurst	01590 616273
Bembridge SC	
Isle of Wight	01983 872237
Benfleet YC	
Canvey Island	01268 792278
Blackpool and Fleetwood YC	01253 884205
Blackwater SC Maldon	01621 853923
Blundellsands SC	0151 929 2101
Bosham SC Chichester	01243 572341
Brading Haven YC	
Isle of Wight	01983 872289
Bradwell CC	01621 892970
Bradwell Quay YC	
Wickford	01268 776539
Brancaster Staithe SC	01485 210249
Brandy Hole YC	
Hullbridge	01702 230320
Brightlingsea SC	
Colchester	01206 303275
Brighton Marina YC	
Peacehaven	01273 818711
Bristol Avon SC	01225 873472
Bristol Channel YC	
Swansea	01792 366000
Bristol Corinthian YC	
Axbridge	01934 732033
Brixham YC	01803 853332
Burnham Overy Staithe SC	01328 730961
Burnham-on-Crouch SC	01621 782812
Burnham-on-Sea SC	
Bridgwater	01278 792911
Burry Port YC	01554 833635
Cabot CC	01275 855207
Caernarfon SC (Menai Strait)	
Caernarfon	01286 672861
Campbeltown SC	01586 552488
Cardiff YC	029 2046 3697
Cardiff Bay YC	029 20226575
Carlingford Lough YC	
Rostrevor	028 4173 8604
Carrickfergus SC	
Whitehead	028 93 351402
Castle Cove SC	
Weymouth	01305 783708
Castlegate Marine Club	
Stockton on Tees	01642 583299
Chanonry SC Fortrose	01463 221415

Chichester Cruiser and Racing Club	01483 770391
Chichester YC	01243 512918
Christchurch SC	01202 483150
Clyde CC Glasgow	0141 221 2774
Co Antrim YC	
Carrickfergus	028 9337 2322
Cobnor Activities Centre Trust	01243 572791
Coleraine YC	028 703 44503
Colne YC Brightlingsea	01206 302594
Conwy YC Deganwy	01492 583690
Coquet YC	01665 710367
Corrib Rowing & YC	
Galway City	+353 91 564560
Cowes Combined Clubs	01983 295744
Cowes Corinthian YC	
Isle of Wight	01983 296333
Cowes Yachting	01983 280770
Cramond BC	0131 336 1356
Creeksea SC	
Burnham-on-Crouch	01245 320578
Crookhaven SC	087 2379997 mobile
Crouch YC	
Burnham-on-Crouch	01621 782252
Dale YC	01646 636362
Dartmouth YC	01803 832305
Deben YC Woodbridge	01394 384440
Dell Quay SC Chichester	01243 785080
Dingle SC	+353 66 51984
Douglas Bay YC	01624 673965
Dovey YC Aberdovey	01213 600008
Dun Laoghaire MYC	+353 1 288 938
Dunbar SC	
Cockburnspath	01368 86287
East Antrim BC	028 28 277204
East Belfast YC	028 9065 6283
East Cowes SC	01983 531687
East Dorset SC Poole	01202 706111
East Lothian YC	01620 892698
Eastney Cruising Association	
Portsmouth	023 92734103
Eling SC	023 80863987
Emsworth SC	01243 372850
Emsworth Slipper SC	01243 378881
Essex YC Southend	01702 478404
Exe SC (River Exe)	
Exmouth	01395 264607
Eyott SC Mayland	01245 320703
Fairlie YC	01294 213940
Falmouth Town SC	01326 373915
Falmouth Watersports Association	
Falmouth	01326 211223
Fareham Sailing & Motor BC	
Fareham	01329 280738
Felixstowe Ferry SC	01394 272466
Findhorn YC Findhorn	01309 690247
Fishguard Bay YC	
Lower Fishguard	01348 872866
Flushing SC Falmouth	01326 374043
Folkestone Yacht and Motor BC	
Folkestone	01303 251574
Forth Corinthian YC	
Haddington	0131 552 5939

Forth YCs Association	
Edinburgh	0131 552 3006
Fowey Gallants SC	01726 832335
Foynes YC Foynes	+353 69 91201
Galway Bay SC	+353 91 794527
Glasson SC Lancaster	01524 751089
Glenans Irish Sailing School	+353 1 6611481
Glenans Irish SC (Westport)	+353 98 26046
Gosport CC Gosport	02392 586838
Gravesend SC	01474 533974
Greenwich YC London	020 8858 7339
Grimsby and Cleethorpes YC	
Grimsby	01472 356678
Guernsey YC	
St Peter Port	01481 722838
Hamble River SC	
Southampton	023 80452070
Hampton Pier YC	
Herne Bay	01227 364749
Hardway SC Gosport	023 9258 1875
Hartlepool YC	01429 233423
Harwich Town SC	01255 503200
Hastings and St Leonards YC	
Hastings	01424 420656
Haven Ports YC	
Woodbridge	01473 659658
Hayling Ferry SC; Locks SC	
Hayling Island	023 80829833
Hayling Island SC	023 92463768
Helensburgh SC Rhu	01436 672778
Helensburgh	01436 821234
Helford River SC	
Helston	01326 231006
Herne Bay SC	01227 375650
Highcliffe SC	
Christchurch	01425 274874
Holyhead SC	01407 762526
Holywood YC	028 90423355
Hoo Ness YC Sidcup	01634 250052
Hornet SC Gosport	023 9258 0403
Howth YC	+353 1 832 2141
Hoylake SC Wirral	0151 632 2616
Hullbridge YC	01702 231797
Humber Yawl Club	01482 667224
Hurlingham YC London	020 8788 5547
Hurst Castle SC	01590 645589
Hythe SC Southampton	02380 846563
Hythe & Saltwood SC	01303 265178
Ilfracombe YC	01271 863969
Iniscealtra SC	
Limerick	+353 61 338347
Invergordon BC	01349 852265
Irish CC	+353 214870031
Island CC Salcombe	01548 531176
Island SC Isle of Wight	01983 296621
Island YC Canvey Island	01268 510360
Isle of Bute SC	
Rothesay	01700 502819
Isle of Man YC	
Port St Mary	01624 832088
Itchenor SC Chichester	01243 512400
Keyhaven YC	01590 642165
Killyleagh YC	028 4482 8250

Kircubbin SC   028 4273 8422
Kirkcudbright SC   01557 331727
Langstone SC Havant   023 9248 4577
Largs SC Largs   01475 670000
Larne Rowing & SC   028 2827 4573
Lawrenny YC   01646 651212
Leigh-on-Sea SC   01702 476788
Lerwick BC   01595 696954
Lilliput SC Poole   01202 740319
Littlehampton Sailing and Motor
Club Littlehampton   01903 715859
Loch Ryan SC Stranraer 01776 706322
Lochaber YC Fort William 01397 772361
Locks SC Portsmouth   023 9282 9833
Looe SC   01503 262559
Lossiemouth CC
Fochabers   01348 812121
Lough Swilly YC Fahn   +353 74 22377
Lowestoft CC   01502 574376
Lyme Regis Power BC   01297 443788
Lyme Regis SC   01297 442373
Lymington Town SC   0159 674514
Lympstone SC Exeter   01395 278792
Madoc YC Porthmadog   01766 512976
Malahide YC   +353 1 845 3372
Maldon Little Ship Club
                        01621 854139

Manx Sailing & CC
Ramsey   01624 813494
Marchwood YC   023 80666141
Margate YC   01843 292602
Marina BC Pwllheli   01758 612271
Maryport YC   01228 560865
Mayflower SC Plymouth 01752 662526
Mayo SC (Rosmoney)
Rosmoney   +353 98 27772
Medway YC Rochester   01634 718399
Menai Bridge BC
Beaumaris   01248 810583
Mengham Rythe SC
Hayling Island   023 92463337
Merioneth YC
Barmouth   01341 280000
Monkstone Cruising and SC
Swansea   01792 812229
Montrose SC Montrose   01674 672554
Mumbles YC Swansea   01792 369321
Mylor YC Falmouth   01326 374391
Nairn SC   01667 453897
National YC
Dun Laoghaire   +353 1 280 5725
Netley SC Netley   023 80454272
New Quay YC
Aberdovey   01545 560516
Newhaven & Seaford SC
Seaford   01323 890077
Newport and Uskmouth SC
Cardiff   01633 271417
Newtownards SC   028 9181 3426
Neyland YC   01646 600267
North Devon YC
Bideford   01271 861390
North Fambridge Yacht Centre
                        01621 740370
North Haven YC Poole   01202 708830

North of England Yachting
Association Kirkwall   01856 872331
North Sunderland Marine Club
Sunderland   01665 721231
North Wales CC
Conwy   01492 593481
North West Venturers YC
(Beaumaris) Beaumaris 0161 2921943
Oban SC Ledaig by Oban
                        01631 563999
Orford SC Woodbridge   01394 450997
Orkney SC Kirkwall   01856 872331
Orwell YC Ipswich   01473 602288
Oulton Broad Yacht Station
                        01502 574946
Ouse Amateur SC
Kings Lynn   01553 772239
Paignton SC Paignton   01803 525817
Parkstone YC Poole   01202 743610
Peel Sailing and CC
Peel   01624 842390
Pembroke Haven YC   01646 684403
Pembrokeshire YC
Milford Haven   01646 692799
Penarth YC   029 20708196
Pentland Firth YC
Thurso   01847 891803
Penzance YC   01736 364989
Peterhead SC Ellon   01779 75527
Pin Mill SC
Woodbridge   01394 780271
Plym YC Plymouth   01752 404991
Poolbeg YC   +353 1 660 4681
Poole YC   01202 672687
Porlock Weir SC
Watchet   01643 862702
Port Edgar YC Penicuik 0131 657 2854
Port Navas YC
Falmouth   01326 340065
Port of Falmouth Sailing Association
Falmouth   01326 372927
Portchester SC
Portchester   023 9237 6375
Porthcawl Harbour BC
Swansea   01656 655935
Porthmadog SC
Porthmadog   01766 513546
Portrush YC Portrush   028 7082 3932
Portsmouth SC   02392 820596
Prestwick SC Prestwick 01292 671117
Pwllheli SC Pwllhelli 01758 613343
Queenborough YC
Queenborough   01795 663955
Quoile YC
Downpatrick   028 44 612266
R Towy BC Tenby   01267 241755
RAFYC   023 80452208
Redclyffe YC Poole   01929 557227
Restronguet SC
Falmouth   01326 374536
Ribble CC
Lytham St Anne's   01253 739983
River Wyre YC   01253 811948
RNSA (Plymouth)   01752 55123/83
Rochester CC   01634 841350

Rock Sailing and Water Ski Club
Wadebridge   01208 862431
Royal Dart YC
Dartmouth   01803 752496
Royal Motor YC Poole   01202 707227
Royal Anglesey YC (Beaumaris)
Anglesey   01248 810295
Royal Burnham YC
Burnham-on-Crouch   01621 782044
Royal Channel Islands YC (Jersey)
St Aubin   01534 745783
Royal Cinque Ports YC
Dover   01304 206262
Royal Corinthian YC
(Burnham-on-Crouch)
Burnham-on-Crouch   01621 782105
Royal Corinthian YC (Cowes)
Cowes   01983 292608
Royal Cork YC
Crosshaven   +353 214 831023
Royal Cornwall YC (RCYC)
Falmouth   01326 312126
Royal Dorset YC
Weymouth   01305 786258
Royal Forth YC
Edinburgh   0131 552 3006
Royal Fowey YC Fowey 01726 833573
Royal Gourock YC
Gourock   01475 632983
Royal Highland YC
Connel   01852 300460
Royal Irish YC
Dun Laoghaire   +353 1 280 9452
Royal London YC
Isle of Wight   019 83299727
Royal Lymington YC   01590 672677
Royal Mersey YC
Birkenhead   0151 645 3204
Royal Motor YC Poole   01202 707227
Royal Naval Club and Royal Albert
YC Portsmouth   023 9282 5924
Royal Naval Sailing Association
Gosport   023 9252 1100
Royal Norfolk & Suffolk YC
Lowestoft   01502 566726
Royal North of Ireland YC
                        028 90 428041
Royal Northern and Clyde YC
Rhu   01436 820322
Royal Northumberland YC
Blyth   01670 353636
Royal Plymouth Corinthian YC
Plymouth   01752 664327
Royal Scottish Motor YC
                        0141 881 1024
Royal Solent YC
Yarmouth   01983 760256
Royal Southampton YC
Southampton   023 8022 3352
Royal Southern YC
Southampton   023 8045 0300
Royal St George YC
Dun Laoghaire   +353 1 280 1811
Royal Tay YC Dundee   01382 477133
Royal Temple YC
Ramsgate   01843 591766

Royal Torbay YC		
Torquay	01803 292006	
Royal Ulster YC		
Bangor	028 91 270568	
Royal Victoria YC		
Fishbourne	01983 882325	
Royal Welsh YC (Caernarfon)		
Caernarfon	01286 672599	
Royal Welsh YC		
Aernarfon	01286 672599	
Royal Western YC		
Plymouth	01752 226299	
Royal Yacht Squadron		
Isle of Wight	01983 292191	
Royal Yorkshire YC		
Bridlington	01262 672041	
Rye Harbour SC	01797 223136	
Salcombe YC	01548 842593	
Saltash SC	01752 845988	
Scalloway BC Lerwick	01595 880409	
Scarborough YC	01723 373821	
Schull SC	+353 28 37352	
Scillonian Sailing and BC		
St Mary's	01720 277229	
Seasalter SC		
Whitstable	07773 189943	
Seaview YC		
Isle of Wight	01983 613268	
Shoreham SC Henfield	01273 453078	
Skerries SC		
Carlingdford Lough	+353 1 849 1233	
Slaughden SC Duxford	01728 689036	
Sligo YC Sligo	+353 71 77168	
Solva Boat Owners Association		
Fishguard	01437 721538	
Solway YC		
Kirkdudbright	01556 620312	
South Caernavonshire YC		
Abersoch	01758 712338	
South Cork SC	+353 28 36383	
South Devon Sailing School		
Newton Abbot	01626 52352	
South Gare Marine Club - Sail Section Middlesbrough	01642 505630	
South Shields SC	0191 456 5821	
South Woodham Ferrers YC		
Chelmsford	01245 325391	
Southampton SC	023 8044 6575	
Southwold SC	01986 784225	
Sovereign Harbour YC		
Eastbourne	01323 470888	
St Helier YC	01534 721307/32229	
St Mawes SC	01326 270686	
Starcross Fishing & CC (River Exe)		
Starcross	01626 891996	
Starcross YC Exeter	01626 890470	
Stoke SC Ipswich	01473 624989	
Stornoway SC	01851 705412	
Stour SC	01206 393924	
Strangford Lough YC		
Newtownards	028 97 541202	
Strangford SC		
Downpatrick	028 4488 1404	
Strood YC Aylesford	01634 718261	
Sunderland YC	0191 567 5133	
Sunsail Portsmouth	023 92222224	

Sussex YC		
Shoreham-by-Sea	01273 464868	
Swanage SC	01929 422987	
Swansea Yacht & Sub-Aqua Club		
Swansea	01792 469096	
Tamar River SC		
Plymouth	01752 362741	
Tarbert Lochfyne YC	01880 820376	
Tay Corinthian BC		
Dundee	01382 553534	
Tay YCs Association	01738 621860	
Tees & Hartlepool YC	01429 233423	
Tees SC		
Aycliffe Village	01429 265400	
Teifi BC - Cardigan Bay		
Fishguard	01239 613846	
Teign Corinthian YC		
Teignmouth	01626 777699	
Tenby SC	01834 842762	
Tenby YC	01834 842762	
Thames Estuary YC	01702 345967	
Thorney Island SC	01243 371731	
Thorpe Bay YC	01702 587563	
Thurrock YC Grays	01375 373720	
Tollesbury CC	01621 869561	
Topsham SC	01392 877524	
Torpoint Mosquito SC -		
Plymouth	01752 812508	
Tralee SC	+353 66 36119	
Troon CC	01292 311190	
Troon YC	01292 315315	
Tudor SC		
Portsmouth	023 92662002	
Tynemouth SC		
Newcastle upon Tyne	0191 2572167	
Up River YC		
Hullbridge	01702 231654	
Upnor SC	01634 718043	
Wakering YC		
Rochford	01702 530926	
Waldringfield SC		
Woodbridge	01394 283347	
Walls Regatta Club		
Lerwick	01595 809273	
Walton & Frinton YC		
Walton-on-the-Naze	01255 675526	
Warrenpoint BC	028 4175 2137	
Warsash SC		
Southampton	01489 583575	
Watchet Boat Owner Association		
Watchet	01984 633736	
Waterford Harbour SC		
Dunmore East	+353 51 383389	
Watermouth YC		
Watchet	01271 865048	
Wear Boating Association		
	0191 567 5313	
Wells SC		
Wells-next-the-sea	01328 711190	
West Kirby SC	0151 625 5579	
West Mersea YC		
Colchester	01206 382947	
Western Isles YC	01688 302371	
Western YC		
Kilrush	+353 87 2262885	

Weston Bay YC		
Portishead	07867 966429	
Weston CC		
Southampton	07905 557298	
Weston SC		
Southampton	023 80452527	
Wexford HBC	+353 53 22039	
Weymouth SC		
Weymouth	01305 785481	
Whitby YC	01947 603623	
Whitstable YC	01227 272942	
Wicklow SC	+353 404 67526	
Witham SC		
Boston	01205 363598	
Wivenhoe SC		
Colchester	01206 822132	
Woodbridge CC	01394 386737	
Wormit BC	01382 553878	
Yarmouth SC	01983 760270	
Yealm YC		
Newton Ferrers	01752 872291	
Youghal Sailing Club	+353 24 92447	

YACHT DESIGNERS

Cannell & Associates, David M		
Wivenhoe	01206 823337	
Clarke Designs LLP, Owen		
Dartmouth	01803 770495	
Giles Naval Architects, Laurent		
Lymington	01590 641777	
Harvey Design, Ray		
Barton on Sea	01425 613492	
Jones Yacht Design, Stephen		
Warsash	01489 576439	
Wharram Designs, James		
Truro	01872 864792	
Wolstenholme Yacht Design		
Coltishall	01603 737024	

YACHT MANAGEMENT

Barbican Yacht Agency Ltd		
Plymouth	01752 228855	
Coastal Leisure Ltd		
Southampton	023 8033 2222	
O'Sullivan Boat Management		
Dun Laoghaire	+353 86 829 6625	
Swanwick Yacht Surveyors		
Swanwick	01489 564822	

YACHT VALETING

Blackwell, Craig		
Co Meath	+353 87 677 9605	
Bright 'N' Clean		
South Coast	07789 494430	
Clean It All		
Nr Brixham	01803 844564	
Kip Marina Inverkip	01475 521485	
Mainstay Yacht Maintenance		
Dartmouth	01803 839076	
Marine Gleam		
Lymington	0800 074 4672	
Mobile Yacht Maintenance		
	07900 148806	
Shipshape Hayling Is	023 9232 4500	
Smith Boat Care, Paul		
Isle of Wight	01983 754726	